CONTENTS

PART 1
Charley Patton and the Mississippi Blues: Origins and Traditions

PART 2
Charley Patton, Mississippi Delta Blues: Comparison with Other Regional Styles
and Mutual Influences

PART 3
Conclusion

CHARLEY PATTON

Voice of the Mississippi Delta

Edited by Robert Sacré   Foreword by William Ferris

University Press of Mississippi / Jackson

www.upress.state.ms.us

The University Press of Mississippi is a member
of the Association of American University Presses.

This volume was originally published in French as *The Voice of the Delta: Charley Patton and
the Mississippi Blues Traditions* by Presses Universitaires de Liège in Belgium in 1987.

First printing 2018

∞

Library of Congress Cataloging-in-Publication Data

Names: Sacré, Robert, 1940–
Title: Charley Patton : voice of the Mississippi Delta / [edited by] Robert Sacré ; foreword by
William Ferris.
Other titles: Revision of: Voice of the Delta.
Description: Jackson : University Press of Mississippi, [2018] | Series: American made music
series | Papers from 1984 symposium sponsored by Université de Liège, Faculté de
philosophie et lettres; revised and updated. | Includes bibliographical references and index.
Identifiers: LCCN 2017049295| ISBN 9781496816139 (cloth : alk. paper) | ISBN 9781496818560
(pbk. : alk. paper) | ISBN 9781496816146 (epub single) | ISBN 9781496816153 (epub
institutional) | ISBN 9781496816177 (pdf institutional)
Subjects: LCSH: Patton, Charley, 1891–1934—Congresses. | Blues (Music)—Mississippi—
Congresses. | African Americans—Mississippi—Congresses.
Classification: LCC ML420.P323 C53 2018 | DDC 781.643092—dc23 LC record available at
https://lccn.loc.gov/2017049295

British Library Cataloging-in-Publication Data available

FOREWORD

Charley Patton and Robert Johnson are arguably the two most important voices of the early Mississippi Delta blues sound. As songwriters and performers, their recordings influenced successive generations of black and white musicians in powerful, enduring ways. The spirit of Patton and Johnson hovers over familiar places in the Delta. Patton is forever linked to Dockery Farms, where he lived and performed regularly. He chronicled Dockery Farms in his "34 Blues." Johnson's blues are associated with the Crossroads, where he is said to have sold his soul to the devil in exchange for his musical genius. The music of Patton and Johnson is etched in the imagination of generations of blues fans who visit historic buildings at Dockery Farms and seek the mythic Crossroads. Apart from their recorded performances, few documents remain to help us understand the lives of either Johnson or Patton. Yet their music continues to burn brightly, like a star in the night sky whose source has long ago been extinguished.

Blues lovers are therefore especially grateful that Robert Sacré assembled a distinguished group of scholars and writers to reflect on Charley Patton's life and his influence on other musicians. Sacré held his International Conference on Charley Patton at Liège University in Belgium in 1984. Inspired by that conference, this volume is an invaluable resource on the life and music of Patton.

Fifty years after the death of Patton, Sacré and his colleagues honored the life and music of a performer who was born in Mississippi around 1887. In Liège, Belgium—five thousand miles from Dockery Farms, where Patton lived and played his blues—Sacré and his international group met and spoke about Charley Patton and his music.

Charley Patton has long attracted music critics. In *Deep Blues*, Robert Palmer acknowledges Patton as a musician who "still informs, entertains and moves listeners all over the world." In his notes to *Patton, Sims, & Bertha Lee: Delta Blues, Bottleneck Guitar Pioneer*, Don Kent calls Patton "the most influential artist of the Mississippi Delta Blues school."

Robert Sacré appropriately describes Charley Patton as a "griot" who serves the role of historian, musician, and songwriter for his people. Sacré argues that Patton uses "blue notes" to conjure the history of black music—from slavery to blues, from country to urban music.

Luther Allison's powerful narrative grounds the origins of both Patton's and his own blues in "the idea of taking a broom wire and a brick and bottle" to create a one-strand instrument that virtually every Delta blues artist—including B.B. King—played as a child. That experience was the first musical step for blues artists. Allison recalled that when he lived "in the country, you hear the crickets at night and the mosquitoes singing, and my dad and my mother would come home and sit out till dark just singing hymns."

Arnold Shaw explores the Mississippi blues tradition and the origins of the blues through the lives and music of Charley Patton, Bukka White, Son House, and Robert Johnson. Shaw argues that these musicians are "the largest and most impressive group of blues singers who have come from Mississippi." Shaw demonstrates the power of Patton's poetic voice in "High Water Everywhere" as he sings of the flood's victims: "I couldn't see nobody home an' wasn't no one to be found."

Mike Rowe follows the Great Central Migration of black families and the influence of the Mississippi Delta style on Chicago's postwar blues. Rowe quotes Otis Spann, who says "Chicago is the greatest blues area there is. It's built from the Mississippi Blues." Rowe shows how Jimmy Reed's 1956 lyrics in "Ride 'em On Down" include Patton's blues phrase "heart like a piece of railroad steel." He then shows the influence of Delta blues on Robert Lockwood Jr., Muddy Waters, Robert Nighthawk, Baby Face Leroy, Johnny Shines, Floyd Jones, Big Joe Williams, Sonny Boy Williamson, Little Walter, Eddie Taylor, Otis Rush, and Jimmy Reed. The musical influence of Charley Patton, Rowe argues, is felt in all of their blues.

Daniel Droixhe focuses on the familiar three-chord pattern with two lines of verse, which he describes as the "elementary blues" in the music of Charley Patton. He connects that pattern with the tonal scale using selections from Patton's Yazoo double album. Droixhe focuses on "Heart Like Railroad Steel," "Mean Black Moan," "Jersey Bull Blues," "Jim Lee," "Mississippi Boweavil Blues," "Hammer Blues," "High Sheriff Blues," "Pony Blues," and "When Your Way Gets Dark."

John Broven compares Louisiana country music with the Mississippi Delta country style of Charley Patton. He describes Patton as "a songster whose all-around repertoire included spiritual songs." While Patton and other Mississippi Delta bluesmen influenced musicians in the Baton Rouge area, Broven finds it "hard to detect 'mutual influences' on the Mississippi blues by

Louisiana artists." Broven suggests that Louisiana musicians lack "the charismatic qualities of Patton" and concludes that there is no "unified early Louisiana country blues around."

Dick Shurman describes his visits with Chicago blues artists Howlin' Wolf and Willie Johnson. Shurman notes the strong influence of Charley Patton on Howlin' Wolf. Wolf knew Patton and recorded a version of Patton's "Pony Blues" as "Saddle My Pony." Shurman suggests we can hear "Patton's growl in Wolf's vocals, and some of Patton's clowning obviously left a strong impression on young Chester."

Jim O'Neal's thoughtful piece on "Modern Chicago Blues: Delta Retentions" deepens our understanding of the rich, complex ties between the Mississippi Delta and Chicago. O'Neal argues that Chicago is the "primary center for the continuation and modernization of the Delta blues traditions." While musicians like Junior Wells, James Cotton, and Sunnyland Slim moved blues from the Delta to the Windy City, more recent influences on Chicago blues include popular soul, R&B, and funk music, as well as the contemporary blues styles of B.B. King, Albert King, Bobby Bland, and Little Milton. O'Neal notes that, while older residents of entire apartment buildings in Chicago may be from a single Delta town like Greenville and Clarksdale, their children were born and raised in Chicago. Reunions of families from these Delta towns are popular social events on the South or West Side that feature blues artists from their towns as the entertainment. A popular blues scene on the West Side is the Delta Fish Market, which is owned by slide guitar player Oliver Davis, whose father was a bandleader in Greenville. The bandstand on the parking lot at the market features blues music as people party and eat fried catfish. Due to the presence of Malaco and LaJam record labels in Jackson, Chicago musicians like Bobby Rush, McKinley Mitchell, and Johnny Littlejohn have moved back to Mississippi where their music is marketed to a young and middle-aged audience. At the same time, in Chicago the children of Willie Dixon, Carey Bell, Eddie Taylor, and numerous other blues artists are exploring the roots of the blues as inspiration for their own music. O'Neal suggests that this latest generation will preserve the legacy of Charley Patton through their blues.

David Evans's magisterial piece "Charley Patton: The Conscience of the Delta" runs a deep plow through both the music and the life of Patton. His research is based on extensive interviews with Patton's family, including his sister Viola Cannon, his niece Bessie Turner, his nephew Tom Cannon, two children, and Tom Rushing, who is featured in one of his songs. Evans stresses that Patton was the first recorded black folk artist to sing about local public events and about white people whom he knew. Patton lived and regularly performed at Dockery Farms. The plantation "was a huge tract of about forty square miles founded in 1895 by Will Dockery, a paternalistic planter who by all accounts treated his tenants very fairly."

Patton's nephew Tom Cannon commented on his uncle's elegant dress. "He always wore a suit every day of his life. . . . He wore his suits and shined shoes, and a different woman every year, two a year sometimes. . . . He didn't go like no working man." Patton's income was dramatically higher than that of Mississippi Delta field workers. Beatrice Gidden of Lula, Mississippi, recalls how between 1916 and 1921, Patton "had a T-Model Ford. . . . Ordinary farm workers, they were getting a dollar and a half a day. They would pay him twenty-five dollars for a party."

Evans notes that Patton had "a sense of *absolute conviction* in his singing and playing. . . . equally in front of black and white audiences, Charley Patton was able to plumb the depths of feeling contained in his blues, spirituals, and other folksongs." It is this "feeling of overwhelming intensity. . . . that Robert Palmer aptly called *deep blues*. . . . The high degree of spontaneity in his songs provides us with a rare opportunity to glimpse a folk blues artist actually *at work* on his songs. . . . He seems to have been determined to have his talent recognized and not to do manual work like an ordinary black man in the Delta. . . . Travel for Patton meant *freedom* and *options*. . . . Patton's very existence was a bold challenge to the status quo in the Delta that was designed to keep him oppressed, to keep him from being a 'great man.'"

Charley Patton would be stunned to see how his life and music are recognized and honored today in his home state of Mississippi. Markers on the Mississippi Blues Trail stand at his birthplace in Bolton, at his grave site in Holly Ridge, and at his home at Dockery Farms. The marker at his grave site reads "Charley Patton—The most important figure in the pioneering era of Delta Blues. Charley Patton. . . . . helped define not only the musical genre but also the image and lifestyle of the rambling Mississippi bluesman." Buildings at Dockery Farms where Patton lived and worked have been restored by the Dockery Foundation, whose members include the Dockery family, T Bone Burnett, Rosanne Cash, Herbie Hancock, Quincy Jones, and Thelonius Monk III. Patton's life and music are celebrated at annual blues conferences at Delta State University, Arkansas State University, and the University of Mississippi. He is also recognized in exhibits at the Delta Blues Museum in Clarksdale, the B.B. King Museum in Indianola, and the Blues Archive at the University of Mississippi, as well as on the pages of *Living Blues* magazine, which is published by the Center for Study of Southern Culture at the University of Mississippi.

This impressive volume further secures the legacy of Charley Patton as the fountainhead of Mississippi Delta blues. Patton's personal life and his recorded music are testaments to how he endured and prevailed in his struggle as a black man who lived in the Mississippi Delta in the early twentieth century. Charley Patton's story is a beacon that offers each of us hope for a better future.

—William Ferris

ACKNOWLEDGMENTS

I am grateful to all the people who gave me their support for the development of this book. Thanks to members of the administration at Liège University, Arthur Bodson, Chancellor in 1984, Dean Paul Delbouille, Professors Pierre Michel, Pierre Colman, Henri Pousseur, and Annette Bragard.

Thanks for the grants I received from various Cultural Offices, from Belgian F.N.R.S. and Department of Education, and from the US Embassy in Brussels. Money is the name of the game, and without all of them, no international conference would have been possible.

A lot of gratitude to friends and musicians who helped me put this project into concrete form. It is a large family and I'm sure I'll forget names, if I try to make a full list, so I will not, but I hope they will forgive me.

To the "inner circle," Professor Daniel Droixhe, Jean Pierre Urbain, Marina Gruslin, Joseph Brems, Robert Vetzburger, Bruno Boulanger, Michel Xhaufflaire.

To the contributors, Professors Eileen Southern, David Evans, Arnold Shaw, Daniel Droixhe, John Broven, Mike Rowe, Jim O'Neal, Dick Shurman, Cilla Huggins, and Luther Allison; their expertise was essential for the success of the conference.

To Sylvain Basteyns, who contributed to the illustrations of the 1987 edition of the book.

To my wife Renée and our sons, Philippe and Pascal; without their love and patience, this project would never have seen the light.

I wish to pay a special debt of gratitude to friends and colleagues who supported me and gave me strength and determination to achieve the project: Dr. William Ferris, Dr. Jeff T. Titon, Dr. Samuel A. Floyd Jr., Doug Seroff, Bruce Iglauer, Dr. Kip Lornell, Dr. Dominique-René de Lerma, Walter Liniger, William Cochrane, Tommy Couch, Dave Clark, Steve Brull, Amy Van Singel, Bruce Bastin, Paul Vernon, Jacques Périn, Gérard Herzhaft, Jacques Demètre, Jean Buzelin, André Fonteyne, Paul de Bruycker, Frank van Rampelberg,

Marcel Vos, Siegfried A. Christmann, Axel Küstner, Jean Philippe Martin-Payre, and all the blues people who were generous with time and friendship.

March 1987

Cover of the first edition of *Charley Patton: The Voice of the Delta* (Liège: Presses Universitaires of Liège, 1987). (Collection of Robert Sacré)

For this 2017 edition, I wish to extend my thanks and gratitude to Craig Gill and the staff at the University Press of Mississippi because they wisely decided to give new life to a book that has been out of print for many years; it's coming out at the right time since I regularly receive requests for copies.

Last but not least, I am indebted to Professor David Evans for his precious assistance and for his expert counsel in the final editing work. Among other problems, there were grammar and punctuation issues, and he solved them all, with patience and determination.

INTRODUCTION

From Africa to the Southern Plantations of America, to the Mississippi Delta . . . and to Charley Patton

The story of black American music started with the black people brought from Western Africa to the New World as early as 1619. The first to arrive were indentured servants, who worked for several years, then became "free people of color." The hundreds of thousands who followed them were slaves with no clothes and nothing in their hands. But they had their oral culture—music especially—in their minds, and over three hundred years they built a subtle mixture of their own musical ideas and views with the psalms and hymns of religious Western music to create Negro spirituals and other styles of religious music (gospel songs), and with white recreational music, which led to blues, ragtime, jazz, and all the various related styles, the story of which is told in the first chapter. But this frame has to be set up first, as Charley Patton is an authentic heir of the African griots and, to quote English researcher Ray Templeton (*Blues & Rhythm* 30, page 9): "He represents a vitally important focal point in the development of the Mississippi Blues . . ."

Robert Palmer wrote: "the music of Charley Patton, a functionally illiterate rounder who sang for common laborers in an isolated geographical pocket that most of the rest of America had forgotten or never knew existed, still informs, entertains and moves listeners all over the world" (*Deep Blues*, New York: Viking, 1981).

Don Kent added: "He was the most influential artist of the Mississippi Delta Blues school. . . . Patton does not merely accompany his vocal with guitar-work, but the two are totally idiosyncratic and hermetic; he forms a duet with himself. . . . [He is] the greatest and most inimitable vocalist and guitar stylist of his or any time . . ." (sleeve notes, *Patton, Sims, & Bertha Lee: Delta Blues, Bottleneck Guitar Pioneer*, Herwin LP 213, 1977).

He was also surrounded by controversy among his contemporaries because you can't satisfy everyone. Some said, "he was a nice guy. . . . everybody liked

Charley Patton circa 1929. (Collection of Robert Sacré)

Paramount advertisement. (Collection of Robert Sacré)

him. . . . A magnificent entertainer." Others said, "Patton was a clowning man with a guitar."

A Symposium? What For?

Patton died in Holly Ridge, near Indianola, Mississippi, in 1934, in total obscurity, epitomizing the cliché of the archetypical bluesman and his hard times. But he had been a legend in his own lifetime, and fifty years later, at the University of Liège in Belgium, a group of scholars and blues collectors and writers thought it was a good opportunity to honor one of the greatest black American bluesmen of all time and to commemorate the death of an artist whose "name and accomplishments are known to many about a century after his birth, whose music was original and remains influential today" (Dr. David Evans).

Patton was born ca. 1887 near Bolton, Mississippi, somewhat before the blues itself came to light as a unique cocktail of African music (with pentatonic scales), field hollers, work songs, ballads, syncopated plantation songs and cake walks, spirituals and Southern white music. Patton played a major role in the development of the Mississippi blues style with followers like Son House, Robert Johnson, Bukka White, Tommy McClennan, Muddy Waters, Howlin' Wolf, and many others. He was called "The Founder of the Delta

Panelists at the International Conference, Liege University, 1984 (left to right): David Evans, Jim O'Neal, Robert Sacré, Dick Shurman, John Broven, Mike Rowe. (Collection of Robert Sacré)

Blues" (Yazoo LP 1020) and, as we can expect from a pioneer, his repertoire was a mixture of blues, ballads, rags, religious songs, and vaudeville pieces.

The fiftieth anniversary of such an artist's death deserved to be honored decently, but when we indulged ourselves in the daydream project of an international conference on this topic in the summer of 1983, we were far from conceiving that we were on the way to actually make a symposium about the theme of Charley Patton, his life, his music, and his influence with such a panel of specialists and scholars and that it would take place in Liège, Belgium, at the University in September 1984 and that it would be the sole event of its kind in the world . . . but it was!

Between Liège and Dockery Farms, Drew, Clarksdale, and the Sunflower River there are more than five thousand miles. Patton himself never imagined or dreamed that people would speak feverishly about him and his music, so much and so far from his homeland, fifty years after his death and one hundred years, or so, after his birth. . . . It is our pride and reward to have been able to make it come true.

The Blues and Charley Patton as Founder of the Delta blues

Professor Arnold Shaw (1909–1989) believed the blues was born following the Reconstruction era that lasted between 1865 and 1877, as a result of psychological changes in Southern black life caused by the economic and sociological atmosphere of the time. In his lecture he demonstrates that the blues was a highly personalized musical form by analyzing blues composed by Patton and three of his best heirs, Son House, Robert Johnson, and Booker ("Bukka") White.

Professor David Evans (University of Memphis) develops the theme of "Charley Patton, the Conscience of the Delta." In his abstract, he says:

Patton was the most extensively recorded early Mississippi folk blues artist and the earliest Mississippi blues artist about whom we have much information. But beyond his importance in the history of the blues, Patton is probably the only black person from Mississippi of his generation who still has a national and international impact, whose name and accomplishments are known to many outside his immediate family and community about a century after his birth and fifty years after his death. This paper will try to answer the question of whether Patton was aware of his potential to communicate outside his community and across barriers of time, class, race, and region, and whether he was consciously trying to communicate anything. New facts about Patton's life revealed by family members show other sides of his personality and career, including his education, his career as a preacher, his associations with white people, and a relatively stable marriage for about the last four years of his life. Most of his songs had personal meaning, often expressing dissatisfaction with conditions of his existence. Many deal with domestic situations, but several deal with Patton's reactions to the world around him. An examination of Patton's life and songs reveals that he tried to live life to the fullest in an extremely oppressive social environment, that he was aware of his unique status during the years of his recording career, and that he did try to reveal his state of mind, his life, and his life style, both to his community and to the world.

Professor Daniel Droixhe (University of Liège, University of Brussels–U.L.B.) analyzes the musical structure, scales, and chords used by Charley Patton, and his lecture "Elementary Blues and Tonal Scale in Patton's Recordings" complements that of Professor Evans.

Charley Patton, Mississippi Delta Blues:
Comparison with Other Regional Styles and Mutual Influences

Author and essayist John Broven says the influence of the Mississippi Delta blues can be found in Louisiana through artists such as Robert Pete Williams and other rural performers, but it seems there was no reciprocal influence from Louisiana to Mississippi.

Author and essayist Mike Rowe examines the influences of Mississippi Delta style on Chicago's postwar blues. A lot of black southern migrants settled in Chicago in the early 1940s—as others did during and after the Civil War, World War I, and World War II. Many musicians were among them, including McKinley Morganfield, better known as Muddy Waters. Born in the Delta and raised on Stovall's Plantation near Clarksdale, he had the same musical roots as Charley Patton and was influenced by the great man. Rowe also describes Muddy Waters's first musical steps in the Windy City from the end of the forties to the early fifties.

Writer-producer Dick Shurman is a longtime Chicago resident who came to know very well, among dozens of blues, soul, and jazz musicians, Chester "Howlin' Wolf" Burnett and Willie Johnson, who are the themes of his lecture, "Memories of Howlin' Wolf and Willie Johnson." Wolf learned directly from Patton; he made his first recordings in Memphis for Sam Phillips (who sold them to RPM), and the first guitarist in his band was Willie Johnson.

Writer, producer, and journalist Jim O'Neal of *Living Blues* magazine fame finds modern Chicago blues men and women using Charley Patton's songs and lyrics, as such or slightly modified.

Mississippi Blues Today and in the Future

Professor David Evans also handles this topic. In his abstract he says:

Mississippi has always been a center of blues activity. The state has a heavy black population, the Mississippi River is an artery of commerce and communication, and the Delta is a great economic and social vortex, drawing people in and forcing them out again. The blues tradition of the state has drawn upon rich older musical resources such as one-string instruments, fife and drum bands, and string bands. Folk blues and these older folk music resources thrived in Mississippi through the forties, and some can still be found in many parts of the state. In the fifties, electric instruments and new styles emerged, including small combos of usually not more than three pieces and "primitive" blues guitarists in a style like that of John Lee Hooker. A small amount of this new music was recorded in the early fifties by southern companies such as Trumpet in Jackson and Sun in Memphis, but we mostly know of this music in forms reflected by artists who moved north and the combinations they formed there. There was an enormous drain of musical talent to the North and a drying up of recording opportunities after Trumpet and Sun ceased recording blues in the mid-1950s. Integration and mechanization of agriculture also brought about many changes. Field recording in Mississippi in the late 1950s, 1960s, and 1970s placed an emphasis on older blues styles characteristic of the 1940s and earlier. These factors have all combined to give the impression that the blues tradition in Mississippi is nearly dead and is bereft of talent and creativity. Recent research, however, shows that Mississippi blues today displays a broad range of styles and that interesting new syntheses are still taking place, building upon developments of the fifties and sometimes older resources. Taped examples will be played of traditionalists like Jack Owens & Bud Spires and Ranie Burnette, neo-traditionalists like Lonnie Pitchford and Jessie Mae Hemphill, and the unusual small combos of Jimmie Holmes and partners, Junior Kimbrough and the Soul Blues Boys, R. L. Burnside and the Sound Machine, and Hezekiah and the House Rockers, as well as the urban synthesis of the Fieldstones, a five-piece Memphis band with three Mississippi-born members. The future of Mississippi blues depends upon the stimulation of present trends from within the blues community and outside forces such as recordings, festivals and tours.

Black Voices

The blues come from right here in America. That is your American music and if
you don't appreciate it, it's like a child being born, don't appreciate his mother.
—**Johnny Shines,** quoted by Barry Lee Pearson, *Sounds So Good to Me:*
The Bluesmen's Story (University of Pennsylvania Press, 1984)

These words run parallel with the fact that the literature of African American
music has been mostly written by white writers and thus has a multiplicity
of problems—the cultural gap, lack of firsthand documentation, etc.—as J. L.
Collier points out in his article "Face to Face: The White Biographer of Black
Subjects" in *Black Music Research Journal* (1985). Until recently, many black
scholars neglected the study and research of black American music, perhaps
because it was old-time music related to Uncle Tom, slavery, and bad times.
But times are changing and an increasing number of African American scholars are taking an interest in their musical heritage, doing research and writing
books and papers for journals and periodicals such as *Black Music Research
Journal, The Black Perspective in Music,* and others.

Professor Eileen Southern (1920–2002) wrote *The Music of Black Americans* and edited *Readings in Black American Music* among other works. A professor at Harvard University, her lecture dealt with that topic; unfortunately,
her paper for the original volume published in French was lost in the mail and
the editor tried to fill in for her. The essay "Black Music USA: From African
to African American Music," written by Robert Sacré, reflects the input and
insight of Professor Southern.

Luther Allison (1939–1997) was a black American bluesman. His interview
by a panel at the conference gives a personal view of the life of a bluesman in
Arkansas and then in Chicago.

To conclude, let us see the future of the blues with confidence and trust,
like *Early Downhome Blues* author Jeff Todd Titon: "Despite predictions of its
impending death, the blues culture continues to flourish."

PART 1

Charley Patton and the Mississippi Blues: Origins and Traditions

Black Music USA: From African to African American Music

—Robert Sacré

When I first got the blues, they brought me over on a ship /
Men was standin' over me and a lot more with a whip
—**B.B. King,** "Why I Sing the Blues"

African Roots and Heritage

Many of the roots of black American music lie in Africa more than four hundred years ago at the start of the slave trade. Slaves shipped to the New World were naked and had been separated from their families, their relatives, and their friends, but their traditions were alive in their minds. These were oral traditions, which explains the paucity of written indigenous archives. But we know a lot about the music of Africa because the oral traditions of modern Africa contain reliable clues to the past—many musical practices of today and yesterday (mid-twentieth century) are remarkably similar to those of the past; and, most of all, we know a lot thanks to the writings of early travelers and traders in Africa.[1]

Many musical instruments of the past are still used today, and a lot of music has been transmitted orally down through the generations.

Most of the African slaves brought to America came from an area in Western Africa now occupied by Senegal, Guinea, Liberia, Nigeria, and Gabon. More precisely, they were captured in the savanna area lying between the coastal lands and the northern desert. Although musical cultures varied from nation to nation, tribe to tribe, they had enough in common to constitute an identifiable heritage for the Africans brought to the New World.

In Africa, songs, music, and dance are of great importance in daily life and on important occasions. There is appropriate music and dance for almost any activity: birth and death, initiation rites, funerals, weddings, agricultural rites,

3

work in the fields, hunting and fishing expeditions, wars, and religious events. The master of ceremonies for musical occasions in some parts of the savanna region is called a *griot*; he is historian, musician, and songwriter. He has a high status in African societies and is much respected.

The instruments most often encountered by early travelers in Africa were percussive—drums of all sizes and shapes played with the fingers or palms, or with wooden sticks, and an endless variety of bells, gongs, sticks, rattles. As well, there were *balafons* (ancestors of the xylophone) and *sanzas* (thumb pianos). Second in importance were stringed instruments including the *mvet* (harp-zither), *lutes* made of gourds or calabashes with strings, the *five-stringed harp*, and the *kora*, one of the most beautiful instruments in Africa, both visually and aurally, which consists basically of a sound-box (a large half calabash) , a neck, a large bridge and twenty-one strings (nineteen in Guinea). Wind instruments included whistles, male flute (longer), female flutes (shorter), and trumpets made from wood, ivory, or the horns of animals, but these were scarcer and only occasionally used.

The instrumentalists were usually men but singers and dancers could be anyone, man, woman, or child. In Africa, music was—and still is—a collective event and all bystanders participated by joining in song refrains, clapping hands, tapping feet, and entering dance rings whenever they wanted to.

The favorite singing style was, and still is, antiphonal, alternating modernity with improvised verses and tradition with unchanging refrains. The style is known as the call-and-response pattern, and it is also a foundation of African American music—improvised solos and unchanging refrains occur in all styles of jazz, blues, and gospel music.

African singers often used vocal effects, including falsetto, shouts, gasps, whispers, and moans; the same techniques are used by African American artists.

There are many types of African scales, but the most common were pentatonic and modal. It is still like that today in Africa.

In Africa, lyrics and melodies were improvised by soloists. But rhythm was usually more important than melody. The superimposition of different rhythms on each other was the rule, creating a polyrhythmic structure. In general, music-making, singing, and dancing were inextricably linked and always associated. Like music, dance was a way to communicate and ring dances were the most common practice.

It is essential to realize that the importance given to music and dance in Africa was reflected among black people in America in the songs they sang, in their dancing, and at their folk gatherings. So every aspect of jazz, blues, and gospel music is African to some degree.

Music in the Colonies and Independent America, Seventeenth to Nineteenth Centuries (till 1865)

When enslaved Africans arrived in the New World they were in chains, naked, separated from families and friends. They were barred from practicing their religion and following their traditions, and no music was allowed. But their minds were free and their music was alive and strong in their heads. As in Africa, they transmitted it to their children and grandchildren who did the same in successive generations. Gradually African American musical patterns emerged, took shape, and grew strong. Sources of information are colonial newspapers, town and court records, diaries, letters, missionary reports, journals, and the like.

In seventeenth-century rural America, music was mostly vocal, focused on church, where psalms were sung a cappella. But there was also instrumental music from fifes and drums in militia and marching bands.

In the eighteenth century, hymns superseded psalms in churches; dance music with violins and percussion was popular, performed in public houses in coastal towns such as New York, Baltimore, Boston, Savannah, New Orleans, and other places. In such towns, music conservatories were also established, and by the end of the century, concert music was popular.

Black musicians were highly valued. They were free men in the North, but remained as slaves in the South, where a tradition of "plantation songs" blossomed when black house servants on plantations were allowed to learn to play violins and/or harpsichord to entertain their masters: ". . . local blacks appear to have been involved in just about every aspect of musical experience available to local whites."[2] On special occasions, they played for other slaves dancing to win a piece of cake—the famous "cake walks," precursors of rags and ragtime, itself precursor of jazz.

Many African Americans fought in the Revolutionary War. A black battalion from Massachusetts, the "Bucks of America," was under the command of a black colonel, George Middelton, a violinist.

The era after the Revolutionary War brought freedom for large numbers of slaves in the North and the community of Free People of Color expanded. But black people in the South stayed as slaves and their only permitted music was work songs, sung in the fields as they tended cotton or tobacco. Change came around 1750, when slaves were admitted in churches and allowed to sing psalms, drawn from the Bible and set to music. These were gradually replaced by hymns—poems built around verses of the Bible, with melodies popular at that time, which started to spread after the First Religious Awakening of 1730. An early hymn writer whose work had strong appeal to African Americans was Isaac Watts, an English nonconformist pastor who in 1707 wrote a compilation of songs popular in England and in America. He had disciples in John Newton and John and Charles Wesley, who preached in private houses, on the street, and other outdoor places instead of waiting for people to come into churches. John Wesley had a methodical approach to the Bible and he was called a "Methodist," the name applied to his new denomination around 1730. From then on, the Baptist Church and the Methodist Church attracted a majority of African Americans (either slaves or free people of color). That is why the first black American music to appear as such was black religious music, and its development can be traced through several stages.

First step: The black church. Beginning in 1775, a movement for the establishment of separate black congregations quickly developed, initially among Baptist and Methodist churches but spreading quickly to Catholic and Presbyterian churches. It appeared first in the South, where black preacher George Liele (also Leile and Lisle) established the African Baptist Church in Silver Bluff, South Carolina, around 1775 before going to Savannah. In the North, it started with an African Methodist Episcopal (A.M.E.) Church in New York in 1787 and a Free African Society led by Richard Allen in Philadelphia, also in 1787. Allen published *A Collection of Spiritual Songs and Hymns selected from various Authors* in 1801, and became the first black bishop in America.

Second step: Independent black denominations. These blossomed at the end of the eighteenth century, led by the Black Baptist Church and the Black Methodist Church, which had black preachers and black congregations with their own rules and liturgy, although these did not differ significantly from their white counterparts. Zion A.M.E. Church in New York in 1796, Black Catholic churches (New York 1807), and Black Presbyterian churches (Philadelphia 1807) were quick to follow.

Third step: camp meetings. A Second Religious Awakening took place at the beginning of the nineteenth century, and extended outdoor religious services were held in fields and clearings. They lasted for days—up to a week—and attracted large crowds of people. The awakening was an interracial institution, but most of the participants were poor and illiterate; the campers had to sing from memory or learn songs during the meeting. At most meetings there was a small majority of blacks and their influence was great. Song leaders added improvised choruses and refrains to official hymns; they also introduced brand new improvised songs with repetitive stanzas and catchy tunes drawing on popular melodies of the time. These were called "tabernacle songs." Physical participation was also encouraged, and people would shout, gesticulate, clap hands, and even dance. This is the origin of the "ring shout": religious dance ceremonies reflecting African form and tradition held by black people after the camp meeting services were finished.

Fourth step: spiritual songs, as pre-Negro spirituals. After 1800, religious black songs began to appear as a distinct genre, covering spirituals, ring spirituals, running spirituals, and shout spirituals. Many black ministers encouraged the singing of these songs, and the performances reflected deep-rooted African traditions. It can be assumed that by just before the Civil War, the foundations had been laid for a characteristic African American folk music. African and European traditions were blended to produce a new style of music. Blacks went on singing African songs and performing African dances, but they learned psalms, hymns, and popular songs—including lullabies, ditties, plantation songs, and marches—from the white man. However, the new black folk music that came out of this was predominantly African in tone. Black religious music was ready to rise from the underground, but a big change in society was necessary. It came with the Civil War.

Politically, it is important to take note of the rise of abolitionist movements in the North. The international slave trade was declared illegal in 1807; this was partially ignored in the South until the first years of the Civil War. Slaves were emancipated in the Northern states in the early nineteenth century.

An American Antislavery Society was founded in 1833, organizing the "underground railroad" to help slaves escape from the South to the North and to Canada. Safe routes were created with guides, "stations" (in which to hide during the day), and station masters. Ex-slaves wrote songs, books, and articles in newspapers and magazines, gave lectures, and tried to make as many people as possible aware of the wretched fate of the slaves in the South and the injustice of their condition . . . and it worked.

From the War Years (1861–65) and the Emancipation Proclamation (1863) to World War I (1917): Pre-Blues and Blues

About 200,000 black men served the Union in the United States Colored Troops, and a couple of regiments were headed by black officers. Large numbers of black musicians served in fife and drum bands, gaining skills they would later use when they returned to civilian life.[3]

In the fall of 1862, President Lincoln issued a preliminary proclamation stating that from January 1, 1863, "all persons held as slaves within any State, or designated part of the State, the people whereof shall be in rebellion against the United States shall be then, thenceforward and forever free" and, in 1865, the Congress added the 13th Amendment to the Constitution abolishing slavery in all states. By the thousands, ex-slaves fled to urban areas South and North and to the plains of the West. But they were not welcomed, and within a few years many were back in the South, engaged in agricultural occupations as before. It had been rumored that each family would receive "40 acres and a mule," but this proved to be a lie. Many were trapped in the sharecropping system, under which the landowner provided land, tools, a mule, and food to a family whose responsibility was to raise crops. When the crop—usually cotton—was sold, a small share of the proceeds went to the workers in return for labor and the rest went to the landowner. It was a vicious system because the black worker virtually never made enough money to repay the cost of goods advanced to him, so his debt increased year after year, leaving him without any hope of clearing it. To escape this new form of slavery, many ex-farmers sought work in lumber and turpentine camps, on steamboats, in coal and iron mines, in factories, in ports as longshoremen, and on railroad gangs. The work songs from slavery times were augmented with new kinds of songs created in these various forms of employment. People who opted for itinerant lives as hoboes and tramps were easily arrested and sentenced to work without pay on levees and roads or on farm or in various industries. Many others were sentenced to prison and prison farms, where song styles were developed to ease the brutal workload. All of these work songs, from the farm, from the factories, and from the prison farms, were the precursors of blues.

Religious Songs

After the Civil War, several Negro institutes and colleges were built in the South and hundreds of black and white teachers came from the North to teach in them, from first grade to university level. Among the more successful were Fisk University in Nashville, Tennessee; the Hampton Institute in Hampton, Virginia; Rust College in Holly Springs, Mississippi; and the Tuskegee Institute in Alabama. To raise money to help develop their university, Fisk's administrators founded a choir with teachers and students. The Fisk Jubilee Singers' programs included hymns and spirituals and they went on tour, initially close to home, singing for cash that went to the university. Their audiences were strictly white, but they had great success and eventually toured the big cities of the US and Europe; they sang before Queen Victoria in London in 1871. Many colleges and institutes followed Fisk's example and sent cash-raising singing troupes on the road. In this way, the white world in the United States, Europe, and as far afield as Australia and New Zealand was introduced to the religious folksongs of black America, the Negro spirituals.

The spirituals sung to white audiences were performed a cappella or with harmonium or piano accompaniment. They were of a classical type, mostly inspired by Bible tests. The ensembles were small groups, singing sophisticated arrangements, without improvisation and with few African retentions, with the exception of the call and response pattern. The Fisk Singers sang in white churches and in concert halls. This style continued to be performed into the twentieth century and beyond by classical opera singers such as Marian Anderson and Paul Robeson before World War II, and more recently by Leontyne Price, Jessye Norman, Wilhelmina Fernandez, Barbara Hendrix, and others.

Jubilee Songs and Gospel Songs

Despite its success in white concert halls around the world, the Negro spiritual style of the Fisk singers and similar groups was not the only popular style among African Americans. In their churches, they followed the traditions of the camp meetings, and their songs had much stronger African influences. At the end of the nineteenth century, after a schism in the Baptist Church, Holiness and Sanctified churches blossomed in Black America. In 1895 the Reverend Charles H. Mason founded the Church Of God In Christ (C.O.G.I.C.) in Lexington, Mississippi, and moved it to Memphis in 1907. Mason's church freely adopted African traditions such as spirit possession, holy dancing, and speaking in tongues. The spirituals became jubilee songs with improvised verses, syncopation, and harmonization of voices, and their inspiration increasingly came from the Gospels of the New Testament. One of the most radical departures was that musical instruments were, for the first time, welcome in churches during services. Initially it was drums and percussion, then guitars, pianos, and sometimes complete jazz bands. This new style of religious music continued evolving until the early 1930s and with it came male "jubilee" groups such as the Dinwiddie Colored Quartet, one of the first black religious groups to make records (in 1902), the very popular Norfolk Jubilee Quartet, and the Birmingham Jubilee Quartet. Also performing the new music outside the church were itinerant evangelists including Blind Willie Johnson, Mother McCollum, Blind Joe Taggart, Sister Cally Fancy, Elder Curry, Bessie Johnson, Reverend Edward W. Clayborn, and many others. All of these were recording artists, but they were not the only religious stylists spreading the word through the new medium of phonograph records. Preachers, such as Reverends A. W. Nix, Emmett Dickinson, J. M. Gates, and F. W. McGee recorded abbreviated sermons, often leavened with snatches of song, and soloists such as C.O.G.I.C. pianist Arizona Dranes and Washington Phillips, with his ethereal accompaniment produced on two zithers, recorded a wide range of sacred song. Many blues and jazz artists also sang religious "gospel songs"; they included Louis Armstrong, Bessie Smith, Charley Patton, Blind Willie McTell, Big Bill Broonzy with the Chicago Sanctified Singers, Thomas A. Dorsey, and many others. All were denying the popular belief that no one could "straddle the fence" by singing secular music—the devil's music—and religious songs.

Thomas A. Dorsey made one of the more dramatic shifts from secular to sacred. He was a pianist and arranger in the band of Gertrude "Ma" Rainey (the Mother of the Blues) in the twenties, a barrelhouse pianist, and the partner of many bluesmen in the thirties. He paired with guitarist Tampa Red and they became the kings of "hokum blues," bawdy humorous songs with double-entendre lyrics. But religion had always been a strong part of Dorsey's life, and in the mid-1930s he ceased straddling the fence, dedicating his life to sacred music. He became a leading gospel composer, writing hundreds of songs and earning the title Father of Gospel Music. Dorsey's compositions set the rules for the new gospel music: religious words with beautiful and catchy melodies, enriched by the rhythms and structures of blues and jazz.

Blues

Work songs and the related prison songs, chain gang songs, hollers, whoops, water calls, arhoolies, ring shouts, and the like are precursors of the blues, the existence of which depended on several factors. These included access to instruments—guitars, banjos, harmonicas, pianos—freedom to travel, and contact with white styles of popular music. The development of blues was gradual, but without written information, we can assume that primitive forms of pre-blues appeared around 1885, mostly in the Deep South and predominantly in the state of Mississippi. But it was several more years before the famous AAB twelve-bar structure appeared, and when it did, one of its leading practitioners was Charley Patton (ca. 1887–1934), the Voice of the Delta who was the focal point of the conference held at the University of Liege in Belgium in March 1984 as a tribute to the greatest bluesman of his era and also as way to honor his death fifty years before.

The rest is history. Before World War II, up to seven blues styles were popular—the classic blues (black female singers with jazz bands or jazz piano players), three rural styles in the twenties (Mississippi blues, Texas blues, East Coast blues), three urban styles in the thirties (Memphis blues, St Louis blues, and Chicago blues). After World War II, more urban, rural, and regional styles developed in Chicago, California, Louisiana, New Orleans, Indianapolis, Kansas City, Houston, Austin, and elsewhere.[4]

Jazz

In its beginnings, jazz was strictly an instrumental style in which musicians tried to imitate human voice with wind instruments. Its forerunners included marches, which had been played by military and civil bands since the early days of colonization, and plantation songs from the eighteenth and nineteenth centuries, which were later transcribed for piano and led to ragtime music by the 1890s. By the end of the nineteenth century, black musicians had access to all kinds of instruments. They formed bands to play blues, spirituals, jubilee songs, gospel songs, cakewalks, rags, marches . . . and jazz was born. Later, the voice came into jazz bands as an extra instrument, and different styles continued to blossom until the present day . . . but that is another story.

Notes

I am grateful to Professor Eileen Southern for the insight she provided me during our discussions about the music of African Americans.

1. Francis Bebey, *African Music, A People's Art*, Lawrence Hill, 1975.

2. Nancy R. Ping, "Black Musical Activities in Antebellum Wilmington, North Carolina," *Black Perspective in Music* 8, no.2 (Fall 1980): 139.

3. Drum and fife bands, marching bands delivering instrumental music, have been popular in rural parts of Mississippi since the nineteenth century, and the tradition was still alive until recently in the hands of musicians such as Napoleon Strickland and Otha Turner. Both men are now deceased, but Otha's granddaughter, Sharde Thomas, is active today with her drum and fife band, playing occasionally with the North Mississippi All Stars; the two bands appeared together at the New Orleans Jazz & Heritage Festival in May 2014.

4. Robert Sacré, *Musiques Cajun, Creole et Zydeco*, Presses Universitaires de France, Que Sais-Je? no. 3010, 1995. Michael Tisserand, *The Kingdom of Zydeco*, Arcade Publishing, New York, 1998. Roger Wood and James Fraher (photos), *Texas Zydeco*, University of Texas Press, 2006.

Bibliography

Bascom, William. *African Folktales in the New World*. Urbana: Indiana University Press, 1992.

Beecher-Stowe, Harriet. *Uncle Tom's Cabin*. 1851; New York: Bantam, 1981.

Bergerot, Frank, and Arnaud Merlin. *L'Epopée du Jazz: a) Du Blues au Bop, b) Au-Delà du Bop*. Paris: Découvertes Gallimard,1991.

Boyer, Horace Clarence. *How Sweet the Sound: The Golden Age of Gospel*. Washington, DC: Elliott & Clark, 1995.

Buzelin, Jean. *Negro Spirituals et Gospel Songs—Chants d'Espoir et de Liberté*. Paris: Ed. du Layeur, 1998.

Charters, Samuel. *The Roots of the Blues: An African Search*. London: Quarter Books, 1982.

Collier, James. *The Making of Jazz: A Comprehensive History*. London: Papermac, 1981.

Darden, Robert. *People Get Ready: A New History of Black Gospel Music*. New York: Continuum International, 2004.

Epstein, Dena J. *Sinful Tunes and Spirituals: Black Folk Music to the Civil War*. Urbana: University of Illinois Press, 1977.

Evans, David. *Big Road Blues*. Berkeley: University of California Press, 1982.

Ferris, William. *Give My Poor Heart Ease: Voices of the Mississippi Blues*. Chapel Hill: University of North Carolina Press, 2009.

Haley, Alex. *Roots*, New York: Dell/Bantam, 1976.

Hamm, Charles. *Music in the New World*. New York: W.W. Norton, 1983.

Harris, Michael W. *The Rise of Gospel Blues: The Music of Thomas Andrew Dorsey in the Urban Church*. Oxford, UK: Oxford University Press, 1992.

Herzhaft, Gérard. *Le Blues*, Paris: Presses Universitaires de France, Que Sais-je no. 1956.

Hinson, Glenn. *Fire in My Bones: Transcendence and the Holy Spirit in African American Gospel*. Philadelphia: University of Pennsylvania, 2000.

King, Stephen A. *I'm Feeling the Blues Right Now: Blues Tourism and the Mississippi Delta*. Jackson: University Press of Mississippi, 2011.

Kubik, Gerhard. *Africa and the Blues*. Jackson: University Press of Mississippi, 1999.

Lomax, Alan. *The Land Where the Blues Began*. New York: Pantheon, 1993.

Lovell, John Jr. *Black Song: The Forge and the Flame: The Story of How the Afro-American Spiritual Was Hammered Out*. New York: Macmillan, 1972.

Marovich, Robert. *A City Called Heaven: Chicago and the Birth of Gospel Music*. Urbana: University of Illinois Press, 2015.

Martin, Denis-Constant. *Le Gospel Afro-Américain—Des Spirituals au Rap Religieux*. Paris: Cité de la Musique, Actes Sud, 1998 (+ CD).

Sacré, Robert. *Les Negro Spirituals et les Gospel Songs*. Paris: Presses Universitaires de France, Que Sais-Je? 2791, 1993.

Seck, Nago, and Sylvie Clerfeuille. *Les Musiciens du Beat Africain*. Paris: Les Compacts Bordas, 1993.

Sernett, Milton C. *Afro American Religious History*. Durham: Duke University Press, 1985.

Southern, Eileen, ed. *Readings in Black American Music*. 2nd ed. New York: W.W. Norton, 1983.

———. *The Music of Black Americans*. 3rd ed. New York and London: W.W. Norton, 1997.

Styron, William. *The Confessions of Nat Turner*. New York: Signet, 1966; in French, *Les Confessions de Nat Turner*, FOLIO 1425.

Turner, Steve. *An Illustrated History of Gospel (Gospel Music from Early Spirituals to Contemporary Urban)*. Oxford, UK: Lion Hudson, 2010. www.lionhudson.com.

Washington, Booker T. *Autobiography: Up from Slavery*. 1901; New York: Penguin Classics, 1986.

Young, Alan. *Woke Me Up This Morning: Black Gospel Singers and the Gospel Life*. Jackson: University Press of Mississippi, 1997.

The Mississippi Blues Tradition and the Origins of the Blues

—Arnold Shaw

Dating the beginnings of the blues is largely an exercise in conjecture and speculation since its origin is shrouded in the foggy days before recordings might have provided documentation. Moreover, as a rural folk art transmitted orally, the blues attracted musicologists later than the spirituals, which began to be notated during the years of the Civil War. Symptomatic is the contrast between *Slave Songs of the United States*, edited by William Francis Allen, Lucy McKim Garrison, and Charles Pickard Ware, which was published in 1867, as against the watershed collection of *Blues: An Anthology*, edited by William Christopher Handy, which appeared in 1926.

But I wish to put forth the idea that we can, with some measure of understanding, and perhaps accuracy, fix the likely beginnings of the blues by considering the psychology and sociology of the form. With this thought in mind I propose to examine the blues of Charley Patton, Son House, Bukka White, and Robert Johnson.

All are part, of course, of what is recognized as Mississippi Delta blues, a style fathered by Charley Patton, who was born in the 1880s, lived and worked on Will Dockery's plantation near Drew in the heart of the Delta, and became one of Paramount and Vocalion Records' leading artists from 1929 until his death in 1934. In a sense, Patton occupied the same charismatic position in the Delta of the 1920s and 1930s that Elvis Presley later did in the rock scene of the 1950s. Like Presley, Patton was a showman whose antics made him an in-demand performer on plantations, in country dance halls, at picnics, and at Saturday night whiskey balls.

Playing the guitar behind his back or over his head, twirling and tapping it, and dancing as he sang, may have made him look like a clown to Son House, one of his principal heirs, but audiences loved him. He had a large repertoire that embraced knife songs, church songs, frailed oldtime dance numbers and popular tunes of the day, all sung in a hoarse, chesty growl of a voice, loud enough to dominate noisy carousers. That he was a commanding figure is evident from the following he attracted among Delta bluesmen, a following that involved in varying degrees Bukka White, Son House, Robert Johnson (whose greatest debt was to Son House), Elmore James (whose inspiration was Robert Johnson), Howlin' Wolf (who literally sat at Patton's feet), and Muddy Waters, a group of bluesmen whose work led to the development of Chicago electric, ensemble blues from Mississippi downhome blues.[1]

Through the ubiquitous talent scout Henry Speir[2]—the John Hammond of his era—Patton began recording for Paramount in 1929 and put on wax some seventy titles, although only fifty-five of those were released before his death five years later. Although these included traditional folk blues, he documented these as well as his originals with details of place, people, and incidents that gave his work a distinctly local, often autobiographical character.

In "Tom Rushen Blues," whose title identifies a local deputy sheriff, we meet a Mr. Holloway and a Tom Day,[3] the latter a town marshal in Merigold who arrested him for drunkenness. In "High Sheriff Blues" liquor also figures in Patton's difficulties, only the scene is Belzoni in Humphreys County, where the sheriff was a Mr. Purvis, who apparently tried to arrange his release.

The floods of 1927 and 1930 provoked Patton's longest blues "High Water Everywhere" in which fear of the onrushing waters leads him to consider and to enumerate the various places to which he might flee—Greenville, Rosedale, Vicksburg, Tallahatchie County, etc. But the water keeps rising ominously, with "families sinkin' down," "fifty men and children, come to sink an' drown," "women and grown men down"—all leading to his crushing final line, "I couldn't see nobody home an' was no one to be found."

More significant than the localization marking Patton's blues is the personalization. "They run me from Will Dockery's," he states in "34 Blues," interweaving his own economic difficulties with those of the Great Depression scourge, which had "women and children flaggin' freight trains for rides." In "High Sheriff Blues" he explains that for him "thirty days seem like years in a jailhouse where there is no booze . . . It takes boozey booze, Lord, to carry me through . . ."

By contrast, when Bukka White is in jail, he does not miss booze. He misses his wife and children. In "Parchman Farm Blues," having indicated that the judge gave him life, he laments: "I wouldn't hate it so bad, but I left my wife and my home." In "Sleepy Man Blues" he describes himself as being "troubled in mind" but once again does not resort to alcohol, as Patton might have. What he wants, instead, is "to sleep all the time" for "he knows if he can sleep all the time, the trouble won't worry his mind."

Born Booker T. Washington White on November 12, 1909, Bukka White learned to sing in church, becoming acquainted with the guitar as a youngster through his father, who was a musician as well as a fireman on the M&O. Bukka spent his teens working on his uncle's farm or carrying water for local construction gangs. Unlike other boys of his age, his secret desire was someday to be as popular as Charley Patton, whom he saw at plantation shows. When he was just 20, he managed to cut fourteen sides for the Victor field studio in Memphis through a white Mississippian, Ralph Lambo, but only four numbers were released.

In the summer of 1937, according to confused reports, he shot a man.[4] Set free on bond, he traveled to Chicago for a September record session for ARC, arranged by producer-publisher Lester Melrose.[5] The two sides that were released sold so well that Melrose worked at getting White out of jail, a process that took two years. But in that period of separation from his family, unhappiness and deprivation at Parchman Farm, White wrote one of the most moving, introspective series of blues about prison life ever produced.

He recorded two songs when John A. Lomax visited the prison for the Library of Congress in May 1939 but did the bulk of the Parchman prison songs in March 1940, after his release. They appeared on the ARC labels OKeh and Vocalion.[6]

Seldom has the dismal sense of being a prisoner been communicated with such deep feeling as in his simple song, "I wonder how long 'fore I can change my clothes." Prison garb was obviously not too protective in the rain and cold. But more consequential was the feeling of shame—in "Walking down the road," he sings, "I could hardly walk with looking down on my clothes." And consider the touching poignance of his closing line: "Never will I forget that day when they taken my clothes, taken my civilian clothes and throwed them away."

Suffering from a fever, he laments the absence of his wife to comfort him— "they don't allow my lover to come and take my hand." But he also fantasizes: "they say it ain't the fever, just your lover has another man." And he concludes: "I want my lover to come and drive my fever away / (repeat) / Doctor says you do me more good than he would in all his days."[7] (Note the internal rhyme.)

Looking at himself in the mirror one day, he decides he is "looking funny in my eyes" and adds, "I believe I'm fixin' to die."[8] Acknowledging his awareness that he is born to die, what troubles him is the effect of his death on his children: "I hate to leave my children crying." He thinks back to his departure for prison and the tears shed for "so many nights" by his wife, "who treated me, children, like I was her baby child." And so in his imagination, he pleads with his wife:

Mother, take my children back
'fore they let me down
Ain't no use of them screaming and crying
on the graveyard ground.

Delta blues reached a high point of artistic beauty in the affecting simplicity of Bukka White's poetry, the result largely of the introspective character of his writing.

I like Peter Guralnick's comment: "White, an uncle[9] of B.B. King, put together one of the most emotionally compelling and moving autobiographical bodies of work, in many ways similar to that of Robert Johnson in its consciously thought-out lyrics, vocal intensity, and taut interplay between voice and guitar."[10]

The major research on Delta blues began in the 1960s. It was then that a number of dedicated students and aficionados of the form went searching and succeeded in locating then still living pioneers such as Skip James and Bertha Lee Patton. Son House was ultimately found in Rochester, New York, by a trio of researchers.[11] Their documentation of Son House's life and work was enhanced by an interview conducted by Julius Lester in 1965.[12]

Born Eddie James House, Jr., on March 21, 1902, on a farm outside of Lyon, a small town near Clarksdale, Mississippi, Son House was brought up in church. He told Lester: "didn't believe in anything else but church, and it always made me mad to see a man with a guitar and singing those blues and things." Nevertheless, his father, who vacillated in his dedication to the church, played bass horn in a little band that included his seven brothers and that entertained at Saturday night balls. Son House did not start playing guitar until he was 26 years old. The impetus came from a chance encounter with bottleneck guitarist Willie Wilson, who in a performance with another guitarist drew such a crowd that Son was overwhelmed. He went and bought himself an $11.50 guitar, which Wilson had to repair for him; and it was from Wilson that he learned his first tune: "Hold Up, Sally, Take Your Big Legs Offa Mine."

Two years later, Son House made his first recordings, through Charley Patton, who also brought him and Willie Brown up to Grafton, Wisconsin, for the Paramount Records date. He received $40.00 for the session. "Forty dollars!" he exclaimed in his interview with Julius Lester. "Making it that easy and quick! It'd take me near about a whole year to make $40.00 in the cotton patch. I was perfectly satisfied. I showed a whole lot with that when I got back to Lula, Miss."

Among the songs he recorded in the session were "Preachin' the Blues" and "Dry Spell Blues." The latter documented the suffering of southerners during a spell that "parched all the cotton and corn," driving people from door to door, forcing some to turn to making moonshine and rye—all at a time when pork chops were "forty-five cents a pound and cotton is only ten." The concluding stanza brought out the churchgoer in House, with his blues ending in a prayer:

> Oh, Lord, have mercy if you please
> Oh, Lord, have mercy if you please
> Let your rain come down and give our poor hearts ease.

House's comment to Lester on how easy and rewarding the $40 payment was, compared to picking and chopping cotton, made it clear that the spell of being a blues singer had taken hold at the time. But it was not a spell without stresses that persisted all through House's life. Samuel Charters cites an unnamed observer who remembered seeing Son in a performance with Charley Patton when "House got drunk and climbed up on a table to give a sermon."[13] Clearly, Son House was unable to resolve the conflict within himself between the "sinful" life of the bluesman and the spiritual rewards of the Christian life. He expressed the ambivalence at one point when he said: "I can't hold God in one hand and the Devil in the other."[14]

The inner turmoil found expression in one of the first songs recorded by House. In "Preachin' the Blues," whose very title would be ambivalent to staunch black churchgoers, House's initial thought is to be a preacher and bring religion to everybody. But then "the blues came 'long and they took my spirit away." Again, he is determined to kneel down in prayer but again the blues came walking "just like a man," forcing him to a new conflicting resolve: "I'm gonna preach these blues and choose my seat and sit down." He finishes with the hope that his listeners will react positively and "jump straight up and down."

Was ever a man trying to delude himself, knowing that for him the blues were antithetical to a deep-seated and irrevocable belief in the church? Thirty years after he recorded "Preachin' the Blues," House was still talking about his indecision. The patent anxiety and mental torment of his ambivalence contributed a heightened emotionalism to his work, characteristic of Delta blues at its best.

The bluesman who brought that tradition to a peak of autobiographical richness and poetic expressiveness was Robert Johnson, who died—was actually murdered—in his twenties. As a youngster, according to Son House (his major inspiration), Johnson would sneak out of a window against his parents' orders, go to where "Willie Brown and I were and sit down on the floor and watch from one to the other."[15] Then, when they went out for a break, he would snatch up a guitar and try feverishly to play it. Of the Delta bluesmen considered in this paper, Johnson recorded the fewest sides—a total of twenty-nine, produced in just five brief sessions, three in San Antonio in November 1936 and two in Dallas in June 1937. When producer John Hammond sought him for another session in 1938, he was already dead.

Just as little is known about his birth, birthplace, and early life, so his death is shrouded in mystery. "He was poisoned," according to Johnny Shines, "by one of those women who really didn't care for him at all.... That was down in Eudora, Mississippi.... And I heard that it was something to do with the black arts."[16] However, Son House heard three different accounts: in one, he was stabbed to death by a jealous husband; in another, stabbed by a woman; and in a third, that he had been poisoned.[17] Dying young, Johnson contributed to the romantic legend, alliteratively described by Peter Guralnick, of the artist "doomed, haunted, dead at an early age, desperate, driven—a brief flickering or tormented genius."[18]

With his limited output and abbreviated life, Johnson has exercised a degree of influence that underlines the awe in which he was held by his contemporaries and his "teacher," Son House. House told Lester: "The first one [of his records] I heard, was 'Terraplane Blues.' Jesus, it was good. We all admired it. Said, 'That boy is really going places!'"[19] And he did. His "Walking Blues" was one of the first songs learned by Muddy Waters. "I Believe I'll Dust My Broom" became Elmore James's theme and James named his group the Broomdusters. "Ramblin' on My Mind" was a Johnny Shines favorite.[20] It is said that rock artist Johnny Winter learned to play the guitar by an intensive study of Johnson's first album. Recovering from a nervous breakdown, the result of a broken love affair, British guitarist Eric Clapton adapted the melody of Johnson's "Love in Vain" to express his still intense love for Patti Harrison.[21] What accounts for this far-reaching impact is not only the power of Johnson's performance but also the immediacy of his poetry. Johnson's songs were introspectively autobiographical: the man who emerges from his blues is the weird, sexually driven, devil-hounded wanderer his contemporaries knew. A shy man who could not face a group of musicians he was asked to play for, he was completely uncontrolled in his aggressiveness toward women.[22] Son House said, "He'd go up to a girl he saw at one of the dances, and try to take her off, no matter who was around; her husband or boyfriend or anybody."[23] The number of girls mentioned in his songs hints at the reach of his sexuality. Beatrice in "Phonograph Blues," Thelma in "I Believe I'll Dust My Broom," Ida Bell in "Last Fair Deal Gone Down," and Bernice in "Walking Blues," whom he describes as having "Elgin movements from her head down to her toes."[24]

In "Terraplane Blues," an extended metaphor linking automotive elements to aspects of sex, is climaxed by a sensually erotic figure:

> I'm gonna get deep down in this connection,
> whoo-well keep on tangling with the wires
> And when I mash down on your little starter,
> then your spark plug would give me fire.

And is there a more extensively and expressly erotic blues than his "Traveling Riverside Blues," with its references to different girls in different places ("I've got womens in Vicksburg clean on in to Tennessee")?

> You can squeeze my lemon till the juice run down my leg
> (that's what I'm talking about now)
> But I'm going back to Friar's Point if I be rocking to my head

Driven by sex, which should, perhaps, not be surprising in a youth of Robert Johnson's years, he was haunted by the Devil. "Hounded" would be a more adequate word, and the Devil was almost a physical presence, not just imagined. Legend has it that Johnson, like Tommy Johnson before him, met a giant black man—the Devil—at a crossroad, who tuned his guitar and handed it back to him, possessed of magical power.[25] But Johnson was not just aided by the Devil; he was terrorized by him, as he sang in "Hellhound on My Trail": "Got to keep moving / I've got to keep moving . . . there's a hellhound on my trail." In "Me and the Devil Blues," he attributes his mistreatment of his sweet little rider to the Devil: "I'm going to beat my woman until I get satisfied." But he tries to console her: "You may bury my body down by the highway side / So my old evil spirit can get a Greyhound Bus and ride."

"I have to ride the blinds," Johnson sings in "Walkin' Blues." Harpist Walter Horton, who wandered with Johnson and Johnny Shines for a period of time, reported: "You couldn't run with Robert for long. He wouldn't stay in one place." To which Johnny Shines added: "If anybody said to him, 'Let's go,' it didn't matter to him where it was they were going; he'd just take off and go. It didn't matter either what time of day or night it was."[26]

The memories that Johnson's fellow bluesmen had of him were underlined in his own songs. He was a man in constant flight, driven by fears, real and imagined, unwilling or unable to elicit any response from women except in sex, paranoid in seeing enemies around him, blocking his passway with stones (as he says in one of his blues), always traveling a road "dark as night." It was a life of terror, but one that produced poetry with an emotional dimension and personal expressiveness unapproached by any of his contemporaries.

The format of classic blues is unique, involving twelve bars of music, arranged in three units of four bars each, with a chordal sequence of I, IV-I, V (or v⁷)-I, and made up of a three-line stanza (AAB). Additionally, the four-bar units generally incorporate a call-and-response pattern, with the melody employing bent notes, especially, the flatted 3rd and 7th of the diatonic scale. Apart from its unique form, the blues is noted for depth of emotion and subjectivity.

Although bluesmen have come from many southern states, the largest and most impressive group of blues singers came from Mississippi. In Delta blues, there was also the ultimate flowering of a personalized, localized style of expression. What has become evident from this brief glance at the work of four Delta bluesmen is that each has to one degree or another employed his songs as a chronicle of his experiences and each has emerged, however sketchily, as an identifiable individual. I would maintain that this type of self-description, self-exploration, self-projection was largely impossible for African Americans in the South until after the Civil War.

During the years of slavery, black folks were not only owned by the slave-holder, as horses and cattle were possessions, but they were attached to the land and part of a conclave in which they had no rights, no power, and literally, no existence as individuals. The children of slaves frequently did not even bear the surname or their fathers, but of the slave-holder. The average slave could not think of himself as "I," except, perhaps, on those rare occasions when out of reach and hearing of the white overseer. A cotton-picker could pretend to be singing but was actually "conversing" with a not-too-distant slave in a type of fragmented melody, later known as a "holler" or "arwhoolie." (And, of course, hollers are regarded as the most likely antecedents of the blues.)

It was not until the slave became self-dependent, not until the family unit superseded the communal structure of slavery, not until "we" became "I" that the door to personalized song was opened. This did not occur until sometime after the issuance of the Emancipation Proclamation and, more specifically, the adoption of the Thirteenth, Fourteenth, and Fifteenth Amendments between 1865 and 1870. These abolished slavery, and guaranteed blacks the rights of citizenship and the right to vote. All these constitutional amendments were adopted during the era of Reconstruction, sometimes also known as "the tragic era."

Now the slave was free—free to own land, free to move about, free to declare his preferences as an individual at the ballot box, free to choose his employer and place of employment, and free to take care of dependents. Can one conceive of the psychological change that occurred in African Americans as a result of this changed status? "Changed outlook" would be more a realistic term, since southern whites, through the Ku Klux Klan, through intimidation and violence, and through discriminatory legislation, sought to prevent blacks from exercising these rights.

As we know, blacks—then known as "freedmen"—were prevented from exercising those constitutional rights not just during the Reconstruction Era but for decades. Yet the potential existed. True, having never worked for wages and lacking finances, he might still be forced to become a sharecropper or tenant farmer, economics depriving him of some of the new freedoms. But now he had dependents, whereas once his dependents were not his but possessions as he was, housed, clothed, and fed as he was. With dependents, he was now the head of a family, facing, like adolescents of all times, the challenge and the fear of being self-sufficient, of making a life for himself, in short, of being an individual.

Was it not inevitable that, in this difficult period of adjustment, African Americans would begin ruminating about their new world, its promises and deprivations? Herein, I suggest, we have the beginnings of the expressiveness of the blues, a rural folk art during the latter decades of the nineteenth century until it exploded after the turn of the century in the incandescent personalized poetry of the Delta bluesmen and others.

W. C. Handy, who called his autobiography *Father of the Blues* and whose creativity as a musician and songwriter was critically affected by his accidental contact with crude, unnamed singers of what later became known as blues, mentions the years between 1892 and 1903 as those in which he first heard and was moved by the sound.[27] This time slot accords with my thought that the sociological and economic atmosphere of the Reconstruction Era, roughly 1867–77, initiated psychological changes in African Americans that found expression in folk blues and ultimately in the creative subjectivity of twentieth-century bluesmen.

Notes

1. Jeff Todd Titon, *Early Downhome Blues* (Urbana: University of Illinois Press, 1979), 56.

2. Samuel Charters, *The Bluesmen* (New York: Oak Publications, 1967), 44. See Peter Guralnick, *The Blues* (New York: Facts on File, 1982), 30–31.

3. Charters, 39.

4. Ibid., 103.

5. Guralnick, 65–66.

6. Charters, 103.

7. Ibid., 104.

8. Eric Sackheim, compiler, *The Blues Line* (New York: Schirmer Books, 1975), 242.

9. Bukka White and B.B. King are sometimes described as cousins or half-brothers. See Arnold Shaw, *Honkers and Shouters* (New York, Macmillan, 1978), 220. In an interview with Shaw, King referred to Bukka White as his cousin.

10. Guralnick, 36.

11. Charters, 38, 57–58.

12. Julius Lester, "Interview with Son House," *Sing Out* XV, 3 (1965): 38–45.

13. Charters, 57.

14. Son House, introduction to "Preachin' the Blues," concert at University of Indiana, November 1964. Reported by Julius Lester and cited by Charters, 65.

15. Charters cites Son House, 88.

16. Pete Welding, liner note, Robert Johnson, *King of the Delta Blues Singers vol.2*, Columbia C 30034. See also Frank Driggs, liner note, Robert Johnson, *King of the Delta Blues Singers*, Columbia CL 1654.

17. Charters, 99.

18. Guralnick, 34.

19. Julius Lester, op. cit. Cited by Charters, 89.

20. Charters, 95.

21. Arnold Shaw, *Dictionary of American Pop/Rock* (New York: Schirmer Books, 1982), 198.

22. Driggs, op. cit.

23. Arnold Shaw, *The World of Soul* (New York: Cowles, 1970), 34.

24. Sackheim, op. cit., 217.

25. Guralnick, 34.

26. Charters, 92.

27. William Christopher Handy, *Father of the Blues* (London: Sidgwick and Jackson, 1957), 71–72.

Charley Patton: The Conscience of the Delta

—David Evans

Charley Patton died on April 28, 1934, some three months after his final recording session. During the preceding five years he had become the most extensively recorded of the early Mississippi folk blues artists, leaving behind a legacy of fifty-two issued songs as well as accompaniments of other artists.

Patton was the first recorded black folk artist to make it a frequent practice to comment in his songs directly and extensively on public events that he had personally witnessed or participated in, and to treat incidents in his own life as *news*. He was also the first recorded black folk artist to mention white people from his own community in his songs, sometimes unfavorably. He did all of this while continuing to live his life in the Mississippi Delta, a region that featured perhaps the most rigid racial caste system in the entire nation.[1]

Charley Patton was almost certainly born between 1885 and 1891, probably in 1885 or 1886, making him more or less a younger member of the first generation of folk blues singers, the originators of this genre. His contemporaries among blues recording artists included Huddie Ledbetter (Lead Belly), Frank Stokes, Gus Cannon, Henry "Ragtime Texas" Thomas, Jim Jackson, and Joshua "Peg Leg" Howell, all of whom, like Patton, displayed repertoires that contained, in addition to blues, such items as ragtime songs, dance tunes, folk ballads, versions of popular songs, and spirituals.

It is known that Patton himself learned some of his music from other artists who were a few years older. He is nevertheless the earliest Mississippi blues artist about whom we have a large body of information, even though much of it comes from the last five years of his life during which he made his recordings. He was extraordinarily influential on other Mississippi blues artists and was a role model in both music and lifestyle for many of them. Among the artists he is known to have influenced or inspired are Willie Brown, Tommy Johnson, "Son" House, Bukka White, Big Joe Williams, Howlin' Wolf, David "Honeyboy" Edwards, and Roebuck "Pops" Staples. Bukka White, a great

Bessie Turner (left) and Viola Cannon (right), 1967.
(Photograph by Marina Bokelman)

Tom Cannon and wife, Cleveland, MS, 1985. (Photograph
by Robert Sacré)

Mississippi blues artist eighteen or more years Patton's junior, recalled saying as a child that he wanted "to come to be a great man like Charley Patton."[2] White was not alone in his respect for the man. It is probably fair to say that Charley Patton is the only black person of his generation to live virtually his entire life in Mississippi who still has a national and international impact and whose name and accomplishments are known to many outside his immediate family and community well over a century after his birth and more than eighty years after his death.

The purpose of this essay is to elucidate certain aspects of Patton's life and personality. It does not purport to be a full-scale biography but is instead mainly concerned with matters of personality and with reaching an understanding of the social context of Patton's life and music. It is based largely on the internal evidence in Patton's songs that contain biographical details and allusions and on interviews with his relatives and associates, particularly his sister Viola Cannon, his niece Bessie Turner, his nephew Tom Cannon, two of his children, and Tom Rushing, a figure in one of his songs.[3] By assessing these sources of information and reassessing previously published information and opinions about Patton, I shall attempt to determine whether Patton was aware of his potential to communicate outside his immediate community and across barriers of time, class, race, and region, and whether he was indeed consciously trying to communicate anything.[4]

Previously published accounts of Charley Patton's life, character and personality have been based on the evidence of his records as well as interviews with fellow blues artists (especially "Son" House), friends, relatives, ex-wives, and girlfriends. The first publication to give much significant information about Patton was a booklet by Bernard Klatzko published in 1964 as the notes to a reissue album of some of Patton's recordings.[5] Klatzko obtained his information during a brief field trip to the Delta in 1963 with fellow researcher Gayle Dean Wardlow. Although their interviews of a number of Patton's relatives and friends were brief and superficial and contained some information that has later been called into question, Klatzko was nevertheless able to piece together an outline of Patton's life that served as a useful starting point for further research. As for Patton's lifestyle and personality, Klatzko revealed that he was popular with women and had married several times, was fond of drinking liquor, and tended to be argumentative. Klatzko also revealed that Patton traveled constantly and was well known in Mississippi, especially in the area between Clarksdale and Vicksburg. His home base appeared to have been Dockery's plantation a few miles east of Cleveland, where his parents lived, but he was also well known around his boyhood home near Bolton, and in Vicksburg, Greenville, Merigold, Lula, Clarksdale, and a host of other

Bertha Lee Patton. (Samuel and Ann Charters Archives, Archives &
Special Collections, University of Connecticut Library)

towns including Holly Ridge, where he died. A subsequently discovered pho
tograph showed Patton as having a rather light complexion and curly hair,
clearly the product of a mixed racial ancestry. Based on the evidence of Patton's performing style on his records, Klatzko speculated that the artist felt
some sense of outrage, stating, "It must have seemed strange to a man like
Patton who looked little different from white men to be relegated to a second
class status. At any rate, Charley's outrage, whatever sparked it, was released
in the blues."[6] Later researchers have largely ignored this speculation or tried
to paint a portrait of Patton as a carefree entertainer.

About the time that Klatzko presented the first factually based outline of
Charley Patton's life, "Son" House was rediscovered. House had known Patton for the last four years of Patton's life and was a Mississippi blues artist of
comparable stature to Patton. House clearly found some of Patton's character
traits hard to comprehend or annoying. He told Stephen Calt and Nick Perls
in an interview published in 1967 that Patton was argumentative, far from
generous with his money, unable to read and write, and careless about his
music, preferring to clown for the audience rather than take care to structure his songs coherently.[7] In an article published in the same magazine issue

as House's interview, Gayle Dean Wardlow and Stephen Calt (writing under the pseudonym of Jacques Roche) proclaimed House's assertions as facts and painted an unflattering portrait of Patton as illiterate, self-centered, a drunkard, a glutton, and a hustler of women who was unfaithful to his wife.[8]

In that same year Samuel Charters, drawing upon Klatzko's booklet as well as an interview with Patton's last wife Bertha Lee, presented a more favorable image of Charley Patton and tried to interpret the meaning of some of his songs.[9] Stephen Calt, however, soon returned to the offensive. In the notes to the then most widely circulated reissue album of Patton's recordings, Calt asserted that Patton "never learned to read or write and passed most of his time . . . in total idleness," that he was a "perpetual squabbler," "extraordinarily tight with money," always courting women and entering sham marriages with them, beating his wives, and "eating out of the white folks' kitchen." Calt added that Patton was "reportedly disavowed" by his daughter from one of his marriages.[10]

In 1970 the first book-length study of Charley Patton's life and music was published. The author, John Fahey, mainly tried to assemble already known facts into a coherent account of Patton's life.[11] Although Fahey actually did some fieldwork in Mississippi as early as 1958, most of his information was supplied by Bernard Klatzko, Gayle Dean Wardlow, and myself. Fahey did subsequently interview a number of other musical figures who knew Patton, including apparently Bertha Lee, Patton's last wife, and Sam Chatmon, who claimed to be Patton's brother. Fahey mentioned Patton's drinking and fighting but did not dwell on these topics. His life history attempted to be factual rather than anecdotal. He did, however, suggest that Patton did not have a particularly profound personality or sensitivity to the world around him. He constantly asserted that Patton was first and foremost an "entertainer" and had a "limited picture of the world."[12]

In the notes to another important reissue album of Patton's recordings, Don Kent mentioned briefly that Patton had a reputation of being a braggart, a tightwad, a clown, and someone who was drunk and rowdy, but Kent preferred to concentrate on Patton's awesome musical talent and genius.[13] A more sympathetic portrait of Patton appeared in Robert Palmer's *Deep Blues*.[14] It was based primarily on Patton's recordings and previously published information as well as new information gained from Joe Rice Dockery, the owner of the plantation on which Patton's family lived, and from several musicians who had learned from Patton, including Hayes McMullen, Howlin' Wolf, and Roebuck Staples. Palmer also drew upon information that I supplied from a 1979 interview of Patton's niece Bessie Turner.[15] Even when discussing Patton's drinking and his less than tender treatment of women, Palmer attempted to see Patton's life in the context of the era and the social system in which he lived. He stated:

> Charley Patton saw a world of changes during the fifty-odd years of his life, but the system was in effect in the upper Delta before he was born, and it outlasted him by several decades. He adapted to it well enough despite his lingering rage, which he tended to take out on his women, sometimes by beating them with a handy guitar. He suffered his dark moods and his occasional repentances and conversions, but he also had fun, or something like it. He rarely worked for whites except to furnish a night's entertainment, and he was never tied to a menial job or a plot of land for very long. He went where he pleased, stayed as long as he pleased, stayed as intoxicated as he pleased, left when he wanted to, and had his pick of the women wherever he went.[16]

The positive effect of Palmer's treatment of Charley Patton was considerably offset by two subsequent works that dealt with this artist, the first being a screenplay by Alan Greenberg about the life of Delta bluesman Robert Johnson.[17] In two fictionalized scenes, based largely on the writings of Calt and Fahey, Greenberg depicts Patton as preaching a comic sermon, drinking furiously, dancing lewdly, talking dirty, fighting with his wife Bertha Lee, who cuts his throat, being dragged off unconscious, later playing music at a riotous house party unconcerned about a murder that has just taken place there, and finally being bested in a musical competition by an upstart Robert Johnson. In another scene Patton has died, and his funeral degenerates into a drunken tribal dance. The overall picture of Patton's character is negative in the extreme, and if the screenplay is ever made into a film, it will do permanent damage to Patton's reputation.

The second of these more recent works is a 1988 book-length treatment of Patton's life and music by Calt and Wardlow, which, while containing much valuable research and analysis, perpetuates the image of Patton as a degenerate sociopath.[18] My original 1987 published version of the present essay was not available to the authors when they wrote their book, nor did I have access to most of their research, which was far more extensive than what they had published in earlier writings. Thus there are substantial differences in our accounts of Patton's life, our interpretations of his life and music, and our assessments of his personality. Both of our accounts of his life are based largely on the oral testimonies of people who knew him, supplemented by the few contemporary official documents that exist, such as census entries, death certificates, and marriage records. Calt and Wardlow mostly relied on fellow musicians and acquaintances, while I relied more on Patton's family members.

While many of Calt and Wardlow's informants knew Patton only briefly or superficially and therefore might be unreliable, there is also the possibility that family members who were around him over an extended period of time might have given accounts distorted by bias in favor of one of "their own." I will not attempt to resolve the differences in our accounts here and leave that task instead to a future biographer of Charley Patton. Calt and Wardlow also included in their book a lengthy critique of my own previously published discussions of Patton as a "folk" or "traditional" blues artist.[19] In my defense, I can simply say that if I did appear in those writings to overemphasize Patton's musical connections and similarities to other blues artists, it was because I was discussing the community of musicians in which he participated and how they handled shared musical and lyrical material. Naturally, artists who participate in a shared tradition can also exhibit individuality, originality, and creativity, and there were, in fact, plenty of these traits in Patton's music. The present article concentrates more on Patton the individualist and balances my earlier treatments of him as a traditionalist. He was, in fact, both a folk musician and a creative artist.

Much else has been written about Charley Patton since the late 1980s, but little of it contains new biographical information or is based on new or previously unpublished interviews. It is thus mostly interpretation and speculation or the reworking of older published material. It is not my purpose to evaluate this literature here except when it contains new information about Patton. I do, however, want to call attention to Alex van der Tuuk's recent (2017) *The New Paramount Book of Blues*, which contains much information on Patton and several of his musical associates, derived especially from public records.[20] I have used his research to modify or correct a few of my own findings.

Many writers have discussed the musical stylistic characteristics of various recorded performances of Charley Patton or transcribed and commented upon lyrics of some of his songs. Fahey attempted to do this in a comprehensive manner for all of Patton's then-extant recordings. While writers like Charters and Palmer have tried to find serious meaning in Patton's song texts, there has been another strain of criticism attempting to show that Patton's songs were often garbled and incoherent and that the artist was merely providing casual entertainment and not attempting to transmit a serious message or meaning. While there are admittedly difficulties in transcribing some of Patton's texts and while some criticism of his compositional technique may be justified, it would appear that the negative view of Patton's lyricism, like the negative view of his character, is based largely on an interpretation and exaggeration of some remarks made by Patton's fellow bluesman "Son" House. House sang with fairly precise diction, his pieces generally maintained consistent musical structures, and his songs display consistent and extended thematic development over several verses or even in their entirety, giving an impression of some degree of lyrical stability and prior rehearsal. House was critical of Patton for not maintaining these same standards in his compositions, saying:

> It's a lot of little foolish songs . . . Charley, he'd try to make a record out of anything, you know, 'cause he'd love to clown . . . "Yeah baby" (imitates Patton) . . . and a lotta kinda funny stuff like that . . . He'd name the record anything . . . , you know, to get away with it . . . He'd take all them old foolish songs and things . . . some of them would sound alright . . . some of them had a meaning to them . . . some didn't. That's the way he played. He'd just say anything, the first thing he could think of . . . "Heh baby" (imitates Patton) "Aw sho" . . . and all that old kind of funny stuff . . . We often . . . tell him, too. Say, "Charley, you outta stop so much that ol' foolish messin' around." (imitates Patton)—"Oh Man, all I want to do is get paid for it. What's the difference?"[21]

Based on House's remarks and his own attempt to decipher some of Patton's recorded lyrics, Stephen Calt characterized the artist as being frequently incoherent and prone to garbling.[22] The most devastating criticism of Patton's lyricism, however, came from John Fahey, who noted the "disconnection, incoherence, and apparent irrationality" and "stanzaic disjunction" in many of Patton's songs, stating that "various unrelated portions of the universe are described *at random*." "Son" House was again quoted, saying, "Charley could make up so many different, foolish monkey junk pieces . . . A lot of Charley's words, . . . you can be sitting right under him . . . you can't hardly understand him."[23] Fahey furthermore trivialized any message that might be contained in Patton's songs, stating, "It is not characteristic of Patton to brood textually for more than a verse or two about his internal feelings regarding women or anything else."[24] Patton was viewed as a mere entertainer with no social message. Fahey stated, "Delta blacks had experienced the 1927 flood of the Mississippi River and probably found Patton's description of his involvement in it quite entertaining. They had experienced the drought of 1928 and 1929 and again were probably entertained by Patton's description of what he and other 'citizens 'round Lula' (in *Dry Well Blues*) did about it."[25] Finally, Patton was portrayed as a man narrowly interested in himself with a limited view of the world:

> If we search Patton's lyrics for words expressive of profound sentiments directly caused by this particular cotton-economy, or for words expressing a desire to

transcend this way of life, if we search for verses of great cultural significance depicting any historical trend or movement, or aspiration to "improve the lot of a people," we search in vain. Such a search would not be fruitful with any blues-singers. Patton could, of course, only sing about his own limited experience. He had a very narrow view of the world. And there was perhaps no intellectual climate available to Patton for the development of significant thoughts or comments about his and his people's status.

Patton was an *entertainer*, not a social prophet in any sense. He had no profound message and was probably not very observant of the troubles of his own people. He was not a "noble savage." Least of all did he try to express the "aspirations of a folk." His lyrics are totally devoid of any protesting sentiments attacking the social or racial *status quo*.[26]

There is, at least, a general agreement among all of the writers on Charley Patton that he was someone important. The known facts about Patton's life and personality, however, have led some of these writers to depict him as a boorish character, constantly arguing, vain, exploitative of women, lazy, frequently drunk, and concerned only with himself. The world has known many great artists who displayed some or all of these characteristics, but almost all such artists also had some special sensitivity to life or their environment that was responsible for their greatness. This sensitivity may have been frustrated, resulting in antisocial or self-destructive behavior, but, frustrated or not, it found expression in art. Those writers who have painted such a negative picture of Patton's character have failed to find much, if any, redeeming sensitivity in the man, and some have even found fault with his art, criticizing him for a kind of sloppiness consistent with his alleged personality. In their view, his greatness, such as it is, is ascribed largely to his role as a consummate entertainer. His recorded musical legacy might contain flashes of brilliance and originality and is to be enjoyed, perhaps even laughed at. It is worth describing and analyzing because it provides a rare and extended glimpse of the music of the first generation of blues performers, but neither Patton nor his music are to be taken too seriously, and we should not look at either beyond the surface. He was an outstanding and innovative musician, but one who primarily entertained dancers with functional music at raucous "frolics."

In the following pages I will introduce new information and interpretations of Charley Patton and his music in an attempt to reveal something of his special artistic sensitivity and thereby to help redeem his reputation as an artist who was serious about his work and whose work should be taken seriously. I do not intend to view him as a saint or to deny the possibility of fault in his work, nor do I downplay the fact that much of his music, including many of his recordings, was created wholly or partly on the spot at the time of performance and was not meant to be taken as his final statement on anything. But I believe it will become clear that many of the criticisms of the man and his work are unfounded, exaggerated, or based on misinterpretations of historical facts, the statements of others who knew him, or Patton's songs. Much will remain unknown about this man and his art, but I hope that the present study may help to lead readers to seek that greater understanding.

There is uncertainty about Charley Patton's date of birth and the proper spelling of his name. According to the 1900 United States Census, the earliest document to mention him, Patton was born in April 1891. But in his September 12, 1908, application to marry Gertrude Lewis, signed by his mark (X), he swears that he is over the age of twenty-one. The August 10, 1917, birth certificate of his daughter Rosetta lists his age as thirty-two. His September 12, 1918, draft registration card lists his date of birth as July 12, 1885, but his age as thirty-four, which would make him even older. We can be reasonably certain that this information came from Patton himself, but it is not uncommon among African Americans to give an age in years that one will reach on the next birthday. On his April 1934 death certificate his age is given as forty-four by an informant who was not a family member. His sister Viola stated in 1963 that Charley was born in 1887, but she listed her own birthdate as January 22, 1887, on her Social Security application, and in the 1900 US Census she is listed as born in January 1887. In 1979 Viola's daughter Bessie Turner stated that Charley was eleven months older than Viola, which would mean that he was born ca. February 1886, but in 1967 she stated that Charley was about two years older than Viola. All of these accounts yield a span of years from 1884 to 1891 for Patton's birth. In my opinion the most likely period is 1885–86, as that period is suggested by information supplied by Patton himself. The information in the 1900 census, in which he is listed as born in April 1891, appears to be an error on the part of either the census taker or the informant for the Patton family. Possibly one or both of them became confused and the information pertains to a sibling, who might have been born in 1891 and died not too long after 1900.

It is not known whether Patton's name was spelled Charley or Charlie. Both spellings occur on the labels of his records and even on his death certificate. There are no documents that would absolutely clarify the issue. The name is spelled Charlie in the 1900 census. If a 1910 census entry in Bolivar County is this same person, he is listed there as Charlie Patter (*sic*), twenty-four years of age. The 1917 birth certificate of his daughter Rosetta lists his name as Charley. His 1918 draft registration card lists him as Charley, but his signature there is Chas. On six marriage applications filed between 1908 and 1926 at the Bolivar and Sunflower County courthouses his name is twice written as Charlie, Chas, and Charles. In a 1934 list of witnesses at the Humphreys County courthouse his name is written as Charles. In all cases except the signature, which is the only one currently known to exist, these names were recorded by white court clerks or other officials, who may have used their own preferred spellings without asking Patton or another informant. The occurrence of Charles and its standard abbreviation Chas in some documents indicates that his given name at birth was Charles, but it would appear that early in life he became known as Charley or Charlie. In this essay I use the spelling Charley, which was found on the Paramount records that first introduced his name to the world.

There is no uncertainty about Patton's place of birth and earliest home. All sources are in agreement that it was near Bolton, Mississippi, which lies about midway between the cities of Vicksburg and Jackson. He was very likely born on the Herring plantation, southeast of Bolton in the direction of Raymond. His parents were Bill and Annie Patton. Blues artist Sam Chatmon, who was born and raised in the same rural community as Charley Patton, claimed that Charley was his "brother," stating that they both had the same father, Henderson Chatmon. Sam was supported in this claim by some other members of the Chatmon family. Possibly Annie Patton had once been the wife or girlfriend of Henderson Chatmon and even had children by him, but the longstanding stability of the Patton family, including the marriage of Bill and Annie Patton, argues strongly for Bill Patton being Charley's father. In any case, Charley remained close to Bill Patton, and there is no suggestion among Charley's surviving relatives that Bill was not Charley's father.[27]

William (Bill) Patton and Annie Martin filed a marriage application at the Hinds County courthouse in Raymond, Mississippi, on December 5, 1882, and were married two days later.[28] According to their granddaughter Bessie Turner, they subsequently had nine daughters and three sons. All but two of the girls died in infancy or childhood, including one who was burned to death in a fire. Of the remaining children Katie (Katherine) was the oldest (b. March 1884), followed by Charley (probably b. 1885–86), Viola (b. January 1887), William (also known as Will, Willie, "Son," and "Buster," b. January 1895),[29] and a brother known as "C" Patton, possibly originally named James, who was evidently born after the 1900 census was taken, probably in 1901. A sister Etha was born in August 1899 but apparently died at a young age.

Family members described Charley's mother Annie Patton as a short, brown-skinned woman with straight hair, of partial Indian ancestry. Charley's daughter Rosetta was told that she looked very much like Annie Patton. According to the 1900 US Census, Annie was born in Mississippi in January 1862. Her grandson Tom Cannon stated that she died before Charley (1934) at

Beaver Bayou east of Merigold and was taken to Bolton for burial. Charley's daughter Rosetta, however, dated Annie's death earlier, around 1918 or 1919. The lyrics of Charley's "Screamin' and Hollerin' the Blues" (Paramount 12805), recorded June 14, 1929, suggest that his mother was still living at the time. His "Troubled 'Bout My Mother" (Vocalion 02904), recorded February 1, 1934, suggests that she was dead by that time. Tom Cannon stated that Annie's father was named Grandeville Martin and that he moved to Dockery Farms for a time but returned to the Bolton area and died there. He was listed in the 1920 census as living alone near Raymond at the age of eighty-four. Besides his daughter Annie he had at least two sons, Jim (b. 1890) and Sherman (b. January 12, 1900). The latter was raised by the Pattons on Dockery Farms and was sometimes known as Sherman Patton. Sherman was thus considerably younger than his sister Annie and had a different mother.

According to the 1900 census, Charley's father Bill Patton was born in Mississippi in March 1864. Tom Cannon stated that he died in 1927 or 1928 in a hospital in Vicksburg, where he had been taken, and that he was buried in Vicksburg. Charley's daughter Rosetta thought he died around 1920, but testimony from other older family members suggesting a later date seems more reliable. He was a very large man weighing about 350 pounds (ca. 114 kg.) and was described by his grandchildren as having a "bright" or "red" complexion.

According to family tradition, Bill Patton's father was a white man from Vicksburg, also named Bill Patton, who was "married" to a "black Indian" woman named Rose. Here it should be noted that the latter expression does not necessarily mean that Rose was especially "black" in complexion, but merely that she was descended from a mix of African and Indian ancestors. Very likely one or more of her ancestors had been slaves in a Native American family in the South. After Emancipation in Mississippi in the 1860s, whether she formerly had been a slave or not, she and any children she had would have been officially classified as Negro. An interracial marriage between the white Bill Patton and the "black Indian" Rose might have been possible in Reconstruction-era Mississippi, but a long-term relationship without a formal marriage could also have been viewed by them or by others as a "marriage," especially by family members on the "black" side of the relationship. Charley's father is said to have had two sisters, one named Mag who was married to a man named Dick Barnes, and the other named Lucy, both of whom lived at Bolton, and possibly one or more brothers. Tom Cannon stated that the younger Bill Patton had two younger brothers named Walter and "X" Patton and that both moved to Dockery Farms and were later killed in separate incidents as a consequence of "fooling with other men's wives." It is not certain whether all or any of these sisters and brothers were children of the same parents or whether they were half-siblings or step-siblings. It has not been possible to trace Charley's father in the 1870 US Census, but he is almost certainly the William Patton, "black" and aged fifteen, listed in the 1880 census living at Bolton as a "stepson" in the family of Thomas and Isabella Jones and their five children, Mary B., Anna B., Walter, Addie, and James. Walter Jones might be one of the "brothers" that Tom Cannon recalled. It is perhaps not surprising that, as the child of a racially mixed couple in post-Reconstruction Mississippi, Bill Patton would have been raised by a black family.

According to Patton family tradition, the elder Bill Patton and Rose lived on the edge of the National Military Cemetery in Vicksburg and between 1866 and 1868 were employed in the exhumation and reburial in cemetery plots of the 18,000 Union soldiers who had died in the 1863 Civil War battle there. The elder Bill Patton is said to have lived until ca. 1915 or 1920 and often visited his children and grandchildren, including Charley. Rose is said to have died in Vicksburg in 1926. She was also very close to her children and grandchildren. In view of other evidence presented below, however, it appears doubtful that either of Charley's grandparents actually lived this long.

It has not been possible to identify positively either the elder Bill Patton or Rose. Their names do not occur together in any census, nor are they listed in any records available at the National Cemetery in Vicksburg. There is an interesting entry, however, in the 1860 United States Census that might help identify them. At that time there were separate enumerations for the free and slave populations. In precisely the same neighborhood where we find the family of Bill and Annie Patton in 1900, there is listed in the 1860 free (i.e., white) census a W. D. Patton. He is described as thirty-seven years old, born in Georgia, and married to Mary S. Patton, aged thirty-five and born in Tennessee. They had five-year-old twin sons, W. D. Patton, Junior, and Robert C. Patton, both born in Mississippi. W. D. Patton owned real estate valued at four hundred dollars and had a personal estate valued at five thousand, four hundred dollars. He was the overseer of a plantation owned by W. Hal Smith, forty-one years old and born in Maryland, whose real estate was worth twenty-six thousand dollars and personal estate worth seventy-one thousand dollars. Smith owned sixty-three slaves living in fourteen slave houses. He had lived there in 1850, when his holdings were approximately the same, sixty-five slaves. W. D. Patton did not live there in 1850. In 1860 W. D. Patton owned one female black slave, aged forty, and one female mulatto slave aged eight. These were very likely a mother and daughter. The actual names of slaves were not recorded in the census. It is possible that W. D. Patton was William "Bill" Patton, Charley Patton's white grandfather, and his female slave was Rose. In turn, the mulatto girl might have been a child of W. D. Patton and his female slave. Although W. D.

Patton had a white wife and two sons, such extramarital liaisons with slave women were quite common. The area around Bolton was occupied by Union soldiers before the fall of Vicksburg, which occurred on July 4, 1863. Bill Patton, Charley's father, was born in March 1864. Possibly W. D. Patton and his wife had separated during the confusion of the war and Patton remained with his newly freed black slave or with another former slave woman. If this was the case, W. D. Patton appears to have reunited with his white wife Mary by 1870, as a William and Mary Patton are listed in that year's census as living in Raymond with their four children. Strangely, William's age is given as 34, perhaps a mistake for 54, while Mary is 43. Their children are William (15), Robert (13), Martha (11), and Charles (3). Despite the discrepancies in ages in the two censuses, this is undoubtedly the same family. In the 1880 census W. D. Patton is still at Raymond, described as a mail carrier, aged 66, born in Georgia to Irish immigrants, with his wife Mary, aged 55, and their son Charlie, aged 12. In fact, W. D. Patton had resided in Raymond since 1865 and between 1867 and 1886 operated a hack service from Cooper's Well through Raymond to Bolton and back, transporting passengers, mail, and freight. Such an occupation could easily have provided opportunities for him to maintain an extramarital relationship. In 1885 he entered the undertaking business in Raymond and before that had dabbled in livestock and local politics. In 1869 he was listed as a member of the National Union Republican Party of Hinds County. The fact that W. D. Patton had a contract with the post office might represent a continuation of federal government employment that had begun around 1866 with work at the National Military Cemetery in Vicksburg. The possibility that W. D. (William) Patton was Charley Patton's paternal grandfather is reinforced by the fact that one of Charley's nephews, a son of his sister Viola Cannon, was named W. D. Cannon (1925–1992). Although his full name was Willie Dockery Cannon and he was named after the owner of the plantation where the Patton and Cannon families lived, he was commonly known simply as W. D. (or "Double-D") Cannon. The name Charles for one of W. D. Patton's white sons could suggest that this name also was passed down in the "black" Patton family, which in turn could suggest that Bill Patton, Charley's father, retained some sense of identity and closeness to his white relatives and transmitted this sense of identity to his own children and grandchildren. W. D. Patton's age (born between 1814 and 1823) and his confirmed death in 1892, however, make it impossible that he survived into the twentieth century.[30]

Charley Patton was about five feet and seven inches in height (ca. 1.7 m.) and weighed between 135 and 160 pounds (61–72.5 kg.) in adult life. He had light brown complexion and curly hair, which he may have oiled. Beatrice Giddens, a lifelong resident of Lula, Mississippi, born in 1909, who knew Patton from around 1916 to the early 1930s, gave the following vivid description of him: "He was a handsome man. He had a light complexion. He wasn't no real dark person. I guess he was about five [feet]—six [inches]. And he was light brownskin. His face was full, but he had clean teeth at the time I knew him. He had kind of dark, sandy hair, but he would have a nice haircut. He said he had Indian in him."

Charley's brother Will was lighter in complexion and heavier in weight like his father. His sister Katie was also large and of light complexion, like her father. Her nephew Tom Cannon described her as "a great big fat Christian woman." Charley was closest in appearance to his sister Viola. Some writers have asserted that Charley Patton was virtually indistinguishable from a white man. This is hardly the case, as any serious look at his one undoubtedly authentic extant photograph reveals.[31] Nevertheless, his physical features were perplexing to many who saw him. Howlin' Wolf, who began his musical career as a disciple of Charley Patton, likened him to a Mexican. Patton's friend Seabron Holloway once asked him if he was kin to a Chinaman, only to receive the reply, "Hell, I don't know. I'm here, that's all I know."[32] The photograph reveals him to be an exotically handsome man of serious demeanor with prominent Indian features below the eyes and evident Caucasian features from the eyes up. Charley's genetic makeup would have been at least one-quarter Caucasian, probably one-quarter to one-half Indian, and the remainder African. The African component in his facial features seems to have manifested itself especially in his complexion being darker than that of most Caucasians and Native Americans and in the curliness of his hair.

It is important to recognize that Charley Patton's cultural and psychological background was as mixed as his racial background. Even though in the post-Reconstruction South he would have been classified officially as Negro, Black, African, Ethiopian, Colored, or perhaps Mulatto, and would have been viewed informally by most whites simply as a "nigger," it is not necessarily the case that Charley accepted and identified with any of these designations. His paternal grandfather, a white man, and his grandmother Rose, who considered herself to be an Indian, remained close to their children and grandchildren and visited with them often. There can be no doubt that the white Bill Patton openly acknowledged his "colored" progeny. He passed on his surname to his descendants, and his first name, William, or its variants Bill, Will, or Willie, remained in the Patton family for at least another three generations. The Indian cultural strain in the Patton family is more obscure, and it would have had less chance to flourish openly in the Mississippi Valley, where the Indian societal presence had been eradicated by the early part of the nineteenth century. Nevertheless, it should be remembered that Rose, the "Indian," is said to have lived until 1926 and had a strong influence on her children and probably on her grandchildren. As for the black cultural element, it was probably absorbed gradually by the family over the generations through the prevailing system of racial classification, which recognized only a distinction between whites and Negroes, and which was designed to force William and Rose's son Bill Patton (Charley's father) and his offspring and descendants to accept the Negro designation and its associated inferior status, i.e., the status of "nigger." As for Charley specifically, it is very unlikely that he had much, if any, awareness of a specific ancestor who had been a slave or that he was descended from any but free people.

There is considerable evidence in the naming practices, migrational patterns, and oral legends of the Pattons, as well as in some of Charley's song lyrics, that he and his family resisted the idea of racial classification and preferred to have an ambiguous status and to be regarded on the basis of their specific mixed ancestry as well as their actual accomplishments and talents. Indeed, it will be my thesis that Charley Patton's entire life and musical output bear witness to this.

The most direct evidence of this sense of racial ambiguity is found in Patton's song lyrics. Besides "Down the Dirt Road Blues," whose lyrics I interpret later in this essay, he alludes to issues of race and skin color in a significant number of his songs. The descriptions of a woman as a "brown" in his 1929 "Shake It and Break It (But Don't Let It Fall Mama)" and the song's 1934 variant "Hang It on the Wall," as well as in his 1934 "Stone Pony Blues," are perhaps rather conventional expressions that shouldn't be given too much weight, but they could indicate a preference for brown skin color in women. In four songs, however, he clearly expresses a rejection of or a distaste for blackness. His "Mean Black Moan" is about a railroad strike in Chicago, and the "moan," which Patton reifies as something lying in front of his door, represents the suffering of the workers and their families. While the workers are very likely African Americans having a variety of shades of pigmentation, and while Patton in his lyrics seems to express sympathy for them, he chooses to call their moans "black" and "mean" and says that he is tired of hearing the moans and wishes that "somebody would kill these black moans dead." In "Mean Black Cat Blues" Patton complains about a "mean black cat" that hangs around his door and his bed. Although a black cat is a conventional symbol of bad luck, there can be no doubt that in this case Patton has in mind a black rival for his woman's affections. He sings:

> It's a mean black cat, Lordy, Lord, it's wearing my clothes.
> It's a mean black cat, Lordy, I mean it's wearing my clothes.
> If you want any more of my loving, let that black cat go.

In another verse he threatens to "kill that black cat dead." In "Pony Blues," the song for which he was best known, he employs a remarkable simile about skin color preference:

And a brownskin woman like something fit to eat.
Brownskin woman like something fit to eat.
But a jet black woman, don't put your hands on me.

Although he doesn't use the word "black" in the song, Patton gives the most nuanced look at his thoughts on the matter in "Jim Lee—Part 1," where he sings:

When I got arrested, what do you reckon was my fine?
Say, they give all coons eleven twenty-nine.

Big Boys and Shines, don't pay me no mind,
'Cause I do not like no coons in mind. (*sic*)

In the first of these couplets Patton obviously resents being classified with "all coons," who receive the standard sentence of eleven months and twenty-nine days. This sentence of just under a full year was customarily delivered in courtrooms of the southern states for various misdemeanors and other crimes that didn't rise to the level of a sentence in the state penitentiary, which held convicts serving a year or more for serious crimes. A prisoner sentenced to "eleven twenty-nine" would have been sent to a "county farm" or workhouse, where he might have been placed on a chain gang maintaining the county roads. Thus, someone convicted of a petty or even bogus crime such as "vagrancy" might serve the same sentence as someone convicted of assault or armed robbery. Jim Crow "justice" made little distinction, since the county needed "all coons" for its public works projects. "Coon" was a term that arose in the nineteenth century, originally to describe a clever or boisterous person, usually from a rural or frontier background, without regard to race. By the 1880s the term was used almost exclusively for African Americans, and a wave of popular "coon songs" by both white and black songwriters depicted the "coon" generally as a young urban black male exhibiting stereotypical traits of behavior, alternately comic and dangerous.[33] The term has remained in use as an ethnic slur, although it is rarely heard today. "Big Boy" and "Shine" were alternate terms with a similar meaning. All of these terms are strongly and negatively associated with the concept of "blackness." It is obvious from his song lyrics that Patton did not want to be placed in any of these categories. In another song, take 2 of "Elder Greene Blues," Patton seems to indicate his actual color preferences:

Well, the creek's all muddy, and the slough's all dry.
If it wasn't for the sweet-mouth colored boy, all the browns would die.

"Colored," which here undoubtedly refers to Patton himself, was a term that became common by the early twentieth century as a designation for anyone with obvious or determinable African ancestry, or even more broadly anyone who was "non-white," thus reflecting the racist climate of the time. It was, however, viewed by all as a polite term and was sufficiently vague to describe complexions ranging from near-white to black. If he had to be categorized at all, Patton evidently preferred the vagueness of this term for himself and "brown" for his women. The latter term was also vague and designated a broad range of complexions between the extremes of "yellow" and "jet black."

While the names Bill, Rose, Annie, Katie, Charley, Viola, and even "C" are unremarkable, there exist some more curious names within the Patton family that deserve to be noted. Charley had an uncle named Sherman Martin, also known as Sherman Patton.[34] He was, in fact, the younger brother of Charley's mother Annie (Martin), and he was raised by Charley's parents. Sherman is a most provocative name, as it was undoubtedly bestowed in honor of General William T. Sherman, the Union army officer in the Civil War who led a division at the siege of Vicksburg in 1863 and whose "scorched earth" policy eventually brought the South to its knees. The giving of this name would mark Annie's parents as strong Union supporters, a viewpoint that became far from popular and even downright dangerous in white-dominated post-Reconstruction Mississippi. The employment of William Patton and Rose, Charley's grandparents, at the National Military Cemetery in Vicksburg might also suggest Union sympathies, as would W. D. Patton's 1869 membership in the National Union Republican Party, if W. D. was indeed Charley's grandfather. In any case, it is hardly likely that a white man with a rather open relationship to a "black Indian" woman would have strongly supported the cause of the Confederacy.

Charley's father Bill Patton gave his children conventional names, but his "baby boy" C. Patton was also known as "X," a name that Tom Cannon said had also belonged to a younger "brother" of Bill Patton. While the use of initials for proper names is not unusual in the South, "X" is hardly a common name or nickname. It is a fundamental symbol of the lack or the cancellation of identity. It serves as the "mark" of one who cannot write his own name, i.e., who cannot claim his legal identity without witnesses. Many years later Elijah Muhammad used this letter as a surname for his followers in the Nation of Islam to indicate the loss of their African surnames and their consequent ambiguous status in America. His most articulate disciple was Malcolm X.

There is a distinct likelihood that Charley's brother "C" (or "X") Patton was severely troubled over his own identity. He was bothered by apocalyptic dreams of red, black, and white horses during that liminal period immediately prior to his baptism when he would assume his identity as an adult.

The following remarkable family legend about his death was told by his niece Bessie Turner. It is confirmed by her brother Tom Cannon, who adds that C. Patton was engaged to be married at the time of his death.

Uncle "Son" [i.e., Will Patton, Charley's brother] went overseas because it was 1918, war. But Uncle Charley wasn't [drafted and sent overseas]. That's when his baby brother got killed, accident. Been hunting rabbits and got shot in the side. They knowed the gun was loaded, and the boy was playing with him, and that gun went off and shot a hole in him. His best friend shot him and killed him, C. He was seventeen years old. He was gonna be baptized that Sunday and got killed that Saturday. But he had saw his death for two months. He'd go to my auntie's place and come home and say, "Mama, a light been following me every night I go over to Kate's,"—my oldest auntie, mama's oldest sister. They had a place out there from Mound Bayou. "Goes right to the step, turns, and goes yonder way." He said, "Every time I go to sleep, I dream of the red horse, the black horse, and the white horse." He said the red horse and the white horse would meet and they would paw together, he say, "and look like I would fall off that red horse and straddle that white horse and it would carry me through the air." Grandmama says, "Well, you got religion now. You getting closer to the Lord. He's just showing you the life that you're living." She said, "Something gonna happen." And they was coming to Mama's that Friday night. They left the house. Grandmama was ironing, she said, on the porch. One of them old hoot owls flew up on her old ironing board and squealed and flew off. She said that something was going to happen. She was thinking that my uncle in the army was going to get killed. She said, "Lord, have mercy." Said she kept on. After a while C came back to the house. He said, "I come after my gun." She said, "What you gonna do with the gun? You going out to the bayous?" He go every Friday night and stay until Sunday night and come home. He said, "I'm gonna have to be baptized on Sunday. I'm gonna try and kill a rabbit." Wasn't gone thirty minutes before he was killed. See, that just show you. When you got to go, you got to go.

The name "X" remained in the Patton family and was given again to the son of Charley's brother Will. X. L. Patton, also known as Exel, Excell, or Excel, was born in 1912 and died in 1972 in Gary, Indiana. If any or all of these X's stood for "Excel," it might indicate a hope on the part of parents within the Patton family that their sons would "do better" in life and overcome the ascribed statuses and limited prospects they had at birth.

The naming practices of Charley Patton himself were perhaps the most curious of all. In what could be interpreted as an incredibly ironic commentary on his own racial ambiguity, he named one of his daughters China Lou. Could this name have symbolized a refusal to allow his daughter to be

The Masked Marvel . . . unmasked. Picture from the sleeve notes of Revenant Records, Album 212. (Collection of Robert Sacré)

classified in a way that made sense within the Delta's rigid social structure? She was not in any way Chinese, though there were some Chinese people in the Delta, many of them in the grocery business. In some towns they were classified with whites, in others with blacks, and in Greenville they were able to fashion a separate classification of their own. Like the Indians before them, they could and did intermarry with both whites and blacks. They thus constituted an ambiguous social category, their threat to the status quo mitigated only by the fact that their numbers were small.

Much later in his life, when Charley Patton made his recording debut in 1929, he had his second record (Paramount 12805) issued under the name of "The Masked Marvel." Although this was done as a promotional device by the Paramount Record Company, it is hard to believe that Patton himself was uninvolved in its planning. While Patton was well known to his Delta audience under his own name, this could have been an attempt by him, either conscious or unconscious, to revert to some ambiguous status as he began to present his music to a much larger audience through the medium of "race" records.

The movement and occupational patterns of the Patton family lend further weight to the idea that they were dissatisfied with the status quo in the post-Reconstruction South. While by the beginning of the twentieth century most Americans of any degree of African ancestry adopted, reluctantly or not, a social status of "colored" (or Negro) and made the best of its accompanying social indignities, it would appear that in many ways both real and symbolic, as exemplified in their naming practices, the members of the Patton family took pains to avoid, as much as possible, adopting this status, and were always seeking a situation of increased freedom and opportunity. All but Charley and the unfortunate "C" Patton, also known as "X," eventually found their place in the system and made a rather successful accommodation.

The white William Patton and Rose the "black Indian," whether they were "married" or living separately, evidently maintained some kind of relationship to one another and looked back to the hopes that were generated by the outcome of the Civil War and Reconstruction. It is not known whether they moved, together or separately, to the area around Bolton and Raymond, but some or all of their children certainly lived there, and so did William Patton himself if he is to be identified as W. D. Patton. This area may have been a haven for upwardly mobile Negroes and families of mixed racial heritage.[35] The large Chatmon family of musicians from this area certainly had such a heritage. Utica Institute, a black college, was located nearby and no doubt served to raise the general educational level of the area. It is interesting to note how many prominent early blues artists came from this general area a few miles to the south and west of the city of Jackson. In addition to Charley Patton and the Chatmons, there were Tommy Johnson and his brothers and cousins, Ishmon Bracey, Walter Vinson, Caldwell Bracy, Eugene Powell, Joe and Charlie McCoy, and many others who moved north to the Delta, such as Dick Bankston, Jack Hicks, Henry Sloan, Jake Martin, and his cousin Fiddlin' Joe Martin.[36]

Despite the relative degree of freedom and opportunity that may have been found in the hills east of Vicksburg and south and west of Jackson, there appeared to be even greater opportunities in the Delta to the north. In the late nineteenth and early twentieth centuries large parts of the Delta were still swampland. Gradually a system of levees and drainage ditches was constructed to control the spring floods. The swamps were drained and timber interests hired mostly black workers to cut down the larger trees. After this the land was carved up into large plantations that had incredibly rich soil deposited by years of flooding. Almost all of the land was bought by whites, but Negro labor was needed to cut the trees, till the soil, and pick the cotton. For people living in the hill country to the South on farms that were eroded and threatened by the advancing boll weevil infestation, the Delta must have seemed like a dream come true, a frontier paradise with plenty of opportunities for work, where a man's labor might earn him a real sense of freedom and dignity.

Like many others from the hills, Charley's father Bill Patton took his family there. The year was between 1901 and 1904, and the place where they settled

Dockery Farms, 1967. (Photograph by Marina Bokelman)

was Dockery's plantation on the Sunflower River between Cleveland and Ruleville.

It was a huge tract of about forty square miles (ca. 104 km²) founded in 1895 by Will Dockery (1866–1936),[37] a paternalistic planter and proponent of "scientific" farming on an industrial scale who by all accounts treated his tenants very fairly and frequently gained their loyalty and residency for stretches of many years. In a biographical portrait compiled in 1940 by Anne McN. McAlpine, it is stated that, besides being "known as the Delta's greatest philanthropist, . . . for seventeen years, he took no profit on handling the cotton of his tenants, but paid them exactly what it brought on the terminal market in even running lots. His books were open, at all times, to all of his tenants, and his commissary prices to them were cash prices, and no interest was charged." His was an extraordinarily well-run and efficient plantation with its own dry goods, grocery, and furniture stores, railroad station, telegraph office, cotton gin, church, graveyard, and picnic ground for the tenants and workers, and many other amenities. It was really more like a "company town" in some northern industrial area run by a rather benevolent "boss." A number of middle-level positions were held by hard-working Negroes, including members of the Patton family.

Although Charley Patton made his mark in the world as an exponent of "black music" and has come to be viewed as the epitome of an early Delta bluesman, it must be kept in mind that his background was far from that of the typical black Delta sharecropper, nor was he a stereotyped downtrodden, illiterate field hand. His father, Bill Patton, led a sober life, made money, and was quite well off by Delta Negro standards. The Patton family in general seems to have been prosperous. There was a cousin, also named Charley, who owned a store in Vicksburg near the railroad depot. Tom Cannon and Bessie Turner stated that their grandfather would rent land from Will Dockery for one-fourth of the crop. Although Dockery probably made most of his sharecropping arrangements with Negro tenants for half of their crop, his deal with Bill Patton was a good one because he did not have the expense and risk of "furnishing" Patton for the year. Instead, Bill Patton had about eight sharecroppers sub-renting the land from him for half of their crop. Patton himself "furnished" these sharecroppers, an arrangement that actually elevated him to some degree to the same "bossman" status that Will Dockery and other white planters enjoyed. Bill Patton also owned four large logging wagons and teams and ran a profitable business hauling timber. On Saturdays he cooked and sold fish in a little shop next to the store at Dockery Farms. There is no doubt that Charley Patton was brought up in a prosperous household. Bessie Turner summed up her grandfather's existence by stating, "He didn't do no kind of work, but he just see to the work being done." Tom Cannon said, "He was a big farmer on Dockery's."

Longtime Dockery resident Ruffin Scott stated that Bill Patton left the plantation in early 1913, the same year Scott's family moved there, and that Bill Patton moved to the Cloud plantation to the north in the direction of Drew, never to return to Dockery Farms, although his grown sons Charley and Will and his daughter Viola continued to live there. But according to his grandson Tom Cannon, Bill Patton bought or rented land on Snake Creek, a few miles west of Mound Bayou, and stayed there about a year before returning to Dockery. He also rented at Blaine for a year or two, but from there he moved to the all-Negro community of Renova, two miles north of Cleveland, where he purchased about three hundred acres adjacent to the land of his son-in-law Eugene Miller. On this land he opened a small country store with a selection of food items and other essential goods. Although this represents an extraordinary lifetime success story, Bill and Annie Patton must have more than once reflected on the irony of seeing their version of the "American dream" come to fruition in the separate-but-equal environment of this black island in a white sea.

Bill and Annie's children generally did well in life also. Katie married Eugene Miller,[38] who owned land at Renova that he had inherited from his parents. Miller had bought more land and eventually owned about seven hundred acres. Their nephew Tom Cannon stated that the Millers "wanted to sell out and go north." In 1925 they did so and made their home in the relative "freedom" of East Chicago, Indiana. They had at least eight children. Katie died in 1944.

Viola stayed on Dockery Farms, and like her sister Katie, she married well. Around 1904 she was wed to John Cannon, the most prominent Negro on the plantation. He was probably born in Coldwater, Mississippi, and was raised in Memphis by the Dockery family after his mother, the family cook, was killed by her husband in a shooting accident. John Cannon finished high school in Memphis, and when the Dockery plantation was established in the Delta, he "ran" the general store there for fifty-six years. In truth, he worked "under" two white men, a Mr. Atkins and a Mr. Jones, but he seems to have had some degree of real responsibility in the operations of the store. John Cannon was also a musician with some formal training, playing saxophone, harmonica, and accordion. He had played in a band in Memphis and may even have played occasionally with Charley, but he is said to have given up music when he became active in the church soon after he was married to Viola, continuing only with the accordion for church songs. Viola was able to bask in the success and exalted status of her husband, a black man who had been raised up in the wealthy white Dockery family. The Cannons had thirteen children, and Viola lived to a ripe old age, dying in 1969. Her daughter Bessie Turner said:

> We never had a hard time. We never knowed nothing about a hard time. All the time of the Depression we never knowed nothing about it. Us fed many a person, my daddy did. See, papa go to Memphis and order all the groceries that come to the store. Mr. Dockery said, "Put your winter supply in." All us had a big storehouse was longer than this and bigger. Everything we wished for was right in there. If it wasn't, papa could bring it to us from the store. His doctor bill didn't cost us nothing. His funeral didn't cost us nothing. He [Mr. Dockery] had a wheel of fortune put on that grave when papa died. It went a whole week playing "Nearer, My God, to Thee" right at his head, and the lights on it turning over. Brought it from Memphis and put it on there, steel casted and everything. Mr. Dockery took care of all that. All the money that was spent at that funeral, he sent it to mama, sent $600 to her the first time, next time sent her $400 more. Said,

"There may be something else she want, 'cause that's my boy what died." All them white folks from Memphis was down there at the funeral.

When Bessie herself got married, Mr. Dockery paid for the wedding and reception that included thirty-six cakes. Her uncle Charley Patton played at the reception. Through his brother-in-law, who was treated as a member of the Dockery family, Charley had access to and a potential claim of patronage from one of the most powerful families in the Delta.

Will "Son" Patton went overseas in 1917–18 to fight for his country and make the world safe for democracy. One wonders how he felt when he returned to the Delta to find things little changed. There had been racial strife at nearby Drew, probably while he was overseas, and in 1923 a black war veteran killed his boss there in a dispute over a sharecropping settlement and was dragged through the town's streets after a pitched battle with an armed mob of whites.[39] Many Negroes left the area following these incidents. Will Patton stayed on Dockery Farms for a while, probably reveling in the role of war hero. He is recalled as a very fine baseball player for the Dockery team, which no doubt added to his stature. He tried to play guitar, but he could never do more than chord and beat out a rhythm behind his brother Charley's playing. As a musician he always remained in Charley's shadow. Tom Cannon stated that his uncle Will married a woman named Mary Torry, and they had a son named William. This marriage probably took place before Will went overseas. When he returned to the Delta, Will Patton "lived a fast life" and sharecropped for a while, sometimes on his father's land. He and Mary split up, and he took another wife, moving around to other locations in Bolivar County. Growing older and probably frustrated with life in the South, and having seen something different in Europe, he moved north around 1940 or a bit later to be with his son William, who had already settled in Gary, Indiana. There Will Patton lived out his days, passing away on September 3, 1957.[40]

The family's "baby boy," C. Patton, also known as "X," never found his niche in the system and was accidentally killed in a senseless "accident" during a crisis period in his life when he was on the verge of manhood and emotionally disturbed. Charley Patton never really found his niche either. He embraced a new form of "black" music, the blues, through which he was able to lead a rambling life, always on the move, very popular among both whites and blacks in the Delta, and never having to commit himself to a permanent status. His "niche" in the system, such as it was, involved placing himself *outside* the system and actually *avoiding* a niche, never permanently accommodating, never letting himself be pinned down. To the end he remained "The Masked Marvel."

In view of his family background, it should not be surprising that Charley Patton had a rather good education. Bessie Turner said that he and his sister Viola both went to the ninth grade together, far higher than the typical share-cropper's son could have achieved. Probably most of this schooling took place before Charley's family arrived at Dockery Farms, and indeed his formal education may have been cut off at that point due to a lack of school facilities close to Dockery in the plantation's early years. Bessie Turner said that Bill Patton stressed education to all of his children and would have whipped them if they neglected their studies. The educational status of children under the age of ten was not listed in the 1900 census, and Charley was listed there as being below that age, but both of Charley's older sisters were described as "at school" with five years of education. Reports that Charley could not read and write, which stem from the testimony of "Son" House, are certainly not true.[41] It would seem, however, that Charley did neglect his education in his later years and probably allowed his literacy skills to decline. As a traveling blues-man he probably had rather little need for reading and writing, other than handling correspondence about playing jobs and recordings. He did read the Bible, but it is not known if he ever read other books or newspapers. While the words of his songs do not display any distinct intellectualism, it must be kept in mind that he participated in a tradition of lyricism that was developed largely by singers far less educated than he. Bessie Turner said of her Uncle Charley's education, "It was good enough to carry him." If Charley Patton was no intellectual, he at least had several years of formal schooling and must have added to it an enormous store of what some black people call "mother wit" to carry him to the heights of success and fame that he reached in his life.

In addition to his education in school, Charley Patton also received a thorough religious education and learned the Bible well. His father Bill Patton was an elder of the church on Dockery Farms and raised his children in a strict manner. Undoubtedly the young Charley was made to attend Sunday school as well as the regular preaching services. His sister Viola and her husband and children were also active in the church, as were no doubt his other brother and sister and their children. Charley's interest in religion continued throughout his life and was not abandoned when he became confirmed in his career as a musician. This fact should be clear from his ten issued religious sides made at three of his four recording sessions. These songs must be considered as a unity with his blues and not as some sort of recording studio afterthought or a mere recollection of songs learned in childhood. Patton continued to perform these songs in family contexts, and in his close-knit family there were many such contexts. He also performed from time to time in church programs, probably alongside local quartets and other soloists.

A church between Dockery and Renova, 1986. The Patton family belonged to this church. (Photograph by David Evans)

A church on Dockery Plantation, Drew, MS, 1986. (Photograph by David Evans)

Patton's recorded church songs concentrate on several distinct themes, all of which were clearly important in his life and most of which are also found in secular guise in his blues recordings. The most important of these themes is death and the afterlife in heaven. Charley had seen a brother and seven sisters die young and had worried about his brother Will dying in battle in France.

He had survived the 1927 flood of the Mississippi River, had been present at
many violent and potentially violent scenes at barrelhouses and house parties,
and came close to dying in 1929 when his throat was cut by a man who was
jealous over the attention his wife paid to Charley at a dance. For about the
last two years of his life Patton was aware of his own impending death from
heart trouble. Heaven was viewed in his church songs as an ideal world, free
from troubles, a world he could never find in all his wanderings on earth.
The second major theme in his religious recordings is the actual journey to
heaven. This preoccupation is paralleled in his blues with their many references to towns, roads, boats, and trains, and travel was certainly part of his
actual lifestyle. Other themes in his spiritual recordings were his personal
dignity and determination, worry about his mother, personal depression, the
troubles of this world and the comfort found in God and Jesus. All of these
were important themes in his own life, and most are reflected in the lyrics
of his secular songs as well. It is of interest to note that none of his recorded
spirituals contains denunciations of various sins, a topic which is otherwise
a common theme in the black spiritual song repertoire. Patton was certainly
self-righteous enough in his blues, but as one who might have been viewed
as a "sinner" by other churchgoers, he probably would have considered it
hypocritical to denounce drinking, fornicating, dancing, and other sins. Bessie Turner recalls several other spirituals that Charley Patton sang in addition to the ones he recorded. All of them dwell on the same themes found
in his recorded spirituals. They include "Nearer, My God, to Thee," "Old Ship
of Zion," a favorite hymn (which he would have sung unaccompanied), and
a song he composed or adapted with reference to the 1927 flood called "God
Will Take Care of You." The lyrics that Mrs. Turner could remember were:

> As you travel in the land, man don't understand,
> But God will take care of you, God will take care of you.

> Through every day, along the way,
> God will take care of you, God will take care of you.

> Your troubles may be heavy, but your burden will be light.
> God will take care of you, God will take care of you.[42]

Charley, of course, also recorded a blues about the 1927 flood with far more
specific detail, "High Water Everywhere, Part 1" (Paramount 12909). He was
also well known for his ability to make the guitar imitate the voice of a man
praying, a virtuoso technique he displayed on "Prayer of Death, Parts 1 and 2"
(Paramount 12799).

Church at Renova where Patton preached, 1986. (Photograph by David Evans)

Charley not only performed and recorded religious songs but for most of his life wrestled with what he thought was a calling to be a preacher. This calling must have been a genuine concern to Patton and should not be dismissed as casual fits of remorse on his part, as some writers have done. Charley preached on a number of occasions, and his sister Viola stated that he even taught others to preach. His niece Bessie Turner stated:

He started to preaching and quit. Let me tell you what happened one time. He was young, and everybody went to hear Uncle Charley, because he done put that guitar down then. He was going to preach up there in Mound Bayou.[43] That night people was at the church like that, you know, because he was a guitar picker that had quit, and he was going to preach. Uncle Charley got right at the church and seen all them people. He looked in there and said, "Sure, I'm gone!" Went out in the cornfield and stayed out there all night long. He did that, and grandmama and them sat out there and waited on Uncle Charley to come in the pulpit to preach and ain't seen Uncle Charley till next morning. He did that. And the next time he preached. The next time he made up his mind, and he went on up there, and he preached like he'd been preaching for ten years. He knowed that Bible just like that. It was the thirteenth chapter of Revelations. He preached it down to the eighteenth, from the thirteenth chapter down to the eighteenth chapter of Revelations. I'll never forget that. I'll never forget his hymn:

Jesus is my God, I know His name.
His name is all my trust.

He would not put my soul to shame,
Or let my hopes be lost.

That was his hymn. He'd sing that hymn all the time when he got up in church.
He could just take his time and say his prayers so good. The next thing you know,
he was back on that guitar.

Patton recorded a brief sample of his preaching in the midst of his singing of "You're Gonna Need Somebody When You Die" (Paramount 13031).
Although he stumbles once in his delivery, the recording shows him to have
been a more than capable preacher. His imagery is excerpted from Chapters
1, 4, 21, and 22 of the Book of Revelation, Patton's favorite book of the Bible,
and dwells on the appearance of God and the holy city of heaven. But Charley Patton ultimately made his greatest mark in blues music. While he was a
sometime churchgoer, gospel singer, and even a preacher, he could not have
been considered a "church worker." His nephew Tom Cannon, who had been
active in church work all his life, stated: "His mother would get at him about
them blues and tell him that he ought to belong to the church. But children
never do like they want . . . So she never did gain it. After he got to putting
out his records and things, she tried to tell him to come by church. He'd go to
church, and he'd sing church songs. He'd get up and preach, but he never was
no famous man in church."

Charley Patton showed an early interest in the guitar, and around the age of
fourteen he obtained his first instrument. This was given to him by his father,
who had at first strongly opposed Charley's interest in music and whipped
him with a bullwhip. Charley first played with members of the Chatmon
family and probably other local musicians around Bolton. His sister Viola
recalled three Chatmon brothers, Ferdinand (born ca. 1875), Ezell (born ca.
1880), and another, who along with their father Henderson Chatmon (born
ca. 1850) comprised a band consisting of mandolin, fiddle, guitar, and bass
violin. In later life Charley frequently returned to his boyhood home and
no doubt continued to play with these musicians if they were still there. The
Chatmons were an important musical family, and a younger set of Chatmon
brothers would later become the famous band and recording unit, the Mississippi Sheiks.

The role of the guitar in the string band music that the Chatmons played
was largely restricted to chorded rhythm and bass runs. Charley's sister stated
that he didn't really learn to *pick* a guitar until he moved to Dockery Farms a
few years later. There he came under the influence of older musicians living
on the plantation who were already developing a blues style of guitar playing:

a Mr. Toby, a man named Wesley Barnes, whose daughter Charley would have a relationship with, and most importantly a man named Henry Sloan. Sloan was born in January 1870, in Mississippi, and in 1900 was living near Bolton in the same community as the Patton and Chatmon families. He moved to Dockery Farms about the same time as the Pattons, between 1901 and 1904. Charley received some direct instruction, observed and imitated the playing of the older men, and played behind Sloan's singing in a "field holler" style. Sloan and Barnes stayed on Dockery a number of years, and Charley had a lengthy opportunity to absorb their music. Evidently at some point he surpassed them in ability and reputation, probably by 1910, as he began influencing other musicians like Willie Brown at that time.

Ruffin Scott, whose family settled on Dockery Farms in 1913, recalled that Charley Patton did some farming there, perhaps helping his father, and in some years even "made a crop" himself, but it seems likely that Charley's farming activity decreased as his music career became well established. He did help his father haul logs, and on these jobs he was apt to carry his guitar in the wagon. Blues singer J. D. Short recalled seeing Charley with his guitar on a logging job near Hollandale, Mississippi.[44] Patton's son Willie Williams was born in Kentwood, Louisiana, a sawmill town where Charley had gone to play music and probably do timber work on the side. Sawmill locations and logging imagery occur in the lyrics of a number of Patton's blues, such as "Down The Dirt Road Blues," "It Won't Be Long," "Hammer Blues," "Joe Kirby," "Green River Blues," and "Jersey Bull Blues," including specific logging camps located at Green River in Tunica County, Mississippi, and Mengelwood in Dyer County, Tennessee. Very likely Patton was able to use his knowledge of the logging industry and his connections within it to build the beginnings of a regional blues touring circuit.

The only other instrument besides guitar that Charley is known to have played is the kazoo. His playing was fondly recalled by his sister and niece. Although he never used a kazoo on any of his recordings, one of his disciples, Tommy Johnson, did record at least one piece with it. It is interesting to note that one of the functions of the kazoo is to disguise the voice. The instrument's origins are in African musical tradition, where it is frequently used to supply the voice of masked dancers and actors in ritual contexts.[45] Charley himself was a master of voice changes, and his recordings are full of interjections in which he imitates the voices of women and members of an audience. It is, then, hardly surprising that The Masked Marvel should have played a kazoo.

Charley's niece gave the following account of how he learned to play guitar and sing blues, pieced together from what her uncle and her mother told her:

He started playing a guitar when he was seven years old, and he growed up on picking that guitar and he went to earning his money. If you called him, and he's a little boy ten years old, and you put on a dance—at that time they had them house dances—they'd send for him. Well, he done made his money that night. Somebody else would hear it, and they liked it. Well, they'd call him, and he be done made his money. Grandmama say, "I can't do nothing with him. I reckon he was called to pick that guitar." His brother couldn't do nothing but second behind him. . . . Uncle Charley said the way he learned, you know, folks in the country would always have Saturday night breakdowns. And Uncle Charley would get up out of the bed at night and go out the window. He was a little boy then, seven years old. Go out the window and sit down there and listen at them. . . . And some of the boys, different ones, had guitars, young men, and they would let him rap on it. The mens would be playing for the womens dancing. He kept on worrying Grandpa, and Grandpapa got him a guitar, and he started to learning then. . . . My Grandmama didn't never like it, but Grandpapa said, "Well, that's all he going to be, 'cause it just worries him to death." Said, "I'm gonna get him a guitar." Said, "I'm gonna let him learn at home, 'cause he gonna be slipping off from home, and I don't want that." Said, "Let him learn. If that's his game he want to play, let him learn just like anybody else. It ain't gonna hurt him." Grandmama scared he's gonna get killed somewhere. She worried over him a lot, but after she see that that's what he's determined to do, let him do it. . . . And the man what learned him how to start to playing a guitar, he was a Barnes.[46] But Uncle Charley started going there. As soon as he got out of school, he'd go on down there. Finally Uncle Charley went to work on it. . . . That's when he got my cousin [i.e., China Lou], by one of the Barnes daughters. . . . He went to going with Miss Millie. . . . See, us wasn't getting out nowhere. We just knowed they was making music. . . . Henry Sloan, he's the one that learned Uncle Charley how to really play the guitar. Henry Sloan, he was a little old brownskin man, low . . . [He played] "Alabama Bound." "Rooster crowed and the hen looked around; if you want anything, you got to run me down," all that kind of song. We weren't mixing in there, you know. We just hear it off, you know. We'd get in the cotton field, get in the back yard, and listen at them over on that hill in that big old house over there. They'd be singing, "You see my black cow, tell her to hurry home; I ain't had no milk since the cow been gone." Lord, I don't know, just some of everything. He sung just like him. Uncle Charley had a good voice. He really could sing. He took after him, Henry Sloan. He was a settled man when he learned Uncle Charley, because he had been playing for years, I reckon, before I was born [1906]. Mama and them knowed him before she married Papa [ca. 1904] . . . Uncle Charley was picking guitar good then. He'd [Sloan] go in and eat, and he'd be walking toward the house, singing, and Uncle Charley'd be picking the guitar. "Cut that out. Go back there." Uncle

Charley'd get on that guitar, and he'd start. See, when Uncle Charley started to pick a guitar, us weren't even thought of. Mama hadn't married. She was a young girl at home. My daddy was courting her at that time.

Charley's relationship with Millie Barnes [later Millie Torry, her married name] is thought to have taken place around 1908. "Alabama Bound" was a popular song published in 1909 and can be considered to be the first blues "hit." A variant of it is heard in Charley Patton's 1930 recording of "Elder Greene Blues" (Paramount 12972). It thus would appear that Patton was performing at house parties and perhaps other venues around 1908–9, when he was in his early twenties, and was viewed as the equal of other local guitarists. He had been gradually working up to this status since he first showed an interest in the guitar at the age of seven.

It is important to realize that Charley Patton considered music to be a career, a profession. It was not a part-time or spare-time activity. It was his livelihood, and he seldom did any other kind of work except to help his father. No doubt, like many other professional musicians, he would have considered it a blow to his dignity to have to do any other type of work. His work for his father was mostly done when he was still developing his reputation prior to the early 1920s and was probably done mainly out of a sense of family responsibility and when his father was short-handed for a logging or farming task. Even beyond his attitude of professionalism, Charley evidently believed that the life of a musician was his "calling." At least, this is the term his mother is said to have used, the same term that is used for the preaching profession. If Charley ever had any doubts about this calling, they were strictly over the issue of whether he had a higher calling to preach the gospel.

Given his position as the eldest son in an upwardly mobile family, it might seem surprising that Charley did not remain at home and eventually take over his father's business interests. We can only assume that at an early stage in his career he became aware of some inherent limitations of his father's apparent success. The supply of timber kept decreasing as Charley grew older, and by 1910 most of the local sawmills had closed. The price of cotton, the Delta's staple crop, was also subject to fluctuation. In 1917, as America entered the World War, the price rose dramatically, only to come tumbling down again in 1920. Many farmers were ruined.[47] Bill Patton's move around this time to Snake Creek near Mound Bayou, where he rented land and would have enjoyed a greater degree of independence, and his return to Dockery Farms not long after, might reflect these fluctuations in the price of cotton. But beyond the economic vagaries of the life of a farmer and logger, there is the fact that such a lifestyle causes one to be tied down to a particular plot of land, a house, and one's farm animals and equipment. For a Negro in the South at this time there was always the possibility that success would invite jealousy and retaliation by whites. There is a widespread belief among blacks, not without considerable justification, that it is useless to accumulate wealth and property because the "white folks" will simply find a way to take it. The only way to prevent this is to have powerful white patrons, which often means subordinating one's sense of dignity and playing the role of "Uncle Tom." Even if his father had a good relationship with Will Dockery and his sisters were married to successful black men, subordinating himself to white people and tying himself down to a plot of land or a steady job were things Charley was not prepared to do.

He could hardly have been naïve about the situation of Negroes in the Delta, and it must have been particularly galling to him. Despite the fact that they comprised over three-quarters of the region's population, the Negroes were politically powerless and had little accumulated wealth. To Charley's father, the nearby all-Negro town of Mound Bayou, and the smaller settlement of Renova where he eventually settled, must have seemed like shining beacons, but they were exceptions to this pattern, beacons in the midst of a hostile sea. In 1923 the main newspaper of Bolivar County, in which Mound Bayou and Renova are located, published a descriptive booklet of the county. It characterized Negroes as "jungle hordes" and "an ignorant and inferior race" and preached against "the idea of mongrelizing the South" while praising "the protecting organization of the Ku Klux Klan."[48] The booklet described every town in the county in glowing fashion except Mound Bayou and Renova, which were ignored completely! The triumph of Charley Patton over this environment and social system was that he was able to live at least as prosperously as his father, probably more prosperously, and have a maximum of physical mobility. A Negro landowner had no mobility in this potentially hostile environment, and a renter or sharecropper could only exercise his mobility once a year following his financial settlement with the "bossman." Charley was his own bossman. His niece described his situation by saying, "He just left when he got ready, because he didn't make no crops ... He was a *free man.*"

There was, of course, a heavy price he had to pay for his freedom. He had to travel frequently to make money, and he was never able to establish a permanent home or a stable family life. One might wonder why he didn't simply move north, as his brother and sister eventually did. The racial climate was milder in the North, and perhaps he could have become a star there like Blind Lemon Jefferson, Big Bill Broonzy, or Tampa Red, or taken a factory job and played music on the side. Probably he would have done this if he thought he could live better up north, but the greatest demand for his services was apparently in the Delta. He could make plenty of money there, and he had plenty of friends and relatives in the region. His decision to remain in the South and pursue the career of a musician must be viewed as a step toward greater freedom than he had grown up with, an extension of a family pattern. Perhaps his parents secretly realized this when they finally acquiesced in his decision.

There were several specific contexts in which Charley Patton played most of his music: cafés, juke houses (also known as juke joints and honky tonks), stores, house parties, wedding and birthday parties, picnics, and medicine shows. A café was a small restaurant catering to black customers, serving sandwiches and hot meals, perhaps fried fish or barbecue. A juke house also served food, but the emphasis was more on music and dancing. In effect, a café by day might become a juke house by night, although most of the latter were out in the country on account of restrictive laws in many of the Delta towns. In the larger towns there might be a black business and entertainment street or "district," but there Patton would have had to compete with pianists and bands. These establishments were usually run by blacks and were located in the towns as well as in populated rural areas. During most of the 1920s and until 1932, it was illegal to buy or sell alcoholic liquor in America. Plenty of illegal drinking took place, but at the cafés and juke joints it was generally done on the outside or in a back room, and the liquor was sold by a bootlegger who was usually not formally associated with the café owner. These places also sometimes provided further illicit attractions such as gambling and prostitution. Such activities, when they occurred, took place in a back, side, or upstairs room. The owner or sponsor was not always involved in promoting these illegal activities, but he or she usually knew of their existence.

During the daytime Patton could play at cafés for tips, as eating was then the main order of business. Saturday and Sunday afternoons would have been the best times, as most people ate at home on weekdays. Tom Cannon specifically recalled the Mississippi Café in Leland, where Charley played on Sundays. On weekend nights a café or juke house owner would probably charge admission at the door, and this would be Patton's payment for the night. When he had to travel any distance, he was probably guaranteed a minimum payment. Although Tom Cannon stated that Charley "had a place to play near about every night in the week," he probably seldom played on weekday nights, unless he was in a large city or was playing at a birthday party in the country that ran late because the adults wanted to dance. Most people, especially in the country, had to go to bed early and work the next day.

Playing at a store was similar to playing at a café or a juke house. Most stores, however, were operated by whites or Chinese. During daytime business

Juke house on Dockery, 1986. Patton often played there for Saturday night fish fries.
(Photograph by David Evans)

hours in the warm months Charley would play outside, usually on the porch,
for tips from the customers, and on the inside during the cold months. The
store owner would probably give him cold drinks and a sandwich and perhaps a little money if he had a lot of customers that day. Saturdays were the
best days, when the farmers and sometimes their families came to town or
to the plantation commissary to shop. Patton is frequently remembered for
playing in front of the commissary at Dockery Farms. A number of rural
stores also had a café/juke house area in a back or side room. For example,
Charley played on the porch and in the back of a white-operated store at
Holly Ridge, his last residence, and the white owner sometimes accompanied
him on the fiddle.

A house party was basically a private home temporarily turned into a juke
house. The head of the house hired the musician, sometimes charged admission, and sold food, with a bootlegger selling liquor outside or in the woods
nearby. House parties were sometimes called "country suppers" or "frolics."
Some houses in the country were more or less permanently open for food,
entertainment, and bootleg liquor, thus serving both as a residence and a juke
house. There were several places like this on Dockery Farms. Albert Walker,
born in 1912, described another such place near his home. Patton was living
at the time about two miles east of Merigold, and Albert picked him up and
took him to the place west of town. He stated:

Charley Patton used to play up there at Merigold, out in the country. That man
had a little place that he used in his house, between Merigold and Six Mile Lake,
six miles from Merigold. One night Charley Patton played, and another fellow
played guitar. They called him A. B. That was my sister's boyfriend. That was in
the twenties. I was about eighteen years old. So they give a little party, and I went
to Merigold and picked him up in a buggy. He wore a starched overall suit, a pair
of overalls and a jumper. That's mostly what people back in there on the farms
had. After the party was over, he spent the night with us.

Eli Pearman, born in 1913, remembered Charley Patton playing around
Mound Bayou with Eli's older brother as well as his own brother. Eli stated:

Him and my brother used to play together, Dallon Pearman [b. 1906]. He used
to second behind him. Him and his brother used to play. They called him "Son."
He couldn't do nothing but second behind him. He [Charley] used to come to
the house all the time, him and my brother, sit there and play together, out in
the country. He was kind of nice. His brother was loud. I was small back in that
time, back in the twenties. He stayed down in Mound Bayou, and I was out in the
country. At these jukes and things he'd play [one song] about five or ten minutes.
Sometimes they had these country parties, they go all night. He'd take breaks.
He'd take his break, and my brother'd be playing. He used to play out here at the
Lawson Store. They used to have a place out there, the white folks did. He'd play
out there. He enjoyed it, 'cause that's where he'd make his money. They was real
nice to him. Just about every weekend he'd be out there playing. He went all the
time. My brother used to play out there at Lawson's store with him.

A picnic was an outdoor version of a café or juke house, but held in the
warm months. It might offer additional attractions, such as a baseball game.
Just as white store owners sometimes operated cafés for blacks, so also the
large white landholders would sometimes sponsor picnics for blacks. These
might be viewed as a treat for their workers, but the sponsors usually made
money as well. People that would not go to juke houses or house parties might
go to picnics and take their families. Sometimes picnics were sponsored by
black social and fraternal organizations, or by churches as fundraisers. Others
were simply given by individuals or families for the purpose of making money
from the sale of the refreshments. Bessie Turner, Patton's niece, described free
picnics given by Will Dockery for his renters and workers:

He [Dockery] liked for all his folks to be nice, lively, have parties. He'd give free
picnics and things like that and got Uncle Charley to play. Had a platform built

for them to dance on the Fourth of July. The dance started about one o'clock and ended up the next morning. Start on the Fourth and end up on the Fifth, dancing out there, right at that grove.... That's where Uncle Charley have made many a tune.... That's where the parties used to be. All through the year they have parties. Mr. Dockery put on big barbecues, and Uncle Charley used to play. All his Negroes would be there. Homer Lewis, and Willie Brown, Mr. Henry Sloan, ... Mr. Barnes. They had a group, some blowing a little old horn [i.e., kazoo] ... and Uncle Charley picking guitar and one playing the accordion, Willie Brown and him picking guitar. Mr. Homer Lewis, ... he played the accordion.

Tom Cannon describes his uncle's playing for house parties, stores, and juke houses:

It'd be hundreds of people at these places. Couldn't half of them get in the house. They had these here juke houses. They'd be so crowded till you couldn't even stir around in there. He played on the inside. Just like on a Saturday a whole bunch would get together, and he'd play at Dockery's at the big store. There used to be a big brick store there at Dockery's. He'd sit out there on the store porch. People all from Lula, Cleveland, everywhere.... Just like he playing for one of them places, they would charge so much at the door. They'd have it in one of these big buildings, and they'd charge 'em at the door.... They'd have a stage. He'd be playing on the stage.

Tom Rushing, who was a deputy sheriff of Bolivar County from 1928 to 1932, describes the juke houses that he patrolled in the towns there:

I heard him a good bit around Mound Bayou, Cleveland, and Merigold. Being the deputy sheriff, we had to systematically watch these places, and we were welcome at any place to go in if we wanted to. In those days we got by with it. I don't know how we did it, but we never had to have a search warrant. We just went ahead and did things our way. The honky tonk is a big room. It's got a little café in connection where they would serve hamburgers and coffee and so forth. Then they had a big area where they could dance, and they had the side room for monkey business.

The police were mainly searching for bootlegging and gambling. The owners and sponsors, musicians, and customers probably had mixed feelings about their occasional unannounced visits, as their presence reduced the chance of random violence and fights breaking out but also probably scared some customers away.

Patton was frequently hired to play at birthday and wedding parties. At these he would be paid a guaranteed fee, and the host would give away refreshments to the invited guests. These parties occurred throughout the year, providing some steadiness to his income. Musicians everywhere have always prized these jobs highly because they can demand a high fee. Sometimes the parties were finished by sundown, making it possible for the musician to book another engagement at night. At other times, however, a children's birthday party in the afternoon might evolve into a dance party for the adults in the night hours. Beatrice Gidden, born in 1909, remembered Charley playing for weddings and especially for children's birthday parties in Lula between 1916 and 1921:

The first time I saw Charley Patterson [sic] it was Richard Sanders, he had twin daughters, and he gave them a birthday party, and he got Charley to play for it. And I was invited to the party. I was about eleven years old then. He sung the blues. Sometimes there would be forty and fifty at some of the parties. And sometimes it would be seventy and eighty at the parties, and it would be a hundred sometimes at the parties. The houses wasn't much large at that time. And some of them would have to go out and come in to see Charley. Everybody wanted to see Charley. He was playing at a party for someone else. That next person that wanted him for a party, he would book them. Now he playing a Wednesday night at this party, and they would book him that Saturday night . . . My mother booked him for a party. I think it was my birthday, the first party she booked him for, on a Saturday night. It was seventy-five [people]. She would have refreshments for the birthday party. She would have all kind of cakes and cookies and oranges and apples and candy. She'd give that away for the birthday party. She never sold anything. We'd two-step, slow drag, and Charleston, and a lot of the boys would buck dance. Sometimes he would get out and show the boys how to do the buck dance. He was by himself. I don't know whether he played in a band in these clubs or not. I wasn't there . . . He seemed to be a nice person. He had a nice personality. And he seemed to like children. He took a lot of interest in children. I never seen him drink at parties or nothing.

Ruthie Mae King relates a similar experience:

I heard him in Boyle. My daddy was giving me a birthday party, and he would get Charley Patton to play. I was, at that time, I guess, about seven or eight years old. I always had a birthday party. He played more than one. He would play in the country for different people. So my daddy would always get him to play for my party. He played alone. Charley Patton was pretty famous around here. I believe

he was in overalls, because he was living out in the country. He played for the
whole entire party. I had a lot of adults, and they brought their kids to the party.
He just sung the blues. I loved his music.

Charley Patton also performed occasionally at gospel programs and church
services, and he is known to have done some preaching, possibly on some of
the same occasions when he performed spiritual songs with guitar. He probably would have received some monetary compensation for both preaching
and performing music from the taking of a "collection" or "offering." Unfortunately, there are rather few reports of this sort of activity because most
researchers have concentrated on his blues career. Beatrice Tripp, who moved
to the Delta around 1916 and used to sell milk and butter to Patton, remembered him performing blues with some other musicians on Main Street in
Cleveland but also preaching and playing "Christian songs" by himself at a
Holiness church there. Holiness (Pentecostal) denominations encouraged the
use of musical instruments to accompany their singing and thus would have
been more welcoming to someone like Patton, in contrast to the more conservative Baptist and Methodist churches, which viewed all instruments, except
possibly the piano and organ, as the devil's playthings.

There were other contexts in which Charley Patton performed occasionally. His sister Viola stated that he played in medicine shows, but he is not
especially remembered for this form of entertainment. In these shows he
probably would have been on salary and under a "bossman," which would
have been against his nature. He could probably make as much money on
most Saturday nights as he could in a week on a medicine show. In the towns,
probably mainly on Saturday afternoons, he could play on the sidewalk or
street corners in business sections, but this activity depended on the tolerance
of the police, preferably officers who knew him. He would have to be careful
not to draw a crowd so big as to block traffic. Patton also made money by giving guitar lessons to youngsters. At one point he moved to the Orange Mound
section of Memphis, a neighborhood of single-family homes on the eastern
edge of the city developed especially for upwardly mobile African Americans,
where he became a guitar teacher.[49]

Between paying engagements Charley Patton would often play for children at the houses where he stayed, as described by his niece:

Uncle Charley could take the guitar and make it talk. He could take a guitar and
put it behind his head and take his fingers.... He could use a guitar any kind of
way and pick it, swing it over, and never lose the tune, pick it on down. Yeah, he
could play it.

What you want with a rooster, he won't crow 'fore day?
What you want with a rooster, he won't crow 'fore day?
What you want with a woman, won't do nothing she say?

He used to sit out on the porch, and us children would be under the shade tree singing right along with him. We used to have some good times with Uncle Charley when mama be gone. Us be dancing down. He said, "Oh, your mama gone. Get out there and shake your hips, ya'll. Let me see what you can do." Mama didn't want us to learn all that. Mama said, "You ain't gonna be a rascal like Charley, on his way to hell." . . . He used to play "A, B, C, D," all like that. He'd play alphabets for the children, and they would dance. Ooh, man, they would shake it up!

It would be futile to attempt to construct a complete chronicle of Charley Patton's movements and residences. Various reports have him living two places at once. We do know that he spent his earliest years around Bolton and then moved with his family north to Dockery's plantation in the Delta. By all accounts these two areas and Vicksburg remained his main "hangouts" for the rest of his life, for the simple reason that he had plenty of relatives and friends in all of these places. His sister Viola lived on Dockery Farms, as did his father and mother and another sister and brother for many years. At other times these family members lived nearby in places like Mound Bayou, Renova, and Blaine. Charley himself is frequently described as living in Mound Bayou and nearby Merigold as well as at Dockery Farms. Around Bolton and at Vicksburg he had aunts and uncles and cousins as well as his grandmother Rose. He was welcome to stay at all of their houses, and some of them no doubt helped him secure work playing music. Another place where he was well remembered from at least the time of World War I was the area around Clarksdale and Lula in northern Coahoma County. His last wife Bertha Lee came from Lula. Probably he had several routes that he followed, between Memphis and Natchez along the Mississippi River, between Memphis and Hollandale along what is now Highway 61, between Drew and Inverness on what is now Highway 49, and between Jackson and Vicksburg on what is now Highway 80. These areas were heavily populated and growing all the time. In his songs he mentions travel by train, automobile, riverboat, horseback, and on foot. By the 1920s transportation by automobile and rail was easy, and there was little likelihood that Patton would become stranded in some unfamiliar place. His nephew Tom Cannon describes his pattern of travel:

[Charley was well known] all over the Delta and the hills [i.e., east of Vicksburg]. He'd go back and forth down in the hills, stay months at a time. He would go all

out in the country on these different plantations. People was on these big plantations then. They would give what you call a supper. They'd come and get him and
carry him back out there to play for 'em. . . . He lived in many different places. . . .
Where he could make the most money at, that's where he would stay for a while.
He'd never stay nowhere a long time, but he did go back and forth to these different places and get his music. Just like he'd have certain nights to play in Cleveland, he'd be there playing. Maybe they'd have him down to Greenville the next
few nights. He'd stay gone near about all the time.

Although Charley's main "beat" was in the northwestern quarter of Mississippi, he was no stranger to places farther afield. His ex-wife Millie Torry
stated that he spent some time at Dermott, Arkansas, across the Mississippi
River from Greenville, after he left her. This may have been around 1910.
Charley also mentions in one of his records having friends around Blytheville
and Joiner, Arkansas, located north of West Memphis toward the Missouri
border. Across the Mississippi River from these towns is the logging camp of
Mengelwood, Tennessee, a location he mentions in another song. He seems
to have developed something of a performing circuit of logging camps and
sawmill towns, as noted earlier, that stretched probably from Mengelwood, if
not further north, to as far south as Kentwood, Louisiana. In the latter town
he fathered two sons by Sallie Hollins, who were born in 1916 and 1918. When
the youngest of these sons, Will Williams, was working at a sawmill in Albany,
Georgia, his co-workers there remembered Charley Patton, as did other sawmill workers across the state line in Florida. As mentioned, for a time in the
early 1930s Patton lived in Memphis giving guitar lessons. He also played in
cities to the north and south where friends and relatives had settled. Feeling
nostalgic for real downhome blues, they would summon him by letter or tele-
gram, as his niece described:

He traveled lots up the road, Milwaukee and Chicago and St. Louis. He used to
get letters from everywhere, all over the world. He'd get letters that they wanted
him . . . They used to call him, send him telegrams and tickets, pay his way on the
train to come up there, him and Willie Brown. They'd be up there for a week's
play, put on programs for the whole week. He couldn't keep a wife for running
so. . . . Charley used to go up to Gary too. He used to put on a week's program
up there. He'd go up there and stay and play. They worried him to death. He just
wasn't contented. . . . He'd go to St. Louis and different places and down in Vicksburg. That was his hangout, was down there in Vicksburg. They'd just worry him
to death. They find out he was at home, they'd just worry him to death. Down
there in Vicksburg and New Orleans, just different places. He was just a traveler.

He didn't farm or nothing like that, because he'd be going all the time. See, he
made his money . . . He never did no other kind of work.

Blues singer David Edwards has confirmed Patton's trips to Chicago, stating that he would be booked there about twice each year.[50] In various songs
he mentions "Dago Hill" in St. Louis, a place called "Shelby" in Illinois, and
the Indian "Nation" in Oklahoma in ways that suggest that he was familiar
with these places. "Rooster" Holloway, the son of Patton's friend Seabron Holloway, said that Patton claimed to have spent some time in Texas, where he
made good money playing music for Mexicans.[51] In addition to these trips,
he traveled to Richmond, Indiana, twice to Grafton, Wisconsin, and to New
York City for recording sessions. It is doubtful that he felt uncomfortable in
cities. In many ways the Delta itself was like a huge city by the 1920s. The
towns were close together, many of them separated by only five to ten miles,
and a large proportion of the countryside was under cultivation and dotted
with sharecroppers' cabins. For many black farmers fleeing the hill country,
the Delta plantations served as a kind of rural factory preparing them for
the eventual transition to true city life in Memphis, St. Louis, Chicago, or
elsewhere in the North.

Charley Patton made a good income from his music. Other blues artists
like "Son" House are in agreement on this fact. Jake Martin, who was about
the same age as Charley and raised in the same area near Bolton, coming to
Dockery Farms himself in 1916, and who played guitar and kazoo in many of
the same contexts as Charley, stated that he himself would make a minimum
of ten dollars a night and once made as much as seventy-five dollars. Martin
did farm work, raised a family, and did not pursue a musical career as seriously as Charley did. Still, he emphasized that one could make much more
"doing nothing" than he could by farming. It is likely that Charley Patton had
an average income between fifty and a hundred dollars per week, all from
"doing nothing." In contrast, a successful sharecropper might be lucky to clear
a few hundred dollars once a year before Christmas at settlement time and
make a little extra money during the off-season for arduous work at a levee,
lumber, or railroad camp. Otherwise the sharecropper had to support himself
and his family on the meager "furnish" provided by his bossman, which was
charged against his settlement at the end of the year. Charley's niece described
the kind of money he would make from music: "He have a sack of money
every time he would go and come back, and he would take that money and
pin it to his pajamas and sleep with it under his legs. Then his wife would call
me and say, 'Come here and look at this sack of money Charley got between
his legs.'"

His nephew describes his prosperity: "After he left his daddy, he didn't do nothing but play music. He made a good living. He stayed in good shape. He made an excellent living, 'cause he would help his sisters. He'd make it and he'd distribute it around amongst them. He'd make 'em all happy. He kept a car. First car he ever drove was a Model T Ford. He'd get a new car every year. He first started getting little old T Models. Then the year he died he had just got a new Chevrolet."

Charley probably gave money to other relatives as well, including his parents, particularly when he stayed with them for several days or weeks. He also no doubt helped his wife or girlfriend of the time and probably his children when he visited them. Besides his car, Charley's main possessions would have been his clothes and his guitars. Tom Cannon adds:

> He always wore a suit every day of his life. I never saw him with nothing but a suit on the whole time I knowed him. . . . He wore his suits and shined shoes, and a different woman every year, two a year sometimes. He just was a special person amongst people. He didn't go like no working man.
>
> He played music in rough places, and then he played a whole lot of music for these here white people. Back in them days they'd give these parties. He played more for them than he did these juke houses, 'cause somebody had him obligated at all times. He'd play through the week, weekends, anytime they got ready for him. He had a place to play near about every night in a week. Sure did. On a Sunday he'd play for them different kind of do's they were giving. Just like it's a big café or something or other in town. He'd sit back in there and play for them there joints like that. Like down there to Leland he used to play at the Mississippi Café all the time. They'd hire him for every Sunday most. He'd be down there playing. He had a car. He'd travel around in his car, drive around mostly by car until he'd get ready to go up north somewhere. He'd leave his car at his brother's, and he'd catch the train back in them days. He started on cars back in the T-Model times. He kept a nice car. He'd get one near about every year. He'd change cars. . . . He first was getting Fords. Then he quit getting Fords. The last car he had was a Chevrolet.
>
> He kept two or three guitars. He had 'em fixed up. On one of his guitars he had a lot of gold pieces plastered all on it. He had 'em real fixed up to play 'em. He kept some special stuff to play with . . . He had gold coins all the way around his main box he used all the time. He had three. He kept his boxes dressed up. He was dressed up hisself all the time. He loved his good clothes and shoes. He wore a Stetson hat.

Perhaps he kept his different guitars in different tunings in order to avoid having to retune at personal appearances, or perhaps he liked to have a spare instrument in case he broke a string or otherwise damaged his first guitar. If he had accumulated any other possessions, he probably kept them stored with his parents or other relatives.

Beatrice Gidden of Lula, Mississippi, confirms this portrait of Charley Patton in the following description of him from around 1916 to 1921:

> He was a nice person. He was a great person. And I really think he brought joy to many persons, to children. I know he did through here.... He would wear a suit to parties when he would be playing. And I can remember that white shirt. He'd wear a white shirt, a pair of shoes on nice and shined. He always dressed nice, and he was always presentable.... He had a T-Model Ford at that time.... Ordinary farm workers, they were getting a dollar and a half a day. They would pay him twenty-five dollars for a party.

There is no doubt that Charley Patton was a famous man in the parts of Mississippi where he lived and made music. His fame was well established there even before he began to record his music in 1929. He is well remembered by other blues artists as well as by thousands of people who comprised his audiences. The list of blues artists who were influenced by him is most impressive, and elements of his performance style were perpetuated by other artists many years after his death. His nephew said:

> This old boy they call Howlin' Wolf, he taught Howlin' Wolf a lot about his playing. This boy they call Will Brown, he taught him. He did have a boy he trained real good called Joseph Harris. I don't know whether he ever put out any records or not, but he was a famous player. He went to playing in larger places.... He lived up in Merigold. He passed years ago.... Some of 'em would do pretty good, but it just looked like everybody fell to Charley. He'd carry Will Brown with him, and he'd play. But the people didn't fall for Will like they did for Charley. They always did fall for Charley's playing ever since he started.... They all was crazy about his singing and playing too. People come from far and near to hear Charley play. Just like he'd come back up here to my mother's house. The whole time he was there it would be crowded with people just to hear him play. He was friendly with everybody. Everybody liked Charley. They kept him going all the time. He was well thought of in Mississippi.

Patton's niece Bessie Turner added:

> I saw the Howlin' Wolf ... Different ones from different places would come and try to learn like Uncle Charley, and they would hang on to him, trying to learn

to play like he could play. . . . Different ones would hang on, but they couldn't
make the music right. When they couldn't learn, Uncle Charley dropped them
and catch on to the best ones. Now him and Willie Brown were really the best out
there, and Henry Sloan . . . Willie Brown was out there at Dockery. That's where
they started at. And Willie Brown learned somewhere else, and then he learned
more when he got with Uncle Charley.

The degree of enthusiasm for Charley Patton in the Delta probably rivaled
that in a later era for artists like Elvis Presley and James Brown. There can
be no doubt that during his lifetime he was the "king" of the Delta blues. If
he had lived into the 1940s, he would almost certainly have been sought out
for field recordings by researchers from the Library of Congress. In the 1950s
he probably would have played a significant role in the American folk music
revival, and in the 1960s he undoubtedly would have become known internationally. Unfortunately he had to leave these achievements to longer-lived
contemporaries like Leadbelly and to his successors such as Big Joe Williams
and Howlin' Wolf.

Even in his own lifetime Charley Patton had established a fame among
Delta whites almost equal to his fame among blacks, and there are sugges-
tions in his recordings that he was reaching for an international fame that
would come to him only posthumously. It was not uncommon for black
musicians to perform locally for white audiences in the South, but it was rare
for them to have a broader regional fame among whites. Only a few, such as
Louis Armstrong, Duke Ellington, and Bessie Smith, were known nationally
among whites at this time. Tom Rushing, the deputy sheriff of Bolivar County,
said, "He was a pretty prominent Negro among the people, and everybody
liked him." Rushing compared Patton's fame to that of the international track
star Jesse Owens, whom Rushing was also proud to have met at a track meet
at Mound Bayou in 1934. (A picture of Rushing and Owens shaking hands
was printed in the local newspaper.) Rushing observed that both Owens and
Patton were southern boys who came from obscure rural backgrounds and
became world famous. Joe Lavene, who had been in the record business in
Clarksdale, recalled following Patton to large picnics where he played and
selling Patton's records there in large quantities. White musicians played with
him, including the fiddler who owned the store at Holly Ridge and a young
harmonica player recalled by his sister Viola. His niece stated:

The biggest he played was white. The white nation would be calling him. They
wanted him. And then he was teaching boys how to play. He done a lot of that
too, young boys, youngsters, how to pick a guitar, you know, white and colored.

But there was more white than there was colored. It was up there in Memphis. He used to be out there, out in Orange Mound. He used to teach them how to pick guitar . . . Uncle Charley had lots of friends, white and colored. He was a man, they loved him. He could say, "I'm broke today." Anybody would run their hand in their pocket and give him twenty-five or thirty dollars. The whites, they was crazy about him. The little school girls, he even had songs for the little children to dance by. He had all them songs. The little kids who would look and see him go, white and colored, they'd be in the streets, they'd start to dance.

Charley's fame was so great that he spawned at least one imposter. A white man was able to tell the difference, however. Charley's niece recalled this incident, which she said took place in 1933:

He went to Chicago, and he was on his way back one Saturday night, and I was on my way up to Cleveland. The colored rode in the front, and the white rode in the back at that time. And this man was so crazy about Uncle Charley, and he knowed he had a good record, he named himself Charley Patton. He was playing for the folks all gathered around him. One man heard the voice, and he came down, a big fine looking white fellow. He said, "I heard Charley Patton was on this train." And he [the imposter] said, "Yes, sir, here I am." He jumped up and stood up. This man looked at him and said, "You're not Charley Patton." "Oh yes." I was sitting across from him, and I said, "No, you're not Charley Patton, 'cause he's my mama's brother, Mister Charley Patton is. He have a daddy named Bill Patton who have a son named Will Patton, a sister named Viola Cannon." And I went to naming 'em all. He sat down. The [white] man said, "No, you ain't Charley Patton. Hit that tune." And he hit it. Said, "'Back Water Blues,' let me hear you play that." And the man got it with his fingers. The [white] man said, "No, you don't even sound like Charley Patton." Said, "Charley Patton is the man! He knows what to do with that. So sing it." And he couldn't sing it. He tried to sing it like Charley Patton, but he couldn't do it. He walked on back in there and said, "Go ahead, boy. Good night!" Gone on away from him. We had a big laugh off it. . . . When I got over there to Leland, the folks was out there to see Charley Patton. He was supposed to be going where he died at down there [Holly Ridge], and the folks were standing out there waiting on Charley Patton. And he [the imposter] come walking out. And different ones walk up and say, "Is Charley Patton here? Did Charley Patton come on this train?" He said, "I can answer in his place." He was scared to say he was Charley Patton that time. He said, "No, Charley sent me to answer in his place." He was slick. And that time Uncle Charley was already there. And Uncle Charley walked up and said, "Here I am." And they had a big laugh over that, you know.

Charley played frequently for white house parties, picnics, dances, and wedding parties. Near the end of his life he was playing for whites on the majority of his jobs, and his widow Bertha Lee stated that his last performance was at a white dance.[52] Even his recording sessions, supervised by white talent scouts and engineers, apparently turned into parties. H. C. Speir, who owned a music store in Jackson and first recommended Patton to Paramount Records, enjoyed being entertained by Patton. Bertha Lee recalled that, after she and Patton finished their 1934 recording sessions, they would have dances in the studio for Vocalion recording executive W. R. Calaway and others.[53] Patton's popularity with white audiences increased after he began his recording career in 1929 and appeared to be gaining a national reputation. His nephew stated: "He played all up yonder around through Lula on back down here [Cleveland]. People come and get him every night! He sung different songs for them. I couldn't tell you exactly what it was. It was sort of like a jazz song. He'd always play for the white people. They liked different songs. They didn't care much about the blues, but he could sing any kind they wanted to hear. I used to go many times to hear him play and sing."

Charley's niece, however, stated that the whites liked his blues as well as his "love songs":

The biggest he played was for whites. [He played] all them kind. That's what they liked, the blues. And then he had love songs too, "I'll miss you, honey, when you're gone," all that, just different things. "I dreamed of you last night; I woke up this morning, the sun was shining bright; I thought about you; You ought to been lying on my right." Just a lot of old love songs. He put out a lot of good songs. He used to sing "Good Morning, Little School Girl." He loved that song. That was for the young folks too.[54]

Charley's popularity among whites was established well before he began his recording career. He was in great demand as an entertainer, and apparently he was reluctant to turn down any request, sometimes booking himself twice in one night. This practice occasionally got him in trouble when crowds wanted to hold him over. There were also problems when whites wanted him on a night when he was already booked to play for blacks. Charley's niece recalled a couple of incidents of this sort from around 1921 in Blaine, Mississippi, where Charley's father had moved:

You could ask him this morning, say, "I want you to play for me two hours or three hours for me tonight." "All right." Well, he'd [the white man] come that evening, come at him. He'd [Charley] say, "Well, I'm going to play for such and such a person, Mr. So and So." "I want you. I told you I was gonna get you." And he'd go there and play. And the man said, "The music be going so good and the folks be gathered in," he say, "play another hour." This other man gonna fight now. They used to fight over Uncle Charley, right down there in Blaine, Mississippi. Grandpapa would come out there with the Winchester and shoot. Boom! "You all cut it out." Them white folks would stop fighting and go to talking up there. "Well, he's supposed to play for me." "Well, he'll play for you. There ain't but one of him." They were just that crazy about him. Wasn't but one of him. He couldn't play in two places at one time. That broke me up. I had just married, and my husband said, "Let's go to the dance. Charley going to play over here." We went over there to the dance, and everybody was just doing fine. Everybody was dancing in the back yard, and Uncle Charley was out there picking. A man come out there and shouted right straight up, "Charley, come on out of there." My husband said, "You gonna have to stop playing music. These folks gonna kill you." Us runned, and I losed one of my shoes. My husband had to go back and get it the next morning. I wasn't but fifteen years old. . . . And Uncle Charley sat on that bridge and played for them white folks until about five o'clock the next morning. All them white folks was all on that bridge dancing. Uncle Charley was sitting there making music for them. They done broke up this other dance, and then they put their dance on the bridge . . . I'll never forget that. He used to have some tough times. He couldn't be but one. They tried to make him be two folks and play so much for this one and so much for this one. If I hired him to play for me, he's going to play my hours out, 'cause I'm paying him. Well, I'm going to speak up then, say he playing for me. Well, you and me get to fighting about it. They really was crazy about him, everybody around there, white and colored. If they had a big wedding, Uncle Charley was going to play for that wedding. He was well thought of.

The idea of a white man in the Delta hijacking Charley Patton from a black dance to play for whites is enough to boggle the mind. It would be as if a white New York cop had hijacked James Brown from a show at Harlem's Apollo Theatre to perform at a policemen's ball. Like the cop, the man in Blaine undoubtedly knew he could get away with it. What is rather incredible is that he wanted Charley so badly, that all the other whites wanted him, and that Charley entertained them until five o'clock in the morning. One wonders whether Charley or any of the whites attached any significance to all this. Were the whites drawing Charley into their world for a night? Or was Charley drawing the whites into some inscrutable world that fascinated them but which they didn't really understand? Was he secretly pleased that the people "were trying to make him be two folks"? The fact that he played on a bridge only seems to add some special symbolic meaning to the whole affair.

The ultimate reasons for Patton's extraordinary popularity in the Delta are hard to pinpoint. Clearly, Fahey was right, in a sense, in stressing Patton's role as a consummate *entertainer*. He could give an audience what it wanted in the way of repertoire and style, and he did many tricks with the guitar, snapping the strings, playing it behind his head and between his legs, flipping it, tapping on it with his fingers, and so forth. But there were plenty of other blues artists who could do tricks and who gave audiences what they wanted. Many, like Willie Brown, were technically better and more versatile guitarists and were judged so by their peers. Others, like "Son" House, had better natural voices. But there is something special that seemed to set Charley Patton beyond the others in his own day and which still exerts a great power through his records some eighty years after his death. There is a special quality of timing in his singing and playing that is hard to define but immediately arrests the attention. Beyond this there is a sense of *absolute conviction* in his singing and playing. To a greater degree than the others, over a longer period of time, on a more regular basis, and equally in front of black and white audiences, Charley Patton was able to plumb the depths of feeling contained in his blues, spirituals, and other folksongs. Even when he garbled his words or meaning or made mistakes on the guitar, as he occasionally did, the feeling is there, a feeling of overwhelming intensity. It is a feeling that Robert Palmer aptly called *deep blues*, a phrase used by blues artists themselves as their ultimate aesthetic criterion for the music and its performers.[55] And despite his occasional mistakes and shortcomings, Patton's records reflect a feeling of intense pride in his work. He may have considered his recording sessions to be just another job, he may not have rehearsed his songs as much as he should have, but underlying this casual approach and willingness to please all audiences there was a strong oneness and wholeness of character and talent in a man that people were trying to make into "two folks." His recordings are like chips from a huge diamond.

One of the most unfathomable aspects of Charley Patton's life is his actual personality. As already noted, several writers have painted a rather negative picture of the man, criticizing alleged failings such as his stinginess, his drinking, his arguing and "squabbling," his treatment of women, his religious hypocrisy, and his casual or chaotic approach to musical composition and performance. This picture, however, is not consistent with the great respect that was accorded to him both as a man and as a musician. We have already noted Tom Rushing's assessment. Charley's nephew stated that he was "friendly with everybody." Reverend Rubin Lacy, a former blues singer, who knew Charley in the Delta around 1929 or 1930, stated, "I thought he had fine ways and actions. He wasn't no bad man . . . He had a good record. He stood good. He had no bad marks on him. Oh yeah, he was a nice guy."[56] Some of Patton's alleged failings might even be viewed another way. For example, "Son" House stated that Patton was tight with his money.[57] This trait, however, might be viewed positively as an inclination to save his money and not spend it foolishly or make risky loans. Unlike most blacks in the Delta, Charley had money throughout the year, and there must have been many "friends" who approached him for loans. Knowing from his father how the credit system worked in the Delta, Charley probably wisely chose not to "furnish" his friends for the year.

There is no doubt that Charley Patton drank liquor. Possibly he could have been classified as an alcoholic. The nature of his profession meant that he would always be in an environment where drinking was a normal activity. He must have had many drinks offered to him. But for all the reports of his drinking, there are none that have him "sloppy drunk" or unable to perform at his best. The main reports of heavy drinking come from the last two years of his life, when he knew he had heart trouble. Possibly in these years his consumption of alcohol was no greater than it had been earlier, but he was simply less able to withstand its effects. His sister Viola stated that "he hardly drank at all."[58] Former blues singer Reverend Rubin Lacy's comment was simply, "Well, his drinking, a lot of us fellows did that."[59] Ruffin Scott, a church man and Patton's neighbor on Dockery Farms for many years, said, "Charley wasn't no trouble maker at all. He had to take a little shot, like that. He just wasn't no drunkard like a lot of 'em was." Perhaps the situation was best summed up by Tom Rushing, former deputy sheriff of Bolivar County whose specific duty it was to arrest the makers of moonshine whisky. Rushing said, "He seemed to be a more or less sober man. I don't think probably he would have ever gotten where he did if he'd been fighting that hundred proof corn whisky."

Charley Patton's argumentativeness seems to have been confined mainly to his relationships with women. These relationships will be examined shortly. His relatives have stated that he was friendly, and most other musicians agree with this assessment. There are consistent reports, however, that Patton argued frequently with Willie Brown.[60] Brown was an outstanding artist and technically may have been a more accomplished guitarist than Patton. He was not as charismatic, however, and perhaps doubted his ability as a singer, preferring to accompany other artists. Charley was undoubtedly aware of Brown's ability and may have felt threatened. Other blues musicians in particular rated Brown highly and tended to compare his playing favorably to Patton's. Patton was proud of his own popularity and may have resented Brown's reputation among their fellow musicians. He and Brown are said to have argued mainly over musical matters. Perhaps, though, their arguments were more in the nature of "lovers' quarrels." Patton and Brown did, after all, perform together off and on for about twenty years, the longest partnership in either musician's career. Patton had partially taught Brown, as he did many other musicians up to the end of his career. Even after Brown moved to Lake Cormorant in the northern part of the Delta around 1930, he continued to play with Patton from time to time. Patton respected Brown enough to bring him to the attention of a record company, something he did also for such artists as Henry Sims, "Son" House, Louise Johnson, and Bertha Lee.

Patton's attitude toward and treatment of women may not have been exemplary in all cases, but they become a bit more understandable when one realizes two facts. One is that Charley clearly believed that the Patton family deserved his primary loyalty. His niece and nephew both have said that he was very generous and helpful to his parents and sisters. He may well have helped other relatives, but this attitude apparently did not extend to his brother. Will "Son" Patton appears to have been the least successful of Bill and Annie Patton's four grown children. Charley may at times have grown weary of supporting him. "Son" House reported that the two brothers had a falling out over Charley's stinginess.[61] As a corollary to his attitude that he should help the Patton family, particularly its women, Charley evidently believed that his own wives or girlfriends should be self-supporting. He made good money himself and must have thought that he deserved a woman who did the same. "Son" House has said that Patton was the kind of man who liked to have a woman who worked in the white folks' kitchen. In this way he wouldn't have to pay for her food, as the woman could bring home enough leftover food from the kitchen to feed them both.[62] House may have been generalizing from the particular example of Bertha Lee, Patton's last wife and apparently the only one House knew. However, even if this was generally the case with Patton, his attitude is quite understandable. As someone with a cash income, Patton was automatically a highly desirable mate. A cook also had a steady cash income, perhaps not a great one, but the leftover food was considered by most southern whites to be a standard supplement to her otherwise low wages. Charley Patton was in a position to have plenty of casual affairs with women, but for his steady woman he probably wanted someone of economic standing similar to his own.

It is important to keep in mind the fact that Charley was extremely attractive to women. He had that special charisma that attaches itself to certain entertainers and causes women to fall at their feet. He was talented and good looking, made good money, came from a well-respected family with good connections, and didn't have to work under a "bossman." Clarksdale bluesman Wade Walton stated that Patton had to hire someone there to beat the women away with a stick![63] Charley's niece described a typical scene:

You know, women will pull up on musicians, won't they? I noticed that on TV. Them boys be out there singing, and they just have to hold them back from them. They just be reaching. That's just the way they was about Uncle Charley. Gather around that buggy. You know, there was more buggies then than there was cars. They gather around that surrey, and they'd just be . . . "Charley, Charley, kiss me, kiss me!" All that stuff. That make his wife jealous, she quit him. Just a mess, you know.

Although Charley's act, with all its movements and guitar tricks, was certainly erotic and his songs are full of references to his enjoyment of women and sex, he must have also been able to convey the impression that it was *an act*. Otherwise his life probably would not have lasted long. Reverend Rubin Lacy, a former Delta bluesman, neatly summed up the situation: "Charley Patton, just like any other musician, he had sense enough not to pay a whole lot of women attention, bragging, and trying to act a fool. If I had did that, I'd have been in trouble long ago, wouldn't have been here now."[64]

Certainly any bluesman who played as much for whites as Patton did had to be especially careful in this regard. He was no doubt as attractive to many of the white women he played for as he was to the black women. However, any display of interest on their part could be very dangerous, and interest on his part could be fatal. No incident of this sort has ever been reported about Patton. There was the problem, though, that he could control his own behavior but could not fully control that of others. There are jealous people everywhere, and Patton ran the danger of becoming the focus of someone's frustrations and jealousy. This was always his mother's fear, and in 1929 this fear was realized. The story was recounted by Patton's niece Bessie Turner:

My uncle, everybody was in love with him. He used to sing, "I got a little old woman, she got two gold teeth." He had a record [i.e., a song] made out of that. And a man got so jealous because his wife was there dancing, and she had two gold teeth. . . . He stood on the outside of the door, up there in Mound Bayou. When they stopped playing and the dance was over, Uncle Charley started out. That man hit Uncle Charley with a razor, hit him there [in the neck] and cut him clean around there. And Uncle Charley was just bowing his head down like that. And they brought him on to Cleveland to the doctor. His shoes was full of blood. They had to scoop that blood out of his shoe. [The man] said, "He was trying to take my wife." . . . He [Charley] had made him a blues about a little old woman got two gold teeth. The man got jealous of Uncle Charley because of the woman. You know how womens do. They just be "Ah, hah, hah," just grabbing at you. And that man just stood out there trying to kill my uncle . . . That was in 1929. It hurt him bad, cut him from here around there. The doctor said it was lacking a hair of cutting that goozle loose. That's right.

I saw him in 1932, that man what cut him. He runned off. He hid, 'cause he knew he wasn't going to live if they could have found him. And I run up on him. I went into the Chinaman's store there in Pace, Mississippi, me and my husband. I was buying some stuff. You know, people used to cut up stuff on blocks, cut the meat up on blocks. Them big knives was laying there. He come in, Mr. Williams. I said, "Hello, Mr. Williams. You the one that cut Charley Patton, but he's doing fine now." "Yeah, he was going to take my wife. She was going crazy over him. I had to put a stop on it." I said, "Sure enough." He didn't know I was his niece. I just walked around by that Chinaman there, and I said, "Yeah, and I'm going to kill you." I throwed that knife, and my husband grabbed me, and I just split him clean on down there. I ain't seen him since. He was going to kill my uncle, and stand up there talking about what he was going to do, and I was standing there and seen something I could use. Bad business to kill my brother, my uncle, or my sister, and then stand before me and say they did it. Now you know that's pretty hard to take. I looked at him, and it looked like a black streak come across my face, and I just reached there and got that knife. And daddy seen what I was going to do, my husband. He seen what I was gonna do, and he hollered, "Look out!" When he looked around and broke to run, I let him have it. That knife swung at him back there and come on down and split that coat off. I mean it, cut it all the way, 'cause he left the coat laying out there on that old wagon. I ain't seen him from that day to this one. He named himself another name, but we knew him well, you know. . . . You can name yourself anything, but you a so-and-so. I know you. All of us had a high temper. I told Uncle Charley about it. He had left Mound Bayou and moved up to Pace. He called himself getting out of the way, dodging the Pattons. Garf Tucker, Old Man Tucker, old tall man.

Charley was lucky to have survived this razor attack, and he bore the scar from it for the rest of his life. Tom Cannon stated that it took place at a house party on the George Carter place near Mound Bayou, and that afterwards Charley frequently wore a scarf to keep the scar from showing. The attack probably occurred early in 1929, for on a Paramount Records publicity photograph, almost certainly taken at the time of his June 14, 1929, recording session, Patton's shirt collar and coat are raised considerably on his left side. He evidently did this deliberately in order to hide the scar, although it made his bow tie look askew. Whether the wound affected his singing is not known, but his voice sounds strong on all three of his Paramount sessions of 1929 and 1930.

We do not know what Charley's criteria were for considering a relationship with a woman to be a "marriage" or how he distinguished a "wife" from a girlfriend. One would presume that in his mind a marriage at least had the characteristics of a common residence over a period of time, a residence Charley would call "home" and to which he would return after his trips to play music, and a reasonable degree of faithfulness to one another. He is said to have argued and fought frequently with his women. Charley himself was notoriously jealous and demanded absolute faithfulness from his wives. His sister Viola stated that if another man even looked at his woman, he would whip her and quit her. Delta bluesman Hayes McMullen stated that Patton would knock women out with his guitar.[65] On the other hand, a number of women are said to have quit Charley, mostly because of the attention he received from other women. No doubt his frequent trips away from home added to his problems. His nephew stated simply, "He didn't stay with his wives too long."

According to Patton family tradition, Charley had eight wives. This was probably his own reckoning. Given his popularity with women, he probably had many casual affairs between his marriages and may even have had more than one wife simultaneously in different locations, not to mention the possibility of brief outside affairs. Two of his known relationships were with women from the hill country around Bolton. Perhaps they were childhood sweethearts or simply women he met on return trips there. The overall picture is confused and will probably never be fully disentangled. It is doubtful that he actually went through the legal formalities of marriage and divorce eight times. In fact, I have been able to trace only six marriage applications, three of which appear to have resulted in legally recorded marriages, but I have not made a complete examination. Research at the Bolivar County courthouse in Cleveland reveals four marriage records, and two more were found at the Sunflower County courthouse in Indianola. None was found at the Coahoma County courthouse in Clarksdale. A thorough search at other courthouses, such as in Tunica, Greenville, Vicksburg, Raymond, and Jackson, might reveal further marriage records. His son Will Williams stated:

> There was, what they told me, I counted about seven wives he had. And they say he had more. Because everywhere he went off from home, any time it was a distance, he'd stay two or three weeks or maybe a month, and then he'd get a woman, and he married her. Fool her that he didn't have no wife, and then he'd marry her and then start a family with her, and then he'd leave and go back home. So I just said he was a rolling stone.... To tell you the truth, I don't think Charley had too many friends.... The people would go to hear him play, but the mens didn't care too much about him, see, 'cause the womens was going for him, see. Them womens really went for him. My brother said, when he died, "Well, he never stayed

Will Williams (Patton's son), Cleveland, MS, 1989. (Photograph by David Evans)

nowhere, but he'll stay where he at now." And so we laughed, and that was it. He never stayed nowhere. I say he had hot foot powder on his shoes or something, 'cause he never would stay.

On September 12, 1908, in Cleveland, Charley and Gertrude Lewis applied for and were granted a marriage license, but a certificate of marriage was never completed. Patton swore that he had reached the age of twenty-one, and Gertrude swore that she had reached the age of eighteen. Patton signed the application with his mark (X), and his name was spelled "Charlie" by the clerk. His sister Viola stated that this was his first marriage.[66] Around this same time Patton also had a relationship with Lizzie Taylor, either in Stringtown in Bolivar County or near Sumner in Yalobusha County, that lasted off and on for several years. The early portrait photo of Patton was preserved by Lizzie Taylor.[67]

Charley's relationship with Millie Barnes (later Millie Torry) must have begun sometime after this, perhaps in 1909 or 1910.[68] She was born ca. 1887–92 and may have lived on Dockery Farms at the time she began her relationship with Charley. Her father, Wesley Barnes, was a musician who helped teach Charley. In 1967 Millie recalled that Charley left her and went to Dermott, Arkansas, with another musician named Tee-Nicey Wade. Millie and Charley had a daughter, China Lou, who was described by Tom Cannon as a "big heavy set bright woman." China Lou later married but had no children. She loved music and operated a café at Boyle with her younger half-sister, who was the daughter of Millie and Cliff Torry. Her cousin Bessie Turner stated that China Lou greatly admired her father, learned to sing just like him, and kept some of his records throughout her life. She died of a stroke around 1962. On visits to his daughter Charley was probably able to maintain a cordial relationship with her stepfather Cliff Torry in part because his brother Will "Son" Patton had been married to a Mary Torry, who was probably a relative.

On April 18, 1913, Charley applied to marry Dela Scott in Indianola, with Will Dockery listed as a witness. It is not known how long this relationship lasted. In 1915, on a visit to the sawmill town of Kentwood, Louisiana, Charley began a relationship with Sallie Hollins that produced a son Johnnie (known as "Son") born on February 2, 1916. Charley maintained this relationship, and on December 25, 1918, another son named Will was born in New Orleans, where Sallie had moved. Patton came there and moved Sallie and the two boys to Sunflower Plantation, a place north of Dockery and east of Merigold run by a woman named Belle Parker. Charley did not live there with Sallie, however, and seldom visited. Later she married a man named Frank Williams, and the two boys took his surname. Will Williams stated that Charley had also settled another wife and some children, five boys and six girls, on the same plantation and had left them 180 acres of land there. Later Will and his mother and brother moved to Meltonia, west of Shaw, and Charley visited them around 1933 when he was playing nearby for the wedding of I. C. Walker. Charley had plenty of money and was making ten dollars for playing at the wedding, but he gave the boys only fifty cents apiece. Will resented this for the rest of his life, as it was all he ever got from his father. Despite this, he still acquired a guitar and tried to learn to play it like Charley.

Around 1916, while Charley was maintaining his relationship with Sallie Hollins, he also took up with Martha Christian. Their daughter Rosetta stated that Charley and Martha were married in Cleveland, but no marriage record has been found at the courthouse there. Nevertheless, Patton listed "Martha" as his wife's name on his draft registration of September 12, 1918, stating that they lived on his father's farm in Renova. Rosetta was born on August 10, 1917. Her birth certificate lists Charley Patton (aged 32, a farmer, living in Bolivar County) and Martha Christian (aged 29, a housewife, living in Bolivar

Rosetta Patton Brown (Patton's daughter), Duncan, MS, 1992. (Photograph by David Evans)

County) as her parents and Rosetta as having a "legitimate birth." Rosetta stated that her mother's family owned land at Renova, and while growing up there she often played with the children of Charley's sister Katie. She said that her parents' marriage lasted only a year or two but that Charley frequently visited her and her mother until around 1929 and would give Rosetta money. On one visit Charley brought a daughter named Willie Mae Turner, slightly older than Rosetta, who lived in Mound Bayou. Charley also told her of a son who died in infancy. Apparently he didn't tell her about his two sons by Sallie Hollins.

Charley's relationship with Martha must have ended soon after his draft registration, because on November 12, 1918, he was granted a license to marry Roxie Morrow, and they were married that very day by Reverend W. C. McCoy, with the marriage certificate filed at the courthouse in Cleveland on November 25. Charley did not sign these documents. His name was spelled Chas (*sic*) by the court clerk. Charley and Roxie stayed together longer than most of his marriages, perhaps about three years. Tom Cannon stated that they lived on Dockery Farms and that Roxie had a child from a previous marriage. The year 1918, during which Charley Patton was involved in serious relationships with three women, was an important year for him in other ways as well. His parents had recently moved off Dockery, his brother Will was fighting in the war in France, and his other brother "C" Patton had recently been killed in a hunting accident. Perhaps Charley felt that he needed the security of married life at this time.

On December 21, 1921, Charles Patten (*sic*) and Minnie Franklin were granted a marriage license in Indianola and were married on January 5, 1922. Charley's sister Viola Cannon stated that Charley met Minnie in Merigold right after he left Dockery Farms.[69] She apparently came from Vicksburg or the hills east of that city, perhaps around Bolton. Tom Cannon recalled Minnie and stated that Charley carried her away from Dockery, a statement that seems to contradict Tom's mother's account of Minnie leaving Charley and moving to Vicksburg, taking his money and pistol. Minnie herself stated that she left Patton in 1924.[70]

A marriage license was granted to Charles Patten (*sic*) and Mattie Parker on June 7, 1924. Tom Cannon recognized the name Mattie Parker but could give no further details. Between 1924 and sometime in 1930 Charley is said to have lived east of Merigold with a woman named Udy or Sudy.[71] It is not known how long this relationship lasted. Perhaps it was an "on and off" affair or an "outside" relationship of some sort, or perhaps this woman was the same person as Charley's next wife. On April 22, 1926, Charlie (*sic*) Patton and Bertha (or Burtha) Reed were granted a marriage license at Cleveland and married by Reverend D. W. Spearman. The marriage certificate was filed on May 8. Tom Cannon recalled Bertha as being "real young" at the time of the marriage. She was from the hill country, near where Charley was born. Tom Cannon said that they had two children, but he might have been confusing them with Charley's children by Sallie Hollins. Cannon said that Charley quit Bertha at Beaver Bayou near Merigold, where they had evidently been living:

He had a wife had two children. He lived up there from Mound Bayou. He married a girl up there and kept her about two or three years. And him and her parted. He sent her back to the hills. He brought her out of the hills and sent her back to the hills. He had three children, I know. There was a daughter he had by his wife on Dockery, and then he had them by this other girl they call Bertha. He had another woman called Bertha from the hills, and he sent her back to the hills where they come from, Bolton. His wife on Dockery, she was called Roxie. He had another wife on Dockery they called Millie. He had the daughter by Millie.

Charley apparently left the area around Merigold and Renova in the latter part of 1929 when his first records were released. At this point he became headquartered around Clarksdale or just to the north in Lula. In February 1930 he brought the fiddler Henry Sims from nearby Farrell to his second recording session. "Son" House recalled that by the middle of 1930 Charley was living at Lula. He left Lula in August of that year for his third Paramount recording session with House, Willie Brown, and a young woman named

Louise Johnson, whom Patton was trying to court.[72] In "Moon Going Down" (Paramount 13014), which he recorded during that session, Patton mentioned a woman from Clarksdale named Rosetta Henry, with whom he may have had a recent brief relationship, but the lyrics state that she told him, "I don't want you hangin' around."

Patton's last wife was Bertha Lee Pate, a tall dark woman whom he had met at Lula. She was born in 1902 and had been previously married to Cleveland Harper, by whom she had a son. By 1930 she was divorced and living with her parents. Charley and Bertha may not have begun living together until 1932 or 1933. They moved south to Holly Ridge, located in Sunflower County between Indianola and Leland. There they lived on the property of a white man, Tom Robertson, for whose family Bertha cooked. Local resident Joseph "Coochie" Howard claimed that they raised a little girl, possibly a child of Bertha from a previous relationship, and that Charley even did a bit of farming. Charley's nephew and niece stated that Charley and Bertha were happy together, although others have recalled them arguing frequently in public. Before settling at Holly Ridge, they might have lived for a time on Dockery Farms, staying with Charley's sister Viola. T. C. Bailey, born in 1909, lived about five miles from Dockery, where Charley and his wife (who was almost certainly Bertha Lee) were staying, and used to pick them up and take them to parties and juke houses. Bailey stated:

> We used to run around together. That was In the thirties, I had a car and he [Charley] didn't. He played out in the country at them houses. Different ones got juke houses, get him to play for 'em. He played for me sometimes. I have run a juke when I was out there in the country too. I carried him to different places. Sometimes he played twice in one night. He played by himself. We drank that corn whiskey. He wouldn't get drunk. He'd get high so he could play good. He'd just sit down in one place where he could watch his wife. He didn't want you to talk to his wife. She could dance. She could sing too. She'd just sing behind him. He'd fight and shoot too. He carried a gun. He got in fights near about everywhere he played.

Bertha Lee herself seemed to have good memories of her brief marriage to Charley Patton.[73] Apparently, unlike any of Charley's previous wives, she was a blues singer and even played some guitar. Charley probably had a kind of respect for her that he didn't have for his other wives and may have treated her as a musical protégée. In turn, she apparently took good care of him at a time when he came to know he was suffering from heart trouble. She also seems to have understood his ways and his moods, which may have given her a special hold on him. At least she suggests this in her probably autobiographical "Mind Reader Blues" (Vocalion 02650), which she recorded in 1934.

1. Baby, I can see just what's on your mind.
Baby, I can see just what's on your mind.
You got a long black woman with a gold teeth in her face. (*sic*)

2. I take a long look right smack down in your mind.
I take a long look right smack down in your mind.
And I'm seeing both womens numb'ring up and down the line. (*unclear*)

3. Don't kid your mama; you ain't fooling nobody but yourself.
Ah, don't kid your mama; you ain't fooling nobody but yourself.
And what I see on your mind, you would not have no friend.

4. I remember a day when I was living at Lula town.
I remember a day when I was living at Lula town.
My man did so many wrong things till I had to leave the town.

5. I caught the Riverside; my man caught the transfer boat.
I caught the Riverside; my man caught the transfer boat.
And the last time I seed him, he had a gal way up the road.

6. Well, I'm worried now and I won't be worried long.
Well, I'm worried now and I won't be worried long.
Well, I'm worried now and I won't be worried long.

If, as the song declares, Charley had caused Bertha Lee to worry, she indeed would not have to worry long, for he died three months after she recorded this song. Charley probably knew that the end was near. One of the songs he and Bertha Lee recorded together was a powerful spiritual titled "Oh Death" (Vocalion 02904), containing the frequently repeated line, "Lord, I know my time ain't long."

Probably a month or two prior to his final recording session, Patton traveled with "Son" House and Willie Brown to Jackson to make some test recordings of "sanctified" songs for talent scout H. C. Speir. The one piece that House later recalled from this session was a song featuring Charley's singing titled "I Had a Dream Last Night Troubled Me."[74] W. R. Calaway, who had worked for the Paramount Record Company in their Artist & Repertoire division, was now working for Vocalion in the same capacity. He would have known the abilities of the three musicians in the blues field, and it seems likely that Speir wanted to demonstrate to him that they were equally capable in the gospel field. House claimed that Vocalion wanted the three men to come to New York, but that he and Brown were unable to make the trip for reasons that are not entirely clear. Patton instead went with Bertha Lee. It is known that Calaway came to Mississippi and managed to get Charley and Bertha released from the Belzoni jail. Possibly, after hearing the bad news directly from House and Brown, Calaway concluded that it would be best for Bertha to accompany Charley on the trip, for he must have come to realize that Patton was not in the best of health.

Patton's death certificate indicates that the onset of his fatal heart trouble occurred on January 27, 1934.[75] This date was just three days before the beginning of his recording session for Vocalion. Probably Charley was experiencing some problems with his health and consulted a doctor, perhaps at Calaway's suggestion, to determine if he should make the trip north. Charley's sister Viola stated that a doctor had told him to stop playing music, a warning that may have taken place at this time. Nevertheless, he made the trip to a chilly New York City, accompanied by Bertha Lee. His performances sound strong, though a few times he can be heard breathing heavily, and he has a little trouble hitting some high notes accurately. In three days he and Bertha Lee recorded twenty-nine songs, a number that indicates that he still had plenty of strength at the time. Bertha Lee remembered that they spent three weeks making records, but this seems unlikely, because they only recorded on three successive days and Patton likely consulted a doctor in Mississippi only three days before their session began. Possibly, however, they stayed in New York for a couple of weeks after their session ended. She recalled that they recorded only in the afternoons when "Charley had his voice ready," and afterwards they performed informally in the studio for Calaway and other personnel from the company. She also recalled that there was plenty of whiskey in the studio.[76] Eight of the songs they recorded were religious titles. These did not include the title Patton had recorded as a test in Jackson with "Son" House and Willie Brown. That song, instead, was assigned by Vocalion to Florida singer-guitarist Louis Washington ("Tallahassee Tight"), who recorded it as "Had a Dream That Troubled Me" (Vocalion 02634) in the same New York studio on January 15, 1934, about two weeks before the session by Charley Patton and Bertha Lee.

In early April 1934, Charley Patton gave his last performance. It was a dance for whites, probably not too far from Holly Ridge. He had been suffering from bronchitis, perhaps from a winter or spring cold. Bertha Lee stated that he returned home hoarse and unable to talk or get his breath properly.[77]

He remained in bed for three weeks and had to sleep with the windows open in order to get enough air to breathe. He was visited by a doctor on Tuesday, April 17, and again on Friday, April 20. Many relatives and fellow blues singers and friends visited him during this final illness. His sister said that an attempt was made to take him to a hospital, but his car was bogged in mud from the spring rains. The end came on the morning of Saturday, April 28, 1934. Some have claimed that Patton was buried the following day at Longswitch cemetery, less than a mile from his last home at Holly Ridge. However, Tom Cannon, his nephew, stated that Charley was buried at Holly Ridge. In December 1986 Michael Leonard and I examined the Longswitch cemetery but found no marker for Charley Patton. Residents of Holly Ridge told me and Marina Bokelman in 1967 that Patton was buried at Holly Ridge, but no marker was found there either.

Charley's niece Bessie Turner described his last days and his death:

And finally one morning he went off and composed some records. And he came home with a shortness at his heart. That was on a Wednesday . . . Saturday morning he called his wife and said, "I'm fixing to leave you now." And he started to preaching. He said, "I've got to preach the text of the Revelation." He started to preaching that morning. He preached all that week, and the next Saturday he passed on. And she called us. I was up there in Shaw, Mississippi, then. She called us and told us that he had passed. Us came down there and looked at him. He had the Bible over there in his hand and his hand up there across his breast. He was gone. They had his funeral that Sunday down there at Holly Ridge. He didn't want to go to no undertaker. He told 'em, "Don't carry me to no undertaker." Said, "Carry me right away from this house to the church and from the church to the cemetery." He died that Saturday, and we buried him that Sunday, 'cause he didn't want to go to a undertaker. That Saturday night they had a big wake for him. A lot of his boys who sang with him was right there too. I'll never forget the last song they sung, "I'll Meet You in the Sweet Bye and Bye." They sung that so pretty and played the music, you know. Couldn't nobody cry. Everybody was just thinking how a person could change around right quick, you know. Changed right quick and then preached Revelation, the thirteenth chapter of Revelation. It says, "Let your light shine that men may see your good work and glorify our Father which art in heaven." I'll never forget it. He said, "Did you hear that? My light been shining on each side. I let it shine for the young; I let it shine for the old." Said, "Count my Christian records and count my swinging records. Just count 'em. They even!" And you know he was just smiling, just tickled to death. Looked like he was happy when he was going.

And he told another boy named Quincely, said, "I want you to take up where I left off." . . . He just gave a lecture there, man. I don't know where Quince went.

You know, he could play second behind him. At the time he was living up there from Indianola, out in the country there somewhere. . . . I would go to see him [i.e., Charley], and I happened to be there when he got low. And he told Quince what he wanted him to do, but I don't know if Quince ever did it or not. . . . I'll never forget Quince, 'cause he called him off the porch . . . And Quince said, "All right, Mister Charley. I'll try it." He was younger than Uncle Charley. Uncle Charley was a settled man when he died.

Possibly Charley preached from the fourteenth chapter of Revelation, a much more appropriate passage for a deathbed sermon than the thirteenth chapter. It is not known whether young Quincely followed in Patton's footsteps. Probably he didn't, as nobody by this name is mentioned anywhere in the literature on blues.

Charley Patton was close to the age of fifty when he died. According to his death certificate, his funeral was conducted by the Central Burial Association of Indianola, where Charley may have had an insurance policy. A man named Willie Calvin served as the informant for Patton's death certificate. Ironically, he gave Patton's occupation as "farmer," a type of work that Charley hated and strove all his life to avoid. It is not known who preached the funeral sermon or what was said. The funeral was well attended, however. Charley's nephew said, "They had a big funeral. It was people from every which way, white and black." Patton's sons Johnnie and Will Williams attended the funeral, and Will later recalled:

My brother had a wife at the time, and he had got him a old car, and we was together. And so he say it was too many hollering "Poor daddy! Poor daddy!" in that church. So, "My poor dad! My poor dad! My poor dad!" And he just got vexed. He said the whole church was hollering, "My poor daddy," and it wasn't no need of him saying nothing but going on with it. So we left. I didn't see him buried. . . . See when they got up and talking and carrying on, the children started to hollerin' and cryin' and carryin' on, so my brother, he just wanted to leave. I left too.

On the day after the funeral Bertha Lee received a check in the mail from Vocalion Records made out to Charley for close to nine hundred dollars. Charley's niece recounted:

When he died, you ought to see. She had a roll of money. Money and checks was sent in there from everywhere when they found out he was dead. And when he got his check, she had to send it back in, 'cause, you see, you couldn't cash a dead man's check. She got it that Monday. Sent it back, and they changed it over to her. Bertha Lee, that was his wife. . . . Went down there, and they said, "Charley's check is here." I think it was eight hundred and some dollars. . . . Then they sent her a bonus too. Then they come down and put the tomb on his grave. They come down from Milwaukee and put that tomb on that grave. When he started to composing records and everything, all that's on the tomb. His picture on that tomb, supposed to be, . . . right at the head.

If record company representatives came to Mississippi to erect a grave marker, they were probably from American Record Corporation in New York, the parent company of Vocalion Records that Charley had recorded for three months before his death, and not from Paramount Records in Port Washington (not Milwaukee), Wisconsin, that he had recorded for in 1929 and 1930. Paramount, in fact, was already out of business by 1934. Such a monument may have been erected, but I have not been able to find it in three searches of the Holly Ridge cemetery since 1967, one of them quite thorough. The cemetery, however, was overgrown with weeds and brambles, and many of the tombstones had fallen over and some had been covered with dirt and weeds. Tom Cannon noted that graveyards are cleaned from time to time and some stones may have been removed in the process. Thus, if Charley did have a gravestone, it may have either fallen over or been removed. Russell Brown, a resident of Holly Ridge, claimed that when the local cotton gin close to the cemetery added a lint burner, it was constructed over some graves including Charley Patton's. If this is true, it would have constituted a sadly ironic "eternal flame" for the King of the Delta Blues.

In the years since Patton's death a number of rumors have grown up about how he died. Some have said that his throat was cut by a jealous woman. This report is probably based on the razor attack he experienced in Mound Bayou, which was actually committed by a man who was provoked by jealousy over a woman and which did indeed come close to killing Patton. Another report has it that he drank whisky that had been poisoned by a jealous man or woman. This is probably based on the death of bluesman Robert Johnson, who was poisoned in this manner four years later near Greenwood, Mississippi. Finally, it has been said that Patton was struck by lightning and killed. This was apparently the fate of Walter Rhodes, an accordion player from Cleveland whom Patton undoubtedly knew. Rhodes's "The Crowing Rooster" (Columbia 14289-D), recorded in 1927, was adapted by Patton two years later as "Banty Rooster Blues" (Paramount 12792) and became a hit record for him. No doubt the two artists became confused in the minds of many people.

An examination of the recordings of Charley Patton can provide some important additional insights to his life and character. In seeking such insights, however, one must use considerable caution and be aware of several variable factors. In the first place, blues singers do not always sing about themselves, even when it appears that they do. In many cases they will describe the thoughts or actions of others as if they were the singer's. Patton did this in at least one song, which will be discussed later, and perhaps in others. Blues singers also borrow verses and whole songs from other singers, frequently by learning them from records. Over a quarter of Patton's blues recordings, both of his popular song versions, and at least one of his spirituals were influenced by earlier commercial recordings of other artists. Finally, many blues singers, including Charley Patton, make use of a body of traditional verses, shared by hundreds of other blues singers, which they individually rework and recombine to create new songs. Although Patton created a number of highly original verses and songs, he relied heavily on traditional verses as building blocks for his compositions. Thus much of his actual language is not his own but is borrowed from the shared tradition of folk blues.[78]

Just how Charley Patton created his blues songs is not known for certain. Nevertheless, in listening to his records, one gets an impression of great spontaneity in his singing. Patton draws heavily upon the body of shared traditional verses, but he seems to do so largely at the time of performance. Many of his songs seem only minimally planned or rehearsed, particularly in their texts. Patton seems to have assembled in advance a "blues core" consisting of a melody, a guitar part, and one or more key verses, which would give the song a certain degree of identity, and then added other verses at the time of performance. Hints of such spontaneity are to be found in the fact that, when alternate takes of a blues exist, there are considerable differences between his two recordings of the same song at a single recording session. It also appears that Patton was often trying to recreate a sense of context and a live audience in the recording studio, especially through his spoken interjections in many songs, often made in the voices of women or other bystanders. This spontaneity and unrehearsed quality is matched in the recordings of only a few other early blues recording artists, among them Patton's contemporary Henry Thomas and two of Patton's disciples and associates, Tommy Johnson and Big Joe Williams.

Excluding his guitar accompaniments of other singers (Henry Sims, Bertha Lee, and possibly "Son" House), and viewing alternate takes recorded at a single session as versions of the same song, but viewing songs recorded as Parts 1 and 2 as separate songs, we can conclude that Patton altogether recorded fifty-two issued songs: thirty-five blues, two folk ballads, three ragtime songs, two popular songs, and ten spirituals. Blues were thus 64 percent of his recorded and released repertoire. It would be impossible to establish percentages of various genres in his total repertoire because of the improvisational and spontaneous character of many of his songs and the fact that some songs might have been dormant in his repertoire or imperfectly known. Also, record companies at this time were especially seeking blues and spirituals from their black artists and therefore might have neglected other material in his repertoire.

Of Patton's thirty-five recorded blues, seven are textually thematic throughout. That is, they concentrate on a single topic over the entire song such that a coherent underlying story or situation can be understood by the listener. Two other blues contain refrains appended to every stanza, which give them a semblance of thematic unity, although the verses themselves deal with a variety of topics that on the surface appear unconnected thematically. Most of Patton's thematic blues are from the latter half of his recording career, suggesting an increasing self-consciousness on his part and an awareness of a need for "original" song material. These traits are typical of blues singers over the course of a recording career. Only one of Patton's thematic blues was recorded at his first session in 1929. Even so, his overall percentage of thematic blues (20 percent) is quite low for a recording artist. At least nine of his blues show some discernible specific influence from earlier blues records by other artists, but in all cases Patton has drastically altered his source material or used only part of it. He did not record any outright "covers" of other artists' blues. He sings fifteen of his stanzas or single lines in more than one recorded blues. There is also some thematic repetition. "Stone Pony Blues" (1934) is something of an updated extension of his earlier hit "Pony Blues" (1929). "Tom Rushen Blues" (1929) and "High Sheriff Blues" (1934) both use versions of the same melody and guitar part and are about two different arrests that Patton experienced. Their close relationship, including a shared lyric stanza, is due to the fact that each song is influenced by the same earlier recording by Ma Rainey. Patton's "Magnolia Blues" and "When Your Way Gets Dark" are simply two rather different takes of the same song recorded in succession at the same early 1930 session but given different titles. Finally, there are lyric and musical similarities between "Bird Nest Bound" (1930) and "Revenue Man Blues" (1934) that are due to the fact that both songs are influenced by Ardell "Shelly" Bragg's 1926 recording of "Bird Nest Blues" (Paramount 12410). The textual differences in these four pairs lead one to think that Patton also composed many of his blues by using the "core" idea and adding additional lines and stanzas at the time of recording. Most of his blues are not thematically coherent but instead are composed mainly from combinations of apparently unrelated traditional phrases, lines, and stanzas that Patton knew and used in any number of different combinations. Quite likely, most of these combinations were made at the time of performance and recording. Son House said of Patton, "Charley, he could start singing of the shoe there and wind up singing about that banana."[79]

Patton's apparent spontaneity, combined with an often imprecise diction and a high degree of surface noise on many of his records, has caused some writers to consider him sloppy, illogical, and sometimes incoherent. He does indeed make occasional mistakes in his singing and playing, but it can be shown that many of his songs have a kind of unconscious structure and coherence based on principles of contrast and association of ideas.[80] Furthermore, the high degree of spontaneity in his songs provides us with a rare opportunity to glimpse a folk blues artist actually *at work* on his songs. Even his blues recordings that are thematic from beginning to end convey the impression that they are *versions* of these songs that happened to be captured in a recording studio, that they are part of a compositional continuum that never resulted in a finished or definitive version. Just as Patton himself was constantly on the move and not content to stay in one place long, so also were his repertoire and his songs constantly shifting. This quality may be annoying to the listener at times, but it allows us an insight into the mind and mental processes of one of the most important blues singers of all time and reveals statements and ideas that other blues artists might have suppressed in an effort to make their songs more polished.

The foregoing discussion should not be taken to mean that Patton's songs and recordings were entirely unplanned and the result of unconscious mental processes. Patton did have a strong interest in composing songs and certainly was capable of doing so in a conscious manner. He simply appears to have had little interest in *finalizing* his compositions. For him the *process* was more important than the *product*. This attitude would explain his apparent casual behavior in the recording studio that so annoyed "Son" House.

Charley's niece stated, "He'd dream a song, and he'd get up and write them." Many folk blues artists have made exactly the same statement about their own compositions. Evidently Charley would write down the ideas he had in dreams and work them out in rough form with the guitar. He probably continued to work with the idea as long as it retained its appeal to himself and his audiences. He seems to have been especially fond of composing topical blues about his own troubles and those of his friends and neighbors. These blues dealt not only with the usual difficulties of the man-woman relationship but also with such subjects as arrests, floods, a drought, a labor strike, and human insensitivity. His niece stated: "Any accidental thing happen, he could take it and make a song out of it and fix it like he want to and make him some money off it too. . . . Anything that come kind of odd, he'd take and make a song out of it. . . . All them hard times, you know, little children walking barefoot, he had a song about that, when their heels cracking open from the hot sand."

Prior to his last recording session he seems to have made an attempt to prepare some songs for the studio. He also used his wife Bertha Lee to help him compose. As a blues singer herself, she was no doubt a sympathetic listener and an intelligent critic. Patton's niece stated:

> I went over to Holly Ridge to see him and spent a week over there, with him and his wife Bertha. And he composed a blues then, "Good morning, little school girl; I want to have a talk with you." That was a good one too. He had a hit on that one, "Good Morning, Little School Girl." He was singing and told us to sit in another room and see how it sounds. You know, he made his own songs. And when he got through with that, a white fellow said, "I'll give you twenty-five dollars for that one right now. That's the first record I want, 'Good Morning, Little School Girl.'" . . . He'd compose, and his wife Bertha would write them as he named it to her. Then he'd get off to hisself, fasten up in a room and give the tune to it. "Bumble Bee, Bumble Bee," I remember I was at his house when he composed that one. "Bumble bee, bumble bee, won't you please come home to me. You got the best stinger of any bumble bee I ever seen."

The first of these songs was not among those that were released from Patton's 1934 session. If he ever recorded it, he did so under another title. Whatever it was that Patton composed on a "school girl" theme, Bessie Turner seems to be confusing it with John Lee "Sonny Boy" Williamson's 1937 hit "Good Morning, School Girl." The second song she mentions was given to Bertha Lee to sing and was recorded by her with Patton's guitar accompaniment under the title "Yellow Bee" (Vocalion 02650). In fact, it is based closely on an earlier recording by Memphis Minnie. In this case, at least, Patton's concept of composing did not preclude a substantial borrowing from another artist's record. And even while his niece's statement seems to suggest a more formal approach to composition, the actual results of the final session reveal just as much spontaneity as on his earlier records. In the case of the song she called "Good Morning, Little School Girl," Patton seems simply to have been recreating the situation of listening to one of his records, probably to test potential audience reaction and sales of a new song. In the case of "Bumble Bee," he seems to have included his wife in his normal process of composition by having her write down ideas as they came to him rather than writing them himself. Perhaps even at that stage he intended that she should be the one to sing the song in the studio.

In addition to singing about his own and his friends' troubles and hard times, Charley Patton had several other favorite themes in his blues and other secular songs. One theme that occurs repeatedly is movement. In Patton's case it was movement out of *necessity*. This necessity was both economic and emotional. Charley had a "home" with his parents or other relatives, but he couldn't stay there and continue to exercise his talent fully and make a good living. He seems to have been determined to have his talent recognized and not to do manual work like an ordinary black man in the Delta. He developed this attitude at a time when Delta society was becoming strictly divided into black and white groups. The kind of ambiguous status that he sought, which would enable him to avoid the status of "nigger," could only be obtained through movement. Travel for Patton meant *freedom* and *options*. It was a bold and potentially dangerous course to take, since it could leave him outside both white and black organized society. Nevertheless, he steered his course quite successfully, choosing a "black" form of expression, the blues, as a means of escaping the lot of being an *ordinary* black man. He was certainly not trying to be white, which was obviously impossible under the circumstances. He simply wanted equality and recognition of his individuality and the freedom that was the exclusive property of the whites, yet he also wanted to remain in the Delta, his home. His dilemma was that, in order to maintain this freedom and be "at home," he had to travel constantly.

Besides travel, Patton sang about women, particularly the difficulty of finding a woman who would stick with him and tolerate his lifestyle. No doubt, women wanted him to settle down. But this would have meant giving up his freedom and becoming more like an ordinary black man. He might have made attempts to settle down in some of his marriages, but he never sustained a settled lifestyle. His attitude seems to have been that his talent and freedom were things that a woman should appreciate. If she would keep the home fire burning and remain faithful to him, he would support her and return to her from his travels. In several of his blues he sings a favorite line, "You've got a home, mama, long as I've got mine." Patton does not seem to have found such a woman until perhaps at the end of his life. He and Bertha Lee were said to be happy together, although there are also reports that they argued and fought. As a blues singer herself, she may have understood Charley better than his other wives had. Still, she had to travel with him sometimes to hold the relationship together.

The difficulty of maintaining relationships with women seems to have produced two other themes in Charley's life and songs: drinking and fighting. These themes had dramatic observable manifestations in his life and seem to have impressed people who knew him. Unfortunately, they also served to obscure his deeper motivations, and they cast a shadow over his personal reputation.

The one remaining great force in Patton's life and music was religion. We have already noted that the subjects of his religious recordings closely paralleled those of his secular songs, particularly the themes of the journey to heaven, his personal dignity, depression, and the troubles of this world. Religion was very much on Charley's mind throughout his life, but it was apparently not part of his frequent daily practice except in his performance of spiritual songs as needed or requested, his few attempts to preach in public, and on his deathbed. His daughter Rosetta stated: "He really wasn't trying to sing the blues to cause trouble. He was doing that because he made more money. And that's what he was out for, making money. Singing gospel songs, they don't pay you much for them. And that's why he went back to singing the blues, because preaching and singing gospel records, he didn't make as much money. But he would mix them in with his blues."

Charley Patton's first recording session for Paramount Records took place on June 14, 1929, in the Gennett studio at Richmond, Indiana. The fourteen songs that he recorded at this session give a remarkable insight into his personality and his main concerns. This is especially true of the first four songs, which make it appear that Patton wanted to tell his audience emphatically who he was and what was on his mind. Curiously, he began his recorded legacy not with a blues song about himself but with a version of a folk ballad titled "Mississippi Bo Weavil Blues" (Paramount 12805). The boll weevil is a little black insect that bores into the cotton bud (known as a "square"), preventing it from blossoming. It swarmed into Texas from Mexico in the early 1890s and, moving at a rate of about sixty miles per year, reached Mississippi early in the twentieth century. It devastated the state's cotton plantations and acted as a great leveler between whites and blacks. Many writers have pointed out how black farmers identified with the boll weevil despite the difficulties the insect created for blacks as well as whites. Despite every effort to control it, the boll weevil survived and spread, defying every force that the rich and powerful planters could muster against it, making its home on their plantations and forcing them to come to terms with it. Charley Patton in particular must have identified with this insect that was constantly on the move, looking for a home. Several of his verses clearly reveal the appeal of this subject for him.

> 2. Boll weevil, boll weevil, where's your native home, Lordy?
> A' Louisiana and Texas is where I was bred and born, Lordy.

3. Well, I saw the boll weevil, Lord, a' circle, Lordy, in the air, Lordy.
And next time I seed him, Lord, he had his family there, Lordy.

4. Boll weevil left Texas, Lord, he bid me fare-you-well, Lordy.
Spoken: Where you going now?
I'm going down to Mississippi, gonna give Louisiana hell, Lordy.

. . . .

7. Boll weevil told his wife, said, "I believe I may go north, Lordy."
Spoken: Boy, I'm gonna tell all about it.
Let's leave Louisiana and go to Arkansas, Lordy.

. . . .

9. Boll weevil told the farmer, "I think I'll treat you fair, Lordy."
Sucked all the blossoms and leaved you a empty square, Lordy.

10. Boll weevil, boll weevil, where's your native home, Lordy?
'Most anywhere they're raising cotton and corn, Lordy.

The title of Patton's next piece, "Screamin' and Hollerin' the Blues" (Paramount 12805), suggests that he viewed the song as a kind of generic blues, a general statement of the things that concerned him. Indeed, it does serve as an outline for the topics on which he would elaborate in many subsequent recordings, topics such as the necessity to travel, his closeness to his mother and her concern about his lifestyle, his search for a "home," his difficulty in maintaining relationships with women, and the conflict between the blues and religion.

1. Jackson on a high hill, mama, Natchez just below.
Jackson on a high hill, mama, Natchez just below.
Spoken: Tell 'em that we know they are.
[If] I ever get back home, I won't be back no more.

2. Oh, my mama's getting old, her head is turning grey.
My mother's getting old, head is turning grey.
Don't you know it'll break her heart, know I'm living thisaway.

3. I woke up in the morning, jinx all around your bed.
And if I woke up in the morning, jinx all around your bed.

Spoken: Children, I know how it is, baby.
Turned my face to the wall, and I didn't have a word to say.

4. No use of hollering, no use screaming and crying.
No use of hollering, no use of screaming and crying.
For you know you got a home, mama, long as I got mine.

5. Hey, Lord, have mercy on my wicked soul.
Oh, Lord, have mercy on my wicked soul.
Spoken: Baby, you know I ain't gonna mistreat you.
I wouldn't mistreat you, baby, for my weight in gold.

6. Oh, I'm going away, baby; don't you want to go?
I'm going away, sweet mama; don't you want to go?
Spoken: I know you want to go, baby.
Take God to tell when I'll be back here anymore.

As in many other folk blues, Patton's verses in this song are arranged in a symmetrical fashion using techniques of association and contrast.[81] The opening and closing stanzas (1 and 6) present images of travel to distant places with the intention or likelihood of never returning. By way of contrast, the central stanzas (3 and 4) portray the singer at home with his woman as they try to deal with their problems, without stating specifically what those problems are. Stanza 3 concentrates on Patton's own difficulties, which cause him to be unable to speak, whereas in stanza 4 his woman screams and cries while he reassures her that they have a home together. The intermediate stanzas 2 and 5 present some causes for the singer's and his woman's unhappiness. In stanza 2 his lowdown way of living is breaking his mother's heart, while in stanza 5 he has to reassure his woman that he won't mistreat her, with an implication that he either has mistreated her in the past or has a reputation for mistreatment ("my wicked soul").[82]

Patton's next song, "Down the Dirt Road Blues" (Paramount 12854), is brilliant both as a performance and as a composition. According to the recording session ledger, the song's original title (and probably Patton's own) was "Over the Sea Blues." This would have been a better title, as it suggests the expansiveness of Patton's imagination that was capable of thinking in universal terms. The song provides an important insight into Patton's deepest concerns about his own identity and purpose in life.

1. I'm going away to a world unknown.
I'm going away to a world unknown.
I'm worried now, but I won't be worried long.

2. My rider got something; she's trying to keep it hid.
   My rider got something; she's trying to keep it hid.
   Lord, I got something to find that something with.

3. I feel like chopping, chips flying everywhere.
   I feel like chopping, chips flying everywhere.
   I've been to the Nation, mmm Lord, but I couldn't stay there.

4. Some people say them overseas blues ain't bad.
   Spoken: Why, of course, they are.
   Some people say them overseas blues ain't bad.
   Spoken: What was the matter with them?
   It must not have been them overseas blues I had.

5. Every day seem like murder here.
   Spoken: My God, I'm gonna sing 'em.
   Every day seem like murder here.
   I'm gonna leave tomorrow; I know you don't bit more care.

6. Can't go down the dark road by myself.
   Can't go down the dark road by myself.
   Spoken: My God, who you gonna carry?
   If I don't carry my high brown, gonna carry me someone's else.

Once again, the structure of the text is symmetrical. The first and last stanzas (1 and 6) serve to create a framework for the song and state Patton's overriding concern. He is going down a "dark road" to "a world unknown." (The latter phrase would have been familiar to Patton from his upbringing in the church, as it occurred in a well-known hymn of the eighteenth century composed by Charles Wesley.) Patton doesn't know what the future holds for him, but he says that he won't let himself be worried. Stanza 2 and the last line of stanza 5 state that his woman is trying to drag him down and that she doesn't really care about him or his concerns. He knows that he needs a woman's company, however, so he will take one with him on his journey. If he can't take his own "high brown," he will take another man's. In the midst of these thoughts about the direction of his life and his relationship to women, he deals with the question of his own identity in stanzas 3–5. He introduces this theme with a remarkable image of frustration and rage ("I feel like chopping"). Then, in a series of extraordinary allusions, he deals with his own racial ambiguity, expressing the problem in terms of racial *homelands*. "The Nation" means only one thing: the Indian Nation, which became part of the state of Oklahoma in 1907. Did Charley make some kind of pilgrimage there earlier in his life, or did his "black Indian" grandmother or his mother with Indian ancestry perhaps take him there for a visit? Or did he simply go there to play music? There actually are communities of black Indians in Oklahoma, and he seems to be suggesting some sort of a sojourn. In any case, whether he really traveled there or only did so in his imagination, Patton seems to be stating that he found it impossible to maintain an Indian identity. No doubt this was actually the case. His racial makeup may have been more Indian than anything else, but his only strong cultural link might have been through his grandmother, and even she had to live out her life in the Deep South, where everything was viewed in black and white. The "overseas" of stanza 4 must refer to Europe, the home of white people. Charley Patton had not been there himself, but his brother had fought there in a "white folks' war" and could hardly have brought back a very favorable report. Charley knew that he couldn't fully participate in white society, and he seems to be saying so obliquely in this stanza. The first line of stanza 5 must refer to the Delta, the Negroes' "home," where "every day seem like murder." Patton certainly could have played the role of a Negro and probably had to do so at times, but throughout his life he seems to have done everything possible to resist this classification. Patton does not really resolve his dilemma. He simply "leaves" and heads for "a world unknown," vowing not to worry about his situation.

Patton's fourth recording was "Pony Blues" (Paramount 12792), his biggest hit and his signature song. It deals with the problem of establishing and maintaining relationships with women and opens with a traditional stanza that seems to take up where the previous song left off:

> Hitch up my pony, saddle up my black mare.
> Hitch up my pony, saddle up my black mare.
> I'm gonna find a rider, baby, in the world somewhere.

In the fourth stanza Patton expresses his preference for brownskin women in a striking simile and spurns black women:

> And a brownskin woman like something fit to eat.
> Brownskin woman like something fit to eat.
> But a jet black woman, don't put your hands on me.

In his sixth and final stanza he opts for temporary relationships with women without the obligations of marriage.

I got something to tell you, when I gets a chance.
Something to tell you, when I get a chance.
I don't want to marry; just want to be your man.

Each of these stanzas reflected real patterns in Patton's life.[83]

Patton's next three blues all deal with relationships with women and elaborate on ideas he had already expressed. The last of these, "Pea Vine Blues" (Paramount 12877), takes its title from the Pea Vine railroad line, so called because of its winding route. This line was originally constructed by Will Dockery to connect his plantation with the nearby town of Boyle.[84] It was taken over by the Yazoo and Mississippi Valley Railroad and extended to Rosedale. Patton merely uses the Pea Vine as a setting for his song and does not elaborate further on it. His second stanza does, however, foreshadow the epic two-part "High Water Everywhere" (Paramount 12909) that he would record at his next session:

And the levee's sinking, and I, babe, and I . . .
Spoken: Baby, you know I can't stay.
The levee's sinking; Lord, you know I ain't gonna stay.
I'm going up the country, mama, in a few more days.

In his next recording, "Tom Rushen Blues" (Paramount 12877), Charley Patton gave the first indication of his propensity for making a song out of "anything that come kind of odd." Here, perhaps for the first time in recorded blues, a singer mentioned *local* white people and even offered some unfavorable criticism of one of them, in this case the town marshal of Merigold, Tom Day. The discussion of major national and world events and political issues is fairly uncommon in the blues, but discussion of local issues and politicians is almost nonexistent. To do so was quite daring for a man who had lived in the Delta a long time and expected to stay there. Perhaps, therefore, it is of some significance that, after his first recording session, Patton seems to have increased his traveling and was seen less often around Dockery Farms, Cleveland, Merigold, Renova, and Mound Bayou.

1. I lay down last night, hoped that I would have my peace . . . eeeh.
I lay down last night, hoped that I would have my peace . . . eeeh.
But when I woke up, Tom Rushing was shaking me.

2. When you get in trouble, there's no use of screaming and crying . . . mmm.
When you gets in trouble, there's no use of screaming and crying . . . mmm.
Tom Rushing will take you back to Cleveland a' flying.

3. It was late one night, Holloway was gone to bed . . . mmm.
It was late one night, Holloway was gone to bed . . . mmm.
Mister Day brought whiskey taken from under Holloway's head.

4. Ah, boozy booze, ah Lord, to carry me through.
It take boozy booze, Lord, to carry me through.
Thirty days seem like years in the jailhouse where there is no booze.

5. Got up this morning; Tom Day was standing 'round . . . mmm.
Got up this morning; Tom Day was standing 'round.
Say, if he lose his office now, he's running from town to town.

6. Let me tell you folkses just how he treated me . . . mmm.
I'm gonna tell you folkses just how he treated me . . . mmm.
And he brought me here, and I was drunk as I could be.

The melody and some of the lyrics in stanzas 1 and 4 are taken from an earlier recording by Ma Rainey, "Booze and Blues" (Paramount 12242), but most of the language is Patton's own. For this song we are very fortunate to have the commentary of one of the persons who is mentioned in it. Tom Rushing was

Tom Rushing, 1985. (Photograph by Robert Sacré)

born in 1898 near Tylertown, Mississippi, and moved with his parents to the Delta around 1910 when the boll weevil devastated the family farm. He was in a Marine officer training program during World War I and served in the Navy during most of the 1920s. During his service he had the opportunity to visit a number of European countries. In 1928 he married and returned to the Delta, settling in Merigold.

He immediately became a special deputy for Sheriff Joe Smith of Bolivar County. His main duty was breaking up moonshine stills and arresting the moonshiners who made whiskey and the bootleggers who sold it. This was during the era of Prohibition, when the sale of all liquor was illegal. Corn whiskey, or "moonshine," was prosecuted especially severely because its makers and sellers paid no taxes and because it was sometimes made improperly and poisoned its drinkers. Rushing received a cash bonus from every still he broke up. He remained a deputy sheriff until 1932, when Prohibition was repealed. Although Mississippi remained officially "dry" until 1966, Rushing's position was probably terminated due to a loss of its federal funding. He took a job as a tractor salesman and around 1944 used his savings to buy a farm east of Merigold on the Sunflower River. He stated:

I was a rum runner, and I was a pretty important figure among the Negroes, being what I had done and being a deputy sheriff and turning in the bootleggers. Charley . . . lived in Mound Bayou, and that's where he first began to be known. He was in demand around the country here in the Delta for his music. . . . One record he cut about myself, about my deputy work and so forth, which I was proud of. I never did arrest him. . . . I never did find out if he was involved in any kind of moonshine deal. . . . He stuck to his music pretty well after he left the farm at Dockery, Mississippi. . . . The way I would get information, really it was a bribery deal where I would have them turn in the bootlegger, and he'd give me the location. Then I would do the rest. I'd generally go out at night when they were brewing the whiskey, which was mostly at night, because in the daytime the smoke would give them away when they was cooking off the mash. They would generally do their cooking at night. . . . They'd sell the whiskey around the honky tonks and places. Charley may be making some music for them. . . . Tom Day was the marshal at that time of Merigold, and he had some work with the Negroes, but only in town was his job. Naturally, being in Merigold a lot, Charley got acquainted with the marshal. Anyway, everybody was on the lookout, and they might spot a lookout to watch for the marshal or the deputy coming around. . . . The aldermen would appoint a marshal. Then if somebody came along and they would say, "I would like to have that job too," then they might have an election for the marshal, a city election for marshal.

When I came out of the Navy, he [Day] was a marshal there then. I never did know really whether he had an opponent or whether he was just appointed.... Any of the city work, I was thinking of him, and if I had something to do with the city, I would generally get him to go with me. I didn't want to have any trouble with the city about bootlegging, so I would take the marshal out with me, and we would have a joint job at the place.... They hardly ever locked people up. The penalty was a heavy fine, which I got a bonus out of. And they'd turn 'em loose, and then more than likely in a month or two or six he'd go back to making moonshine. Some of them I turned in as much as three times. Holloway had a little still out east of Merigold. He was turned in.... He didn't own land. He was a sharecropper out in the country. At that time a lot of Delta land wasn't cleared up on the bayous and around in different low places. And we had a lot more woodland in those days, everywhere. And maybe the people he was living with wouldn't know what he was doing. And he would sneak into the woods and set up everything and get going, unbeknownst maybe to his tenant owner. It was the time of my life. I'd break a still, and nobody asked any questions. I did what I wanted to do with the corn whiskey, and I would take the sacks of sugar. And that was one of my deals I had at Christmas time. I gave my friends a sack of sugar.

Holloway has been identified as Seabron Holloway, a friend of Patton who lived near Merigold.[85] Unfortunately Rushing did not recall the details of his arrest, but he was emphatic that he did not arrest Patton. He thought well of Patton, and the feeling was probably mutual, as Patton gave Rushing a copy of the record that he kept for many years. It would appear that Rushing was indeed "a pretty important figure among the Negroes," and Patton wanted to honor him in a song. On the other hand, Holloway the moonshiner was a friend of Patton's and probably an "important figure" in his own right. Patton probably sympathized with his plight and wanted to call attention to it in a song. He apparently did so by merging his own character with Holloway's in stanzas 1, 4, and 6, which are sung in the first person as if Patton were singing about his own experiences. This is a common technique of blues composers, but Patton may have been induced to compose in this way because Ma Rainey's record, which influenced his own record in stanzas 1 and 4, is also composed in the first person. Patton's text thus appears confusing to us but probably was not to his Delta listeners who knew the circumstances of the case. What the text appears to be saying is that Tom Day, the town marshal of Merigold, obtained some whiskey that Holloway had made and/or sold. Holloway evidently had kept his whiskey hidden under the head of his bed. Rushing's statement noted that Holloway was "turned in." Day may have learned of

Holloway's activities through an informer or "snitcher," or he may have simply arrested someone in town for public drunkenness and given him the "third degree" to trace the whiskey back to its source. Since Holloway lived outside of town, it would have been Rushing's job to arrest him and destroy the still. Rushing, typically working at night, apparently found Holloway in a drunken sleep and brought him to the county jail in Cleveland. Contrary to the usual practice described by Rushing, Holloway seems to have drawn a jail sentence. Perhaps he was a repeat offender. Rushing recalled that he only arrested Holloway the one time, but Holloway could have been arrested previously by Rushing's predecessor. A thorough search of courthouse records in Cleveland in December 1986 turned up no further information on this case, but many cases of this sort were tried by judges in their homes or offices outside the courthouse. Holloway probably spent some time in the jail before he was brought before a judge, and he may have been simply fined and released. The "thirty days" jail stretch may well have no basis in reality, as Patton's source was Ma Rainey's "Booze and Blues," which states:

> Sixty days ain't long when you can spend them as you choose.
> Sixty days ain't long when you can spend them as you choose.
> But they seem like years in a cell where there ain't no booze.

In the song Patton does not seem to show any indignation at Rushing, who was after all simply doing his job. He does seem to be upset that Holloway spent some time in jail and sympathizes with his plight in a cell where he can't obtain whiskey. The most serious and cryptic statement comes in the last line of stanza 5, where Patton suggests either that Tom Day had an opponent for his office or that the aldermen of Merigold may have been unhappy with his performance on the job. In a biting conclusion, Patton reduces the potentially jobless marshal to the status of a common vagrant, the kind of person that Day probably arrested without compunction. In fact, itinerant musicians like Patton himself were commonly viewed as vagrants by the more settled elements of Delta society. In effect, Patton has put Tom Day on the same level as himself. As a final ironic footnote to this story, Tom Rushing's farm in 1977 became Mississippi's first legal winery since Prohibition, specializing in fine wines made from Mississippi's native muscadine grape. Patton probably would have understood this turn of events and had a good laugh over it.[86]

Charley Patton followed this topical blues with two lighter pieces in a ragtime style, both of them dealing primarily with the pleasures of sex. In one song he states that he will fight and kill for his "spoonful." Patton concluded the session with four spiritual sides, including the two-part "Prayer of Death"

(Paramount 12799), in which he demonstrated his technique of making the guitar say prayers. These songs cover the full range of his favorite religious themes, including death and the journey to heaven, the troubles of this world, depression, trust in God, and his personal dignity.

Patton's first records sold rather well, and he was called back to a Paramount studio in February 1930. In the meantime he seems to have relocated his base of operations from the Merigold, Renova, and Mound Bayou area north by about forty miles to the Clarksdale area in Coahoma County. His second recording session was held at Paramount's main studio in Grafton, Wisconsin, and Patton brought fiddler Henry Sims with him from the little rural community of Farrell near Clarksdale. Sims (1890–1958) had earlier lived at Mound Bayou and by 1910 was living at Renova, where Patton first met him. Patton's total of twenty-four recorded songs at this 1930 session, combined with fourteen from his first session, made him Paramount's most prolific recording artist in this period, an indication of the confidence that the company had in his sales potential.

Most of Patton's songs at the second session were blues and spirituals, but he also recorded two older folk ballads and versions of two popular songs that had been hits earlier in the 1920s and were probably especially popular with white audiences. One of them, "Runnin' Wild Blues" (Paramount 12924), may have had a certain autobiographical application to Patton's lifestyle, but his text is rather garbled. The folk ballads, "Elder Greene Blues" (Paramount 12972) and "Frankie and Albert" (Paramount 13110), along with "Jim Lee, Parts I and II" (Paramount 13080 and 13133), all draw heavily from the black folk-song tradition and may represent an early stylistic level in Patton's music, the kind of material he learned from Henry Sloan and other mentors. "Elder Greene Blues" is, in fact, related melodically to versions of "Alabama Bound," a song that appeared in a published version in 1909 and which Patton's niece identified as being in Sloan's repertoire.[87] "Frankie and Albert," based on an actual murder and trial in St. Louis in 1900, is a thoroughly traditional song. Patton may have felt some personal identification with its theme, which deals with the violent conclusion of a lovers' triangle, but his text is rather confused as a narrative account. "Elder Greene Blues," about a backsliding churchman, is also quite traditional, but it too contains verses that Patton could have identified with, particularly this one:

> I love to fuss and fight,
> I love to fuss and fight,
> Lord, and get sloppy drunk off o' bottle and bond,
> And walk the streets all night.

Most of Patton's blues from his second session deal with the usual themes of travel and women troubles. In some of them, however, are embedded a few topical references. In "Circle Round the Moon" (Paramount 13040) and "Hammer Blues" (Paramount 12998) there are brief mentions of serving a sentence on a road gang and being shackled in preparation for a train ride to Parchman Penitentiary, which is situated in northern Sunflower County. It is not known whether these verses refer to experiences of Patton or of one or more of his friends. If he did serve a jail sentence, it was probably a brief stretch on a county road gang for something such as public drunkenness or simply possessing liquor, not a sentence at the state penitentiary at Parchman, which was for more serious crimes. If the Charlie Patter (*sic*) listed in the 1910 census in Bolivar County is indeed Charley Patton, that person is described as a laborer on a "county road" and employed by F. O. Bennett, owner of a "road company." It is possible that Patton was a prisoner who had been leased to Bennett by the county or state, but the census entry appears to suggest that he was an actual employee. It would also be unusual for Patton to sing in 1930 about an experience that had occurred twenty years earlier. In all of the information on Patton's life gathered so far, no one has mentioned a serious crime or long jail sentence on his part. Another blues, "Joe Kirby" (Paramount 13133), contains a cryptic reference to the owner of a plantation near Tunica, Mississippi. According to "Son" House, Mr. Kirby was a popular figure among the local blues artists, but it is at present impossible to know what Patton meant when he sang, "Some people say them Joe Kirby blues ain't bad."

Out of all of Patton's blues from his second session on the themes of women and travel, perhaps the most interesting for its lyrics is "Rattlesnake Blues" (Paramount 12924).

1. Just like a rattlesnake, I say, mama, Lordy, every minute I'm in a coil.
I say, I'm just like a rattlesnake, baby; I say, every minute I'm in a coil.
I ain't gonna have no hard time, mama, rolling through this world.

2. When I leave here, mama, I'm going further down the road.
I said, when I leave here, mama, I'm going further down the road.
So if I meet him up there, I'm going back to the Gulf of Mexico.

3. I'm gonna shake glad hands, mama, I say, Lord, with your loving boy.
I'm gonna shake glad hands, I say, with your loving boy.
Fixing to eat my supper in Shelby, Illinois.

4. Vicksburg on a high hill, and Louisiana, Lord, is just below.
   Vicksburg on a high hill, mama, you know, Louisiana just below.
   If I get back there, I ain't gonna never be bad no more.

5. And my babe got a heart like a piece of railroad steel.
   Babe got a heart like a piece of railroad steel.
   If I leave you this morning, never say, "Dad, how do you feel?"

While the precise events underlying this song are unknown at present, Patton's general meaning is clear enough. The song opens with a remarkable simile. The coiled rattlesnake is the perfect symbol for someone who is both ready to defend himself against attack and ready to strike without warning. No doubt Patton saw himself as a man who was always *ready*. One should also not fail to recognize the latent sexual symbolism of the rattlesnake. Patton's readiness, then, enables him to "snake" his way through the world around all obstacles. In the next two stanzas he suggests the southern and northern limits of his world. Shelby, Illinois, must be the town of Shelbyville in that state's Shelby County. It is not known what connection Patton had with this town, but for his audience it no doubt served more as an expression of great distance than of a literal place on the map. In fact, Patton had already been farther north than Shelbyville, which is in the middle of Illinois. In these two stanzas Patton also states that he travels because his woman keeps company with another man, perhaps while he is absent. Nevertheless, he seems to have no particular animosity toward the rival and is even willing to shake hands with him. Evidently his rage is reserved for the woman with "a heart like a piece of railroad steel." Vicksburg, in stanza 4, is an image of "home," a safe place where Patton had friends and relatives and would be treated well. It is meant to contrast with the distant places mentioned in the two preceding stanzas. The final stanza contains another remarkable simile, this time applied to his woman and meant to balance the simile in the first stanza as well as provide further motivation for his travel. This is a brilliantly structured and brilliantly performed blues, all the more extraordinary if it was composed spontaneously.

Patton's best-known recording from his second session is the epic two-part blues on a flood theme, "High Water Everywhere, Parts I and II" (Paramount 12909). Both parts of the song were long thought to refer to the flood of the Mississippi River and its tributaries that took place in April and May 1927. It is now known that only Part I, which is set in Mississippi, is about the 1927 flood, while Part II, set in Arkansas, is about another flood that occurred only a few weeks before Patton made his recording in February 1930. The two parts of "High Water Everywhere" are therefore two different songs, and, in fact, they have different melodies, guitar parts, and moods, as well as different geographical settings. Probably the recent flood in Arkansas described in Part II was the main reason why Patton recorded on this theme at this time. Most topical blues are composed and recorded shortly after the event. It is likely, however, that he had composed and sung another blues about the 1927 flood shortly after that flood occurred. Perhaps he had stopped singing it by the time of his first recording session in June 1929, and only the opportunity at his second session to record a blues about a more recent flood prompted him to recall his other song about the earlier flood. He might not have made it clear to Paramount Records executives that the songs were about two different floods, with the result that they were listed as Parts I and II of the same song.

The 1927 flood was the worst on the Mississippi River in modern history. Heavy winter and spring rains had caused the river and its tributaries to swell up and eventually burst the levees. The first breaks came at Dorena, Missouri, Hickman, Kentucky, and Pendleton, Arkansas, the latter sending waters swirling through much of eastern Arkansas. Perhaps the worst break occurred on April 21 at Mounds Landing, eighteen miles north of Greenville, Mississippi, flooding much of the Delta. Further breaks occurred in Louisiana, as the waters rushed toward the Gulf of Mexico. In all, sixteen and a half million acres of land were flooded in seven states, over 162,000 homes were flooded and 41,000 buildings destroyed, over 600,000 people were made homeless and without food, and between 250 and 500 people were killed including officially 78 in Arkansas and 125 in Mississippi.[88]

Twenty blues about this flood were recorded by such popular artists as Bessie Smith, Sippie Wallace, Blind Lemon Jefferson, Lonnie Johnson, Laura Smith, Kansas Joe McCoy, and Barbecue Bob, among others. One gospel song and a sermon were also recorded, along with three topical songs by white artists in a hillbilly style.[89] Charley Patton and Greenville-based blues singer Alice Pearson, along with Elder Moses Mason, likely also from Greenville, are probably the only artists to make recordings on this theme who actually lived in the flood zone and experienced the flood firsthand. But there is a directness and sense of personal involvement and real drama that is found in Patton's recording and nowhere else. While the other artists expressed sorrow and sympathy for the victims, Patton's narrative conveys a very real sense of fear, confusion, menace, and rage. His nephew Tom Cannon placed Patton at the little community of Gunnison near the Mississippi River, when the flood struck, while his niece Bessie Turner placed him about ten miles further east at the town of Shelby. Blues artist "Son" House stated that Patton told him he was at Rolling Fork, about eighty miles to the South.[90] Perhaps he was in all of these places at various times shortly before, during, or after the flood, although none is mentioned in the song. All of these locations were affected by the flood, though not as severely as towns like Rosedale, Greenville, and Leland, which he does mention. Patton's home territory of Dockery Farms, Renova, Mound Bayou, and Merigold did not experience any significant flooding. Although Patton himself may not have felt the worst effects of the flood directly, he did know hundreds of its victims and had traveled all over the territory that was devastated. Thus he could compose and sing about the flood from a level of personal experience that most of the other blues recording stars could not muster.

1. The backwater done rose all around Sumner, Lord, drove me down the
line.
Back water done rose at Sumner, drove poor Charley down the line.
And I'll tell the world the water done struck Drew'ses town.

2. Lord, the whole round country, Lord, creek water is overflowed.
Lord, the whole round country, man, it's overflowed.
Spoken: You know, I can't stay here. I'm ... I'll go where it's high, boy.
I would go to the hill country, but they got me barred.

3. Now looky here now at Leland, Lord, river was rising high.
Looky here, boys around Leland tell me river is ragin' high.
Spoken: Boy, it's rising over there. Yeah.
I'm gonna move over to Greenville. Bought our tickets. Good-bye.

4. Looky here, the water dug out, Lordy (*Spoken*: levee broke), rose most
everywhere.
The water at Greenville and Leland, Lord, it done rose everywhere.
Spoken: Boy, you can't never stay here.
I would go down to Rosedale, but they tell me it's water there.

5. Lord, the water now, mama, done struck Shaw'ses town.
Well, they tell me the water done struck Shaw'ses town.
Spoken: Boy, I'm going to Vicksburg.
Well, I'm going to Vicksburg on a high[er] mound.

6. I am going on dry water where land don't never flow. [*sic*]
Well, I'm going on a hill where water, oh, it don't never flow.

Spoken: Boy, Sharkey County and Issaquena's drowned and inched over.
Bolivar County was inchin' over in Tallahatchie's shore.
Spoken: Boy, I went in Tallahatchie. They got it over there.

7. Lord, the water done rushed all over that old Jackson Road.
Lord, the water done raised up over the Jackson Road.
Spoken: Boy, it got my clothes.
I'm going back to the hill country. Won't be worried no more.

The song portrays the sense of confusion and mounting fear of someone caught in the Delta with the water rising around him in all directions. Patton's description is not tied to any one location. Instead he becomes a kind of Delta Everyman constantly changing his mind about where to go as he hears fresh reports of rising water. This must have been the real experience of thousands of people like Patton. His phrase, "I'll tell the world," in the last line of stanza 1 should probably be taken quite literally. The attention of the world was fixed on this disaster, and Patton here sets himself up as a spokesman for thousands of Delta residents who had no other voice to tell their story to the world. Following an amusing mistake in the first line of stanza 6, he introduces a remarkable image of entire counties literally being carried away by the water and deposited on the shores of other counties. Patton's performance is especially intense, as he growls the lyrics, beats on his guitar, snaps the strings, stomps on the floor, and carries on a conversation with an imaginary audience of fellow flood victims. From towns on the periphery of the flood zone in stanzas 1 and 2, Patton takes listeners to the hardest hit areas in stanzas 3 and 4, finally in stanzas 5–7 painting a more general portrait of devastation in three entire counties and mentioning places of refuge (Vicksburg and Jackson). Overall it is a frightening image of confusion, truly of "high water everywhere," with the singer not knowing which way to go. This must have been the reality for many of the flood's victims. The logical places of refuge were in the "hill country" to the east and south of the areas hardest hit. There was a large refugee camp set up in Vicksburg, and Patton's original home, where he could have taken refuge, was in the hills between that city and Jackson. Many of the Delta's black refugees, however, were settled in a Red Cross concentration camp set up on the top of the levee at Greenville, where they were confined under awful conditions, policed by white National Guard troops, often forced to do clean-up and repair work, and ultimately returned to white-owned plantations where they had been renters or sharecroppers. Patton's allusive statement in stanza 2, "I would go to the hill country, but they got me barred," seems to refer to these conditions. There is no evidence that

Patton himself was confined to the camp at Greenville, but he seems to be speaking up, albeit cautiously, for those who were. It would have been dangerous for him to be more specific.

Part II of "High Water Everywhere" is about a flood in parts of Greene and Mississippi Counties, Arkansas, and adjacent sections of Missouri, that occurred on January 16, 1930. This area was a vast, low-lying floodplain just west of the Mississippi River, protected by levees. The Mississippi River itself did not flood at this time, but its tributaries, the Saint Francis and Little Rivers, did, and Big Lake overflowed its banks. The heavy rains in the Mid-South area at this time also caused flooding of the Tallahatchie and Coldwater Rivers in Tallahatchie and Quitman Counties, Mississippi. That flooding became the subject of Mattie Delaney's "Tallahatchie River Blues" (Vocalion 1480), recorded in Memphis around February 21, 1930.[91] The flooding was far worse in Arkansas. Several people died there and an estimated five hundred families, most of them poor black farmers, were stranded for a week or longer in bitter cold with dwindling provisions. As the rivers and lake overflowed and the water spread through 200,000 acres of the Arkansas lowlands, the weather quickly turned extremely cold. The flood water froze into a gigantic ice sheet to the point where small boats could not pass, yet the ice was too thin to allow the flood victims to walk across it safely. The water and ice rose up to and, in some cases, over the floors of cabins in the area, and many residents were forced to wait for rescue in their homes or on rooftops, exposed to the elements. Airplanes were sent out to locate victims, assess danger and damage, and drop badly needed provisions. Finally, around January 24 the weather turned warmer and the ice began to melt, allowing rescue boats to break their way through and carry victims to safety. Some of them had to be housed temporarily in railroad boxcars and tents in Blytheville and other nearby locations. There is no accurate accounting of the damage and the number of lives lost.

Since the flood in northeast Arkansas was relatively localized and most of its victims were black people, it was quickly forgotten by the mass media and by historians. A. G. Little, president of the First National Bank of Blytheville and chairman of the Mississippi County Red Cross, seemed to be relieved that the area's plantation owners would likely be able to plant their crops in a few weeks once the flooding had receded. He insisted to a newspaper reporter that

Flood conditions in Northeast Arkansas are only a little worse than those of the same period in past years. . . . The situation is not unusual and has been overplayed by the newspapers. There is suffering and tragedy. They always go hand in hand with flood conditions, but it is little worse than is experienced every year. . . . The

WITH A ZERO WAVE adding more misery to the suffering already caused by the high waters, 2,000 families have been driven from their homes in Dunklin county, Missouri, and Mississippi county, Arkansas, where 200,000 acres of land are under water from the overflow of St. Francis river and Big lake.. One of the many families who have been forced to use a box car for their home.

Flood victims temporarily housed in railroad boxcars, Blytheville, Arkansas, 1930. From the Chicago *Defender*.

prosperity of the section has not been affected, and will not be if the water goes down in time for crops to be planted. Airplane surveys are useless.... The natives of the district know the country and the situation. It is an old story with them, and every sufferer will be located. When a group waves at a passing plane, it does not always mean that they are refugees calling for aid.[92]

Charley Patton knew better and would tell the world. If it were not for his "High Water Everywhere, Part II," we would have little understanding today of the impact of this flood.

1. Back water at Blytheville, backed up all around.
Back water at Blytheville, done struck Joiner town.
It was fifty families and children. "Tough luck, they can drown."

2. The water was rising up in my friend's door.
The water was rising up in my friend's door.
The man said to his womenfolk, "Lord, we'd better go."

3. The water was rising, got up in my bed.
Lord, the water was rolling, got up to my bed.
I thought I would take a trip, Lord, out on the big ice sled.

4. Oh, I hear the horn blow, blowin' up on my shore.
Spoken: Blowin'; couldn't hear it.
I heard the iceboat, Lord, was sinking down.
I couldn't get no boat, so I let 'em sink on down.

5. Oh-ah, the water rising, islands sinking down.
Sayin', the water was rising, airplanes was all around.
Spoken: Boy, they was all around.
It was fifty men and children. "Tough luck, they can drown."

6. Oh, Lordy, women is groanin' down.
Oh, women and children sinkin' down.
Spoken: Lord, have mercy.
I couldn't see nobody home, and wasn't no one to be found.

The mood of fear and confusion found in Patton's Part I has changed to a mood of stark terror in Part II. No longer is one able to compare reports and ponder where to go to find higher ground. Now the water is up to the singer's bed, and the only hope is for rescue. Part II evidently is based on the experiences of friends of Patton (cf. stanza 2), although typically he sings some verses in the first person as if he himself had experienced the events. It is not known whether Patton himself was actually in Northeast Arkansas at the time of this flood, but he seems at least to have known people in the area and possibly had played music there in the past. Besides posing as a reporter and a purported eyewitness, he alternates between the viewpoints of a rescuer and one of the rescued. In truth, there wasn't much difference: those with access to boats became rescuers; those without boats hoped to become the rescued. Patton paints a grim picture of islands being created and then submerged by the rising water, rescue boats blowing horns and people unable to hear them, a lifeboat itself sinking in the flood, and reconnaissance airplanes flying overhead unable to offer direct assistance. The mood of helplessness that Patton depicts of both the victims and the rescuers is awesome and terrifying. The final chilling stanza, with its imagery of complete devastation and an absence of life anywhere, is one of Patton's greatest musical moments and one of the greatest in all of recorded blues. It stands in stark contrast to A. G. Little's callous assessment of the flood's impact and significance.

Charley Patton recorded one more topical blues at his second recording session, a piece accompanied by his fiddle partner Henry Sims called "Mean Black Moan" (Paramount 12953). It deals with the consequences of a railroad strike in Chicago, making it the only topical blues by Patton not set in the South. The specific events underlying the song are not entirely clear, but it almost certainly concerns a massive railroad shop workers' strike that occurred in 1922.[93] Under the administration of President Woodrow Wilson, a Democrat, the railroads were nationalized as an emergency measure during World War I. Some 420,000 railroad shop workers throughout the country, who built, maintained, and repaired freight and passenger cars and locomotives, were given government recognition of their union rights as members of the Railway Employees' Department (RED). By 1919, following the war, the original railroad owners and managers were starting to take steps to regain their former power and control. A wave of labor strikes, race riots, and the "Red Scare" in that year created an anti-union climate in much of the country. The Republican Warren G. Harding was elected president in 1920 and inaugurated early in 1921. In late 1920 and 1921 thousands of railroad workers, including shopmen, were laid off, and by late 1921 management was back in control. At the April 1922 RED convention in Chicago a vote was taken to strike if management did not end its practices of contracting out and piecework. These demands were not met, and on July 1 nearly 400,000 shopmen walked off their jobs, including 14,400 in Chicago and many more in the greater Chicago area. Chicago itself, served by close to a dozen railroad lines, was the major center of strike activity. Between July and November 1922, railroad passenger traffic was at its lowest level since 1916. Management quickly moved to hire armed guards and strikebreakers. President Harding expressed his opposition to the strike, and in September a federal judge issued an injunction that forbade many of the activities of the strikers. With no salaries and faced with the need to pay food and house rent bills, some workers began to return to their jobs. By the end of October about 150,000 had returned. The strike continued to collapse in November, although some strikers around the country held out well into 1923 and a few into 1924, with the last ones holding out until 1928.

Whether Patton composed this song in 1922 or in 1930, or at some point between these dates, is not known. Most topical songs are composed shortly after the event and continue to be sung only as long as public interest in the event lasts. Surely by 1930, in the midst of a worsening economic depression, there was little residual interest in a labor dispute that had occurred almost eight years earlier. Patton recorded the song at the very end of his session with Henry Sims. In fact, their session was interrupted by the recording of six songs by St. Louis blues singer Edith North Johnson. "Mean Black Moan" was the only song that Patton recorded after Johnson's session. It would appear, then, that Patton and Sims had stayed at the Paramount studio in Grafton while Johnson recorded. Perhaps some discussion in the studio about Patton's other topical recording, "High Water Everywhere," prompted him to recall "Mean Black Moan" from his dormant repertoire.

1. It's a mean black moan, baby, lying front of my door.
When I leave Chicago, Lord, I ain't coming back no more.

2. Ninety men were laid off at a railroad shop.
Ninety men were laid off, Lord, at a railroad shop.
And the strike in Chicago, Lordy, Lord, it just won't stop.

3. I'm tired of mean black moans, baby, lying front of my door.
I'm tired of mean black moans, baby, lying front of my door.
But when I leave Chicago, Lord, I ain't coming back here no more.

4. There are hungry men, Lordy, all around my bed.
There are hungry men, Lordy, standing around my bed.
I wish somebody might be able to kill these black moans dead.

5. Every morning, Lord, rent man is at my door.
Every morning, baby, rent man is at my door.
And my man hasn't worked, Lord, in two or three months or more.

6. It's all I can do, Lord, ah, spare my life.
All I can do, Lord, if You can spare my life.
But when the strike is over, I will be all right.

7. Ninety men were laid off, Lord, at a railroad shop.
Ninety men were laid off, Lord, in a railroad shop.
It's a wreck in Chicago, Lord, it just won't stop.

It is not certain whether Patton understood the issues that provoked the strike or whether he even cared. It is also not certain whether he is singing specifically about black strikers or all of the strikers, who were overwhelmingly white Americans or foreign immigrants. Blacks constituted only about one or two percent of all shop workers and were concentrated in the less skilled occupations such as carman and blacksmith. If Patton is referring only to black shop workers in Chicago, as seems likely, his figure of ninety men in stanza 2 is probably roughly accurate. Whether or not Patton understood the issues underlying the strike, he seems much more concerned about its consequences for himself and the strikers. In the first place, the strike inconvenienced him, perhaps interfering with his travel plans, as he suggests in stanzas 1 and 3. But he is also concerned about the plight of the workers who are hungry and unable to pay their rent. They seem to be literally oppressing Patton with their "mean black moans," lying in front of his door like hungry stray dogs and standing around his bed. The language of this piece is remarkable, as the striking men are merged with their own complaints or "moans" and Patton himself in stanzas 5 and 6 assumes the persona of a striker's wife and then of one of the strikers. We have seen this technique before in "Tom Rushen Blues" and "High Water Everywhere—Part II." Patton, the Masked Marvel, was a master of changes of voice and character, imitating the voices of women, friends, and members of an audience in his vocal asides and jumping from one persona or perspective to another in his song lyrics. It is a compositional technique that completely defies all the logic of Western literary and artistic expression, yet it is remarkably effective in Patton's hands.

Patton's third recording session occurred in August 1930, again in the Paramount studio at Grafton, Wisconsin. Sometime prior to this session he had moved to Lula, but he did not immediately take up with Bertha Lee, his last wife, who was living there. He brought with him to the session singer/pianist

The Lula well, 1991. (Photograph by David Evans)

Louise Johnson, along with "Son" House and his old partner Willie Brown. Patton only recorded four songs. All have Willie Brown playing second guitar, and they are among Patton's finest performances. This is the only session where he recorded no spiritual songs. Paramount was feeling the Depression and experiencing financial difficulties. Perhaps they wanted to stick with Patton's blues, which had enjoyed the greatest success in the past.

Two of Patton's blues from this session deal with the usual themes of women troubles and travel. "Moon Going Down" (Paramount 13014) is mostly about travel, but it does contain a reference to the burning of a mill in Clarksdale. It also mentions Rosetta Henry, a woman in Clarksdale that Patton had been trying to court. These themes are not developed, however. "Bird Nest Bound" (Paramount 13070) draws some of its lyric material from an earlier recording by Ardell Bragg, "Bird Nest Blues" (Paramount 12410), but Patton greatly transforms the original into a song that expresses a longing for a permanent home. A third blues, "Some Summer Day" (Paramount 13080), also draws its melodic and some of its lyric material from another record, the Mississippi Sheiks' "Sittin' On Top of the World" (OKeh 8784), recorded earlier in the year. It mentions a woman's man who went off to prison, but the theme's relation to Patton's life remains a mystery.

Patton's fourth song from this session, "Dry Well Blues" (Paramount 13070), deals with another natural disaster in the Delta, a drought that was taking place at the time. It was also a theme that "Son" House would handle in his

"Dry Spell Blues—Parts I and II" (Paramount 12990), recorded at the same session.[94] An examination of the Clarksdale *Daily Register* newspaper for the months of June–August, 1930, sheds some light on the events underlying "Dry Well Blues" and incidentally helps in dating the Paramount recording session. The paper begins to take notice of continued unusually hot and dry weather on June 26, but only in a rather lighthearted editorial. Not until July 8 is there a front-page article with a tone of alarm, "Dry Spell For Delta Without Any Surcease." Headlines continued to recount the disaster through August, with the August 8 headline reading "Crop Is 500,000 Bales Short" and a story on August 15 reading "Drought Takes Huge Farm Toll." There can be little doubt, then, that Patton's recording session took place no earlier than late June and most likely in July or August. "Son" House stated in 1964 that it was in August.

Meanwhile, the *Daily Register* on July 15 ran an official notice of intention to issue $5,000 in municipal bonds. It was titled "Bond Issue for Improvement, Repair and Extension of the Water Works System of the Town of Lula, Coahoma County, Mississippi." On July 20 the newspaper published a short article titled "Lula Booms," which stated, "In keeping with the progress of Lula, one of the most progressive of the small towns of the Delta, officials have added a street sprinkler, that is keeping the streets dust free and adding much to the pleasure of living in that wide-awake town. The town has recently issued a few thousand dollars in bonds and is boring a second artesian well to supply the demands of a growing town." On the same day the paper's headlines read "62-Day Drought Hangs On." On August 1 it reported that the water lines of Vicksburg had gone dry, and on August 10 it ran an editorial titled "When the Well Goes Dry." It must have been around this time that Patton recorded his "Dry Well Blues."

1. When I was living at Lula, I was living at ease.
When I was living at Lula, I was living at ease.
Lord, the drought come and caught us and parched up all our trees.

2. Oh, today over in Lula we'll bid the town good-bye.
Today in Lula bidding you and the town good-bye.
Well, we have come to know the day, Lord, the Lula well was gone dry.

3. Lord, the citizens around Lula all was doing very well.
Citizens around Lula all was doing very well.
Lord, they all got together, and they done bored a well.

4. I ain't got no money, and I sure ain't got no home.
Lord, I ain't got no money and sure ain't got no home.
The hot weather done come in, scorched all the cotton and corn.

5. Oh, look down the country. Lord, it'll make you cry.
Look . . . country. Lord, it'll make you cry.
Most everybody, Lord, had a water bayou.

6. Lord, the Lula women, Lord, putting the Lula men down.
Lula men (*sic*) all putting Lula men down.
Lord, you ought to been there, Lord; the womens all leaving town.

Patton views the situation, as usual, in personal terms while at the same time identifying with the people of Lula. His concern is with the breakup of a happy domestic situation. The text alternates between scenes of "before" and "after," while Patton's voice moves between that of his own persona and that of the residents of Lula. Prior to the drought he was "living at ease" and the (white) "citizens around Lula all was doing very well." It is highly unlikely that Patton himself was raising cotton and corn or tending trees at Lula, but he uses the imagery of farming in order to give the song greater appeal to his Delta audience. Both the wealthy white plantation owners and the poor black renters and sharecroppers were engaged in farming, and all were affected by the drought, just as they were by such earlier disasters as the 1927 flood and the boll weevil pestilence. Ultimately their suffering would have affected Patton's income from music, though it is doubtful that he became completely broke and homeless as he states in stanza 4. He himself didn't exactly fit into either group. Despite his partial white ancestry and his living "at ease" from his musical earnings, he could never hope to be accepted as a social equal by the "citizens." As a successful musician, he was also somewhat above the economic status of most of the black residents of Lula. In his song, the dry spell causes all of the farmers, white and black, to lose their homes, their money, and their women. These were all things that Patton valued highly, and they were important themes in his life and his songs. Against the background of the worsening drought we can possibly detect a subtle subtext of social criticism in Patton's song. While the white "citizens" are adding to their "pleasure of living" by keeping their streets dust-free with a sprinkler, maintaining their individual irrigation channels (stanza 5), and confidently buying municipal bonds to bore a second well (stanza 3), the ordinary men and women, perhaps even some of the "citizens," are losing their trees, crops, homes, and families.

As in previous disasters, everyone seems to be temporarily on the same level. For the most part, Patton's lyrics simply report facts, but it is hard to imagine that he was not struck by the contrast between the confidence shown by the "citizens" and the devastation wrought by God's hand. By reporting on a topical event, Patton makes literal truth out of one of the most common traditional blues stanzas:

> You never miss your water until the well goes dry.
> You never miss your rider until she says good-bye.

In the blues from Patton's second 1930 session there is a suggestion that he is tiring of the constant travel and tempestuous relationships with women. He seems to want to find a permanent home and a woman with whom he can settle down and "live at ease." Apparently, however, he found it impossible to make Lula his home. The drought that he sang about may have had something to do with this, but we have elsewhere noticed in Bertha Lee's 1934 recording of "Mind Reader Blues" that he apparently got in some kind of trouble there and was forced to leave town, as was Bertha Lee herself. Just what happened and when this took place are not clear. The years 1931 and 1932 are an obscure period in Patton's life story. He probably tried to settle in Memphis sometime during these years and make money giving guitar lessons and performing locally. The Depression had set in, however, and money was extremely scarce. The recording industry had virtually collapsed, and his last recordings from 1930 had sold poorly. His career as a recording artist might have seemed to him to be at an end. Patton probably suffered some tough times, at least to a moderate extent, and he apparently returned to his usual pattern of moving about the Delta. He occasionally played with "Son" House and Willie Brown, who had settled in Robinsonville and Lake Cormorant respectively, in the northernmost part of the Delta.

If Patton failed to find a permanent home during this period, he did find a rather compatible mate in Bertha Lee, one who could both create a home life for him as well as sometimes travel with him to perform music. In 1933 they settled in Holly Ridge, in the southern part of Sunflower County, in a house owned by a white man named Tom Robertson for whose family Bertha Lee became the cook. By 1934 the record industry was beginning to make a comeback from the worst effects of the Great Depression. W. R. Calaway, who had formerly worked for Paramount, was now working for the American Record Corporation and contacted Patton about recording once again. Charley and Bertha Lee traveled by train to New York and between January 30 and February 1 recorded twenty-nine songs. Only twelve of these were ever released, probably because of Patton's death three months after the session and the poor sales of the initial releases. Unfortunately, the remaining masters were lost or destroyed. Two of the twelve issued songs are spiritual duets by Charley and Bertha, and two others are blues vocals by Bertha. The remaining eight pieces are blues and a ragtime dance piece sung by Charley.

There are two main topics of Patton's blues from this last session. One is Bertha Lee herself and Charley's evident satisfaction with her. Unlike the women in most of his earlier blues, he has a consistently positive attitude toward Bertha throughout the session. The second main topic is Patton's relationships with important white people. This topic had emerged in "Tom Rushen Blues" at his first recording session, but in that song he was adopting another man's situation as his own. In his songs about the boll weevil, floods, and the dry spell he was a spokesman for the entire Delta population, black and white. Even in "Mean Black Moan" he did not take sides in a labor dispute that had racial implications but concentrated instead on the hardships of the workers out on strike. In his last session, however, he is definitely singing about his own personal experiences and frequently with a tone of bitterness. It may have seemed to him that the delicate balance of forces that had preserved his ambiguous social status was crumbling. He was aware of his heart trouble and was trying to settle down more and stay in one place. This inevitably weakened his social position and pushed him toward the typical status of a Delta Negro. At the same time, he was performing increasingly for white audiences yet finding increasing difficulties in his relationships with whites. Throughout the songs of his last session there is not only bitterness but a sense of an impending great crisis in his life, a sense that the threads that had held his life together up to now were beginning to unravel. Perhaps he knew he was about to die and did not care what the consequences of his song-statements might be.

Patton was far more directly outspoken at his last session than he had ever been before. This is the case both about the subject of sex and about local characters and events. It was also the case about the subject of death itself. Charley had recently witnessed a horrible axe murder at a country supper at Four Mile Lake. According to Big Joe Williams, who claimed to have witnessed the event along with Patton, a gambler named Henry Freeman had killed another gambler named "Quicksilver" over a woman. Patton and Williams, who was playing music with him, were called as witnesses, and Charley made up a song about the event.[95] This was probably the song he recorded titled "The Delta Murder," which remained unissued. Williams recalled one of the verses:

I know poor Quicksilver gonna hear Gabriel when he sound.
He gonna raise up in the grave, but the poor boy got to lay back down.

Four Mile Lake is located in Humphreys County a few miles northeast of Belzoni. Courthouse records reveal that James Manuel (evidently the man that Williams knew as Quicksilver) was accused of murdering Henry Freeman. Williams stated that the two men, whose identities he evidently reversed, fought over a woman named Velma Larry, whose name appears in an official list of witnesses for the defense. Charles Patton [sic] and Bertha Lee Patton are listed as witnesses for the state, but Joe Williams was not listed as a witness for either side. An indictment was filed against Manuel and a bench warrant issued for his arrest on March 6, 1934, in the Circuit Court of Humphreys County. He was arrested the following day. Subpoenas were issued for the state's witnesses on March 7 and served on March 10. On March 12 Manuel entered a plea of not guilty, and on the following day eight witnesses for the defense were subpoenaed. Charley and Bertha Lee and the other state's witnesses were called to Belzoni on March 12, and the trial was apparently held on March 15. There is no record of a verdict, so it is likely that the case ended in a hung jury or mistrial due to conflicting evidence. There are no newspaper accounts that would clarify the situation. Although the indictment was issued in March, the crime could have been committed any time after December 20, 1933, when the court was last in session in Belzoni. The court next met on March 6, 1934, the day that the arrest warrant and subpoenas were issued. In 1985 the then current court clerk, Robert Doyle, surmised that Manuel had a white man speak for him when he was first arrested and that he was let go, perhaps because his labor was needed, only to be indicted and arrested again when the court next met in March. Thus, it is quite possible that the murder took place before Patton's recording session began on January 30 and that his unissued recording of "The Delta Murder" refers to this event.

Patton used the image of an axe in his recording of "Jersey Bull Blues" (Vocalion 02782), but here its symbolism appears to be purely sexual. Nevertheless, it is perhaps of some significance that Patton at this point had merged the imagery of sex and violent murder. Charley and Bertha Lee also recorded a spiritual at this session called "Oh Death" (Vocalion 02904). Their version is based on an earlier recording, "I Know My Time Ain't Long" (Paramount 12948), made by Charley's friends from Lula, the Delta Big Four quartet. "Oh Death" is one of the most powerful and chilling songs on this subject ever recorded. Patton's involvement with the song is total, and he must have known that his own time was indeed not long.

Bertha Lee is the focus of several songs from Patton's last session. Her own singing of "Yellow Bee" (Vocalion 02650), a song based on an earlier recording by Memphis Minnie and one that Charley apparently taught to Bertha prior to the recording session, is frankly sexual and employs imagery of a long stinger, making honey, and buzzing around a hive. Charley's recording of "Hang It On The Wall" (Vocalion 02931), a remake of a ragtime dance song that he had recorded at his first session in 1929, is also quite sexual, and in it Charley calls out to Bertha Lee, who was probably dancing in the studio. Immediately before this piece Patton recorded "Poor Me" (Vocalion 02651), a tender love song in which he mentions Bertha Lee by name. In "Stone Pony Blues" (Vocalion 02680), recorded earlier in the session as an updated follow-up to Patton's 1929 hit of "Pony Blues," Charley seems to be saying in a metaphorical way that he has given up other women and settled down: "I got me a stone pony and I don't ride shetland no more." His "stone pony," which refers to a male pony that has not been castrated, can be found "hooked to his rider's door" and "down in Lula town somewhere." The latter phrase is an obvious reference to Bertha Lee, whom he had first met in Lula. Later in the song there occurs a stanza that declares that he is not interested in any of the women in his audience:

> Well, I didn't come here to steal nobody's brown.
> Didn't come here to steal nobody's brown.
> I just stopped by here, well, to keep you from stealing mine.

No doubt Patton found these lines useful at his live performances for avoiding dangerous situations. They contrast markedly with the verse he addressed to the women in his earlier "Pony Blues": "I don't want to marry, just want to be your man." But there is also a hint of trouble in "Stone Pony Blues." Twice Patton sings the line, "And I can't feel welcome, rider, nowhere I go." Patton's settling down was probably beginning to limit his opportunities and forcing him to accept conditions that were not entirely to his liking, conditions that he could always avoid in the past simply by leaving. This same contrast of apparent bliss and ominous foreboding is found in "Love My Stuff" (Vocalion 02782). The first three stanzas border on being positively lewd, as Patton sings of his delight in his hot "jelly," his "stuff," and his rider's way of shimmying. But then the mood suddenly turns grim for the last half of the song. In stanza 4 he mentions an apparition of the devil, but his full meaning is not clear. Then he states that he feels compelled to leave in a hurry, drawing his imagery from the 1927 flood that he had sung about in an earlier record.

5. Oh, I'm gonna leave Mississippi now, babe, 'fore it be too late.
I'm gonna leave Mississippi 'fore it be too late.
Spoken: Boy, you know I got to leave Mississippi.
It may be like Twenty-Seven high water; swear it just won't wait.

6. Oh, I once had a notion; Lord, I believe I will.
Spoken: Oh sure.
I once had a notion; Lord, I believe I will.
I'm gonna boat 'cross the river and stop at Dago Hill.

Dago Hill was a neighborhood in St. Louis originally settled by Sicilian immigrants and known as a center of whisky making and good times. By the 1920s a number of blacks had moved there, and it is mentioned in several blues recordings from that era. We don't know whether Patton meant the devil in his stanza 4 to be taken for a spirit or a real person, and we don't know why he wanted to leave Mississippi, but there are strong hints of causes in some of the other songs he recorded in 1934.

Several of Charley's songs from his last session mention the activities of white people and Charley's relationships with them. Big Joe Williams told me in 1979 that Patton made up "Jersey Bull Blues" (Vocalion 02782) about a bull belonging to his landlord in Holly Ridge, Tom Robertson. The record's lyrics, however, never mention Robertson. They merely develop a sexual metaphor of a bull for three stanzas before introducing the axe imagery that was discussed previously. Patton probably told Robertson that the song was about his bull as an easy way of paying him a compliment. He also seems to have paid a compliment to a favorite railroad engineer in "Charley Bradley's Ten Sixty-Six Blues," a piece that remained unissued. "Son" House stated that Bradley drove Engine Number 1066 on a route from Memphis to Vicksburg, and everyone liked the way he blew his whistle as his train sped through the Delta.[96] Patton had probably ridden the Ten Sixty-Six many times.

Another unissued song, "Whiskey Distillery," may have mentioned local white people. Its title perhaps suggests a theme like the one Patton had developed earlier in "Tom Rushen Blues." Illegal activities had been very much in the news in the two years prior to Patton's last recording session. The Depression was at its worst, and many people, desperate for money, turned to careers of crime. People like Al Capone, "Machine Gun" Kelly, "Pretty Boy" Floyd, "Baby Face" Nelson, John Dillinger, Ma and Pa Barker, and Bonnie and Clyde became household names to millions of Americans and heroes to many as they flamboyantly defied the law. Revenue agents seeking unpaid taxes and the Federal Bureau of Investigation's notorious "G-Men" pursued such criminals relentlessly and were not above using ruthless methods to hunt down or wipe out these fugitives from justice. Things had changed from a few years earlier when an officer like Tom Rushing could quietly arrest a moonshiner or bootlegger and take him to the county courthouse to pay a fine. Criminals were now more apt to carry and use weapons, and law officers were more likely to get tough first and ask questions later. Charley Patton was evidently concerned about this situation and recorded "Revenue Man Blues" (Vocalion 02931) as a kind of warning to others on the danger of police brutality. "If he hollers and you don't stop, you will likely be knocked out," he sings, and "If they see you with a bottle, they will almost break your neck." The theme is not developed further, however, as Patton reverts to some verses he had previously sung in 1930 in "Bird Nest Bound." He concludes with a stanza that hints at bad luck and trouble and seems to suggest a series of personal failures.

Oh, I wake up every morning now with the jinx all around my bed.
Spoken: Oh sure.
I wake up every morning with the jinx all around my bed.
Spoken: You know, I had them jinx hangin' out.
I have been a good provider, but I believe I've been misled.

If Patton's references to whites are brief or obscure in these songs, they are quite explicit and detailed in "High Sheriff Blues" (Vocalion 02680). It contains the melody and guitar part and a few of the verses that he had used in 1929 in "Tom Rushen Blues." It also deals with a jailhouse experience, but this time it is Patton's own. Bertha Lee stated that she and Charley were both jailed in Belzoni following a row at a house party and that it was none other than W. R. Calaway of the American Record Corporation who bailed them out.[97] Belzoni is the county seat of Humphreys County, which lies just to the south of Sunflower County, where Patton was living at the time. Humphreys County has a rather unsavory reputation among blacks for race relations, and it had not been one of Patton's more frequented parts of the Delta. Unlike the case in some of the other Delta counties, Patton was probably not very familiar with the law officers there.

1. Get in trouble at Belzoni, ain't no use of screaming and crying . . . mmm.
Get in trouble in Belzoni, ain't no use of screaming and crying . . . mmm.
Mister Webb will take you back to Belzoni jail a' flying.

2. Let me tell you folks just how he treated me . . . eeeh.
Let me tell you folks just how he treated me . . . eeeh.
And he put me in a cellar; it was dark as it could be.

3. It was late one evening, Mister Purvis was standing 'round . . . mmm.
It was late one evening, Mister Purvis was standing 'round . . . mmm.
Mister Purvis told Mister Webb to let poor Charley down.

4. It takes boozy booze, Lord, to carry me through . . . mmm.
Takes boozy booze, Lord, to carry me through . . . mmm.
Thirty days seem like years in a jailhouse where there is no booze.

5. I got up one morning feeling awful . . . mmm.
I got up one morning feeling mighty bad . . . mmm.
And it must not have been them Belzoni jail I had. (*sic*)
Spoken: Blues I had, boy.

6. Got in trouble, ain't no use of screaming and . . . mmm.
When I was in prison, it ain't no use of screaming and crying.
Mister Purvis the onliest man could ease that pain of mine.

In the song Patton protests his treatment in the jail. He evidently needed either whiskey or medical treatment, or both. He knew by this time that he had heart trouble, and he had increased his drinking, perhaps to try to blot his troubles out of his mind. The jail in Belzoni was a two-story brick structure having cramped cells on both floors with bare walls and strong steel bars. The cells surrounded a small space on three sides. On the ceiling above this space on the second floor was an iron ring, and directly below it was a drophole operated by a lever. This device was designed for hangings of criminals convicted of capital offenses. The rope passed through the ring, and the victim fell through the drophole to the first floor when the lever was released. Thus prisoners on both floors would have observed a hanging from a few feet away. As late as 1985 the system was still occasionally "tested" with weighted bags for the edification of prisoners, even though actual hangings had long ceased and executions were transferred to the state penitentiary at Parchman.

The incident referred to in this song probably stems from the murder of Henry Freeman. As suggested earlier, this murder, to which Patton and Bertha Lee were witnesses, could have taken place before Patton's recording session. My guess is that James Manuel and all of the witnesses were arrested at the scene of the crime and brought to the Belzoni jail until the details could be sorted out. Thus Charley and Bertha would have spent some time in jail until Mr. Calaway got them out. R. Carlos Webb, known as "Hopalong" because one of his feet was shorter than the other, was a deputy sheriff of Humphreys County and probably the man who made the arrests at Four Mile Lake and

Humphreys County Court House in Belzoni, 1986. (Photograph by David Evans)

Belzoni jail house, 1986. (Photograph by David Evans)

brought Manuel and the witnesses to the jail at Belzoni. John D. Purvis was the county sheriff. He was probably convinced by Calaway that the Pattons were of good character and not directly involved in the crime, and he evidently ordered Webb to release them ("let poor Charley down"). The Pattons were thus likely incarcerated on the upper floor, and the "cellar" in stanza 2 is probably a mistake for "cell," as the jail had no cellar. Patton's attitude seems to be critical of the fact that he was placed in jail by Mr. Webb, but he apparently is grateful to Sheriff Purvis for letting him off to travel to his recording session. As in his earlier "Tom Rushen Blues" the reference to thirty days in jail should probably be taken merely as a figure of speech and not literally.[98]

Patton must have been demoralized by being thrown in jail in a relatively unfamiliar place like Belzoni, but he was probably hurt far worse by being told to stay off Dockery's plantation. The man who told him to leave was Herman G. Jett, who was a good friend of Will Dockery and served for forty years as the general manager or overseer of the plantation. The incident evidently took place at the end of 1933 or in January 1934, not long before Patton's final recording session, for he describes it in his "34 Blues" (Vocalion 02651). Charley's nephew Tom Cannon, who lived nearly his entire life on Dockery Farms and as of the late 1980s still occasionally did work there, stated that Charley was living at Holly Ridge when the incident took place. He must have been visiting his sister Viola, who still lived on Dockery Farms. Cannon described what happened:

He [Charley] would go around and play for different places through the community, and he would come in [i.e., to Dockery Farms]. He'd be coming in some days, and Mr. Jett would be riding, tending the farm. And Mr. Jett got at him one day, after his daddy had left the farm, told him that he didn't want him hanging around Dockery 'cause everybody was at work and he didn't want him hanging around Dockery Farm. And he put out a record about that. He had done lived on Dockery, was growed up on Dockery, had been there for years. After he [Charley's father] moved off, Charley come back in there. Sometimes he would pick a little cotton on Dockery, but the biggest he did was put out music. As long as his daddy was there on Dockery, he didn't say anything to him about coming back and forth on Dockery. But he [Charley] carried a couple of men's wives off from Dockery, and they were tore up about that. And when Mr. Jett met him coming on the place, Mr. Jett told him that he didn't want him hanging around Dockery no more. Then he put out that record about Herman Jett.... He [Charley] carried off one of the tenant's wives. She followed him off. She was crazy about that music he was playing and followed him and his wife [Bertha Lee] off. She just followed them off. When he come back on the place, this old boy had been on the place all his days. And he [Jett] asked Charley how come he taked the boy's wife off. The boy was named Floyd Williams, what he took the wife off. But she was following him and his wife off her own self. That's the reason Mr. Jett told him like he did. She just wanted to be around with that music. He put that song out after Mr. Jett met him and told him that he carried the boy's wife off and he'd rather for him not to be fooling around on the place. He went on and put that record out and then sent Mr. Jett one. Mr. Jett used to talk about him. . . . He had fun out of Mr. Jett when he sent him that record back after Mr. Jett told him that. He had been around Mr. Jett ever since he was a boy up until a man. Mr. Jett laughed. He wasn't mad at him. They didn't have no falling out.

Longtime Dockery resident Ruffin Scott told the story somewhat differently, stating: "You know, he put out a record about Mister Jett, Herman Jett. He was the manager of the place, Dockery Farm. He was a great big man, you know. Got mad about the record Charley putting out, ha ha, about him. It's just the way he was speaking on, you know, putting that record out. That's what he didn't like about, you know, ha ha."

Jett may or may not have laughed about the record, but he probably considered it to be all in a day's work when he banned Charley from the plantation, and as a lifelong Dockery worker, Tom Cannon perhaps underestimated his uncle's reaction. Patton's "34 Blues" is anything but mild in its description of Jett, although the criticism is indirect. Only someone who knew the background and circumstances of the incident would really understand the meaning of the lyrics.

1. I ain't gonna tell nobody . . . Thirty-Four have done for me.
I ain't gonna tell nobody what Thirty-Four have done for me.
Christmas rolled up; I was broke as I could be.

2. He run me from Will Dockery's; told my brown, "I want you to stop."
He run me from Will Dockery's; told my brown, "I want you to stop."
Spoken: Wonder what's the matter.
Herman told Papa Charley, "I don't want you hanging 'round on my job no more."

3. Further down the country it almost make you cry.
Further down the country it almost make you cry.
Spoken: My God, children.
Women and children flagging freight trains for rides.

4. Herman got a little six Buick, big six Chevrolet car.
Herman got a little six Buick, little six Chevrolet car.
Spoken: My God, what solid power!
And it don't do nothing but follow behind Harvey Parker's plow.

5. And it may bring sorrow, Lord, and it may bring tears.
It may bring sorrow, Lord, and it may bring tears.
Oh Lord, oh Lord, spare me to see a brand new year.

Charley is saying that the year 1934 had started badly for him. We don't know if he really was broke at Christmas time. It seems unlikely, as the workers on the farms had just received their settlements, and there were probably plenty of parties where Charley could have made money. The white folks, too, had sold their cotton and were probably in a mood to celebrate with music. But the general economic climate of the country was bad. It was still a time of severe economic depression, and Patton's general level of income was probably lower than it had been in earlier years. In the opening stanza he was most likely taking the role of spokesman for the poor people of the Delta. This view is strengthened by his third stanza, in which he calls attention to the pathetic plight of women and children who can't afford to buy a railroad ticket and are forced to try to bum rides on freight trains. Herman Jett, on the other hand, owned two cars and could afford to burn up his gasoline on something as trivial as riding around in the fields behind one of the farm workers. (Harvey Parker was a tenant on Dockery Farms and an old friend of Charley Patton.) Jett had also insulted Patton's dignity by speaking first to his wife and then treating him like a common vagrant. Obviously Jett didn't consider Charley's profession as a musician to be a real job. The only job that he probably considered suitable for black people was work on a plantation. In other words, he was implicitly telling Charley to reduce himself to the status of "nigger." Charley had been driven from the home where he had grown up, and his pride had been wounded. Rather than swallow this bitter pill in silence, he contradicted his opening line and "told everybody." This song was on the first record that Vocalion released from the session, at a time when Patton was still living. We must admire his bold move in referring to Mr. Jett by his first name and sending him a copy of the record. Tom Cannon stated that Will Dockery also heard this record. But it was definitely Jett's idea, not Dockery's, to keep Charley off the plantation, as Dockery was very fond of Charley's music.

Charley Patton did not leave Mississippi, nor was he spared to see a brand new year. In his last years his music had become very popular with Delta whites, and the difficulty he had in maintaining the same freedom and

Charley Patton's new grave marker, Holly Ridge, MS, 1991. (Photograph by David Evans)

Roebuck Staples and John Fogerty at Patton's grave,
1991. (Photograph by David Evans)

security that whites enjoyed must have weighed heavily upon him. During his final recording session he was openly criticizing the social status quo in the Delta. His last playing job was for whites, and one wonders what songs he performed there. Did he sing "High Sheriff Blues" and "34 Blues"? Did the white folks understand what he was singing about? Did they care?

On July 20, 1991, a stone monument was erected by the Mt. Zion Memorial Fund at the supposed site of Charley Patton's grave in the Holly Ridge cemetery to mark what was thought to be the centennial of his birth (based on the probably erroneous information in the 1900 US Census). Famed gospel singer and guitarist Roebuck Staples, who was born in 1914 and raised on Dockery's plantation, was the special guest at the memorial service held nearby at New Jerusalem Missionary Baptist Church. It was attended by local black and white residents, blues/rock star John Fogerty who had paid for the stone, and various other guests and officials, among them Patton's daughter Rosetta Patton Brown, Patton's nephew Tom Cannon and his wife, and a large delegation of her children and grandchildren who sang a piece called "Memories."

Local white resident Billy Robertson recalled seeing Patton play his "banjo" (sic) on his father's store porch in Holly Ridge. Then Staples said that in his boyhood he had seen Patton and said to himself, "If I ever get to be a man, I'm gonna get me a guitar and play the blues." Later, in fact, Staples did so and played blues on a local circuit before moving with his family to Chicago and switching to gospel music. Fogerty related how he had been influenced by Staples and inspired by Patton's recordings. Finally, the church's pastor, Reverend Ernest J. Ware, preached a funeral sermon from Philippians III: 12–14, on the subject of "Pressing On." He compared Charley Patton to Saul of Tarsus on his journey to Damascus, noting that Patton was not a perfect man but that he pressed on toward his goal and "made it" and "made a way for some of us."[99]

Charley Patton has been dead for over eighty years, and it is over a century and a quarter since he was born. He was practically one of the originators of the blues, one of the first generation of blues artists, yet he also seems to have anticipated the international interest in blues that is now taking place over a hundred years after he and others began to create this music. Patton was truly the Masked Marvel, someone who was able to "tell the world" and create the "Over the Sea Blues." His fame lives today, not only undiminished but grown greater. Charley Patton was indeed the "great man" that the young Bukka White thought he was. He will be remembered and discussed worldwide for his own brilliant accomplishments, while the other "great men" of the Delta that he sang about will be remembered only because they figured in Charley Patton's life and songs. Patton's very existence was a bold challenge to the status quo in the Delta that was designed to keep him oppressed, to keep him from being a "great man." Charley Patton knew his own greatness and was proud of it. He would have been proud of a conference of blues scholars over the sea in honor of the fiftieth anniversary of his death and the memorial service at the place of his death to honor the hundredth anniversary of his birth, but he also would have expected these honors.

Notes

This is the third version of this essay to be published. It first appeared in the original 1987 edition of this book as an expanded version of a paper I had read at the 1984 international colloquium in Liège, Belgium, commemorating the fiftieth anniversary of Charley Patton's death. After preparing the paper for publication, I discovered some new information on Patton and managed to have it inserted rather awkwardly as addenda to my main text. In 2002 the essay was included as a component in an elaborate box set reissue of all of Patton's recordings along with many of the recordings of his musical associates and contemporaries: Revenant 212, *Screamin' and Hollerin' the Blues: The Worlds of Charley Patton*. The addenda in the first published version were incorporated into the text along with some other new material. Some sections of the original essay, however, were deleted, including my lyric transcriptions of several of Patton's songs. Instead, reference was made to transcriptions appearing elsewhere in the production's notes. These transcriptions were not my own, and in some cases they differed from my own versions. My essay in the box set won a Grammy award in 2003 for Best Album Notes and has been posted on the Paramount Records website (http://paramountshome.org). For the present publication I have reverted to the full 1987 text, including my lyric transcriptions, but have integrated the addenda into the main text and have retained additions and revisions from the 2002 version, while also incorporating a substantial amount of new material from my fieldwork and the research of colleagues. I have made other alterations in the text for the sake of clarity or to correct errors, and I offer some new and revised interpretations. I have not, however, attempted to assess, incorporate, or reconcile all of the new information and interpretation of Patton's life and music that has appeared since 1987 in the writings of other researchers.

1. For insight into the social conditions and caste system of the Delta during the 1930s, see the following works: Hortense Powdermaker, *After Freedom* (New York: Russell and Russell, 1968); John Dollard, *Caste and Class in a Southern Town* (New Haven: Yale University Press, 1937); Allison Davis, Burleigh B. Gardner, and Mary R. Gardner, *Deep South* (Chicago: University of Chicago Press, 1941); and David L. Cohn, *Where I Was Born and Raised* (Notre Dame: University of Notre Dame Press, 1967). See also James C. Cobb, *The Most Southern Place on Earth: The Mississippi Delta and the Roots of Regional Identity* (New York: Oxford University Press, 1992).

2. Samuel Charters, *The Bluesmen* (New York: Oak Publications, 1967), 34. For similar statements by other Delta bluesmen see Robert Palmer, *Deep Blues* (New York: Viking, 1981), 61–63.

3. Eddie "Son" House interviewed by David Evans and Alan Wilson, Cambridge, Massachusetts, November 4–6, 1964; Viola Cannon and Bessie Turner interviewed by David Evans and Marina Bokelman, Greenville, Mississippi, August 22, 1967; Tom Cannon interviewed by David Evans and Marina Bokelman, Dockery, Mississippi, August 25, 1967; Bessie Turner interviewed by David Evans and Bob Vinisky, Greenville, Mississippi, March 10, 1979; Tom Rushing interviewed by David Evans, Robert Sacré, and Bob Groom, Cleveland, Mississippi, April 9, 1985; Tom Cannon interviewed by David Evans, Robert Sacré, and Bob Groom, Cleveland, Mississippi, April 9, 1985; Tom Cannon interviewed by David Evans and Michael Leonard, Cleveland, Mississippi, December 8, 1986; Ruffin Scott interviewed by David Evans, Dockery, Mississippi, April 24, 1989; Will Williams interviewed by David Evans, Cleveland, Mississippi, June 27, 1989; Joseph "Coochie" Howard interviewed by David and Marice Evans, Holly Ridge, Mississippi, July 20, 1991; Rosetta Patton Brown interviewed by David and Marice Evans, Duncan, Mississippi, August 10, 1991; Beatrice Gidden interviewed by David Evans for Mojo Working Productions, Lula, Mississippi, February, 1992; Rosetta Patton Brown interviewed by David Evans for Mojo Working Productions, Duncan, Mississippi, February, 1992. I am grateful to Michael Leonard for further help in research at the courthouses in Belzoni and Cleveland, Mississippi, in December 1986, and for interviews of Ruthie Mae King, Albert Walker, Beatrice Tripp, Eli Pearman, Leroy Marshall, Caddie Carter, and T. C. Bailey in Cleveland, Mississippi, June 1989. I offer my sincere thanks to those who collaborated with me in the interviews and those who willingly gave information about Charley Patton. The 1989 interviews were made possible by a faculty research grant from the University of Memphis, whose support is gratefully acknowledged. I would also like to acknowledge and thank Alex van der Tuuk, Bob Eagle, Eric LeBlanc, Chris Smith, Jim O'Neal, Steve LaVere, Terry Barkley, Ed Payne, Chuck Roscopf, Paul Garon, Gayle Dean Wardlow, T. DeWayne Moore, Dick Spottswood, Jerry Zolten, Luigi Monge, and Guido van Rijn for supplying further information on Charley Patton and/or commenting on my research, and Dean Blackwood, Susan Archie, and Lynn Abbott for help and cooperation in preparing this revised version of the essay.

4. For my earlier assessment of Patton's career and music see "Charlie Patton's Life and Music" in *Charlie Patton*, Blues World Booklet No. 2, ed. Bob Groom (Knutsford, UK: Blues World, 1969), 3–7 (reprinted in *Blues World* 33 [August 1970]: 11–15). See also David Evans, "Blues on Dockery's Plantation: 1895 to 1967," in *Nothing But the Blues*, ed. Mike Leadbitter (London: Hanover, 1971), 129–32; and David Evans, *Big Road Blues: Tradition and Creativity in the Folk Blues* (Berkeley: University of California Press, 1982).

5. Bernard Klatzko, notes to *The Immortal Charlie Patton*, Origin Jazz Library 7, LP, 1964.

6. Klatzko, *Immortal Charlie Patton*.

7. Nick Perls, "Son House Interview—Part One," *78 Quarterly* 1, no. 1 (Autumn 1967): 59–61.

8. Gayle Dean Wardlow and Jacques Roche, "Patton's Murder—Whitewash or Hogwash?," *78 Quarterly* 1, no. 1 (Autumn 1967): 10–17.

9. Charters, 34–56.

10. Stephen Calt et al., notes to *Charley Patton: Founder of the Delta Blues*, Yazoo L-1020, LP, ca. 1967.

11. John Fahey, *Charley Patton* (London: Studio Vista, 1970).

12. Fahey, 26, 29.

13. Don Kent, notes to *Patton, Sims, & Bertha Lee*, Herwin 213, LP, 1977.

14. Palmer, 48–92. R. Crumb published "Patton," an illustrated biography of Charley Patton, in *Zap Comix* 11 (1985), based largely on the account in Palmer's book. Subsequently this and other Crumb strips on blues figures were collected in *R. Crumb Draws the Blues* (San Francisco: Last Gasp, 1993).

15. This information was transmitted hastily to Palmer from memory in order to meet a publication deadline. Palmer's account contains a few errors of fact, for which I take responsibility and which I will endeavor to correct here.

16. Palmer, 56–57.

17. Alan Greenberg, *Love in Vain* (Garden City, NY: Doubleday, 1983), 38–45, 95–105, 109–18.

18. Stephen Calt and Gayle Dean Wardlow, *King of the Delta Blues: The Life and Music of Charlie Patton* (Newton, NJ: Rock Chapel Press, 1988).

19. Calt and Wardlow, 301–18.

20. Alex van der Tuuk, *The New Paramount Book of Blues* (Overveen, NL: Agram Blues Books, 2017).

21. Perls, 60.

22. Jacques Roche, "The Words," *78 Quarterly* 1, no. 1 (Autumn 1967): 51–52, 54; Stephen Calt, "The Country Blues as Meaning," in *Country Blues Songbook*, ed. Stefan Grossman, Hal Grossman, and Stephen Calt (New York: Oak Publications, 1973), 22.

23. Fahey, 60, 62, 65.

24. Fahey, 66.

25. Fahey, 63. The drought actually occurred in 1930.

26. Fahey, 67. In 2002 Fahey modified his views somewhat in "Charley Reconsidered, Thirty-Five Years On," in *Screamin' and Hollerin' the Blues: The Worlds of Charley Patton*, Revenant 212, 7-CD box set, 46–53.

27. Calt and Wardlow also reject the idea that Henderson Chatmon was Charley Patton's biological father, although they state that he could have been the father of Charley's brother Will "Son" Patton. This and other aspects of Charley Patton's birth, family, and youth in the area around Bolton are discussed in their *King of the Delta Blues*, 44–51. Some of their information and interpretation differs from what is presented here. See also van der Tuuk, 245–47.

28. Calt and Wardlow, 45, without citing a source, claim that the marriage took place in 1884 and "must have been something of a shotgun wedding." Presumably they are referring to daughter Katie's birth in March of that year.

29. On his World War I draft registration form he listed his birthdate as August 4, 1893.

30. "Strayed or Stolen," *The Vicksburg Herald*, Nov. 26, 1865; list of National Union Republican Party members, *Jackson Clarion-Ledger*, Sept. 2, 1869; *Vicksburg Evening Post*, July 4, 1883; "W. D. Patten Undertaker," *Hinds County Gazette*, July 25, 1885; *The Vicksburg Herald*, Sept. 26, 1886; death notice, *The Weekly Democrat*, June 1, 1892. An alternative possibility is that Charley's paternal grandfather was not named William/Bill but was instead a John

Patton or Patten. In the 1870 census a white man named John Patton, aged sixty-five and born in North Carolina, is listed as married to a black woman named Rose, aged fifty-two and born in South Carolina, with their three children, George (7), William (5), and Ida (3), all described as black, along with a mulatto girl named Ella Hussey (11). Their residence, however, is in Lauderdale County near Meridian, Mississippi, far from any region of the state associated with Charley Patton. In the 1880 census the family is found in the same part of Mississippi without Ella Hussey, but now John is listed as black and aged 66; Rose is mulatto and aged 45; George mulatto and aged 18; Willie black and aged 17; and Ida black and aged 14. If this John and Rose are the grandparents of Charley Patton, it could be the case that they relocated to Lauderdale County for economic reasons after the work at the Vicksburg cemetery was finished in 1868 and that John chose to pass for black in the volatile post-Reconstruction climate of 1880. On the other hand, it is possible that the description of this John Patton as "white" in the 1870 census is simply an error. Calt and Wardlow, 44–45, assert that Charley's grandfather was yet another John Patten (*sic*), a black man listed in the 1880 census as aged 40 and living in Coahoma County, Mississippi, with his children Anderson (18), Rosa (15), and Bill (14). Next door to them is Ether Patten, aged 25, with her daughter Marriah. In the 1870 census John Patton (*sic*) is listed in DeSoto County, Mississippi, black and aged 29, with wife Susan, black and aged 42, and their children Andy (16, mulatto), Martha (14, mulatto), Anderson (10, black), Rose (6, black), and Billy (5, black). The names Rose/Rosa, Bill/Billy, and Ether/Etha all figure among those associated with Charley's family, but the first two are also found in the family of the other John Patton. None of these candidates for Charley Patton's paternal grandparents is entirely satisfactory in respect to name, age, location, or even racial identity, and their sons named William/Willie/Bill/Billy appear to be different from the William Patton listed in the 1880 census as living in Bolton and who is almost certainly Charley's father.

31. This photograph exists in both full-length and head-shot forms and was taken in 1929 by Paramount Records for publicity purposes. Another heavily retouched photo discovered by Gayle Dean Wardlow in the home of one of Patton's ex-girlfriends cannot be authenticated as being an image of Charley Patton. If it is Patton, it shows him about twenty years younger than the other photo, with a moustache, and looking more like a white man. Patton family members and friends that I interviewed about this photo did think that it looked like Charley Patton as a young man. On these two portraits, see van der Tuuk, 259.

32. Jim O'Neal, booklet notes to *The Complete Recorded Works of Charley Patton*, Pea Vine Blues PCD-2255/6/7 (1992), 34. See also O'Neal's chapter in the present volume.

33. For a discussion of this term and its use in African American folklore, see John Minton and David Evans, *"The Coon in the Box": A Global Folktale in African-American Tradition* (Helsinki: Academia Scientiarum Fennica, 2001).

34. This is confirmed in Pete Welding, "David 'Honeyboy' Edwards," in *Nothing But the Blues*, ed. Mike Leadbitter (London: Hanover Books, 1971), 135. Edwards also mentioned an Ed Patton, Charley's brother. This name is otherwise unknown and might be a mistaken identification of Charley's brother Will or another relative who was not actually a brother. See also Palmer, 89.

35. Calt and Wardlow, 51, paint a picture of the nearby town of Edwards as a haven for African Americans in the 1880s and 1890s.

36. For more information on these artists see Evans, "Blues on Dockery's Plantation: 1895 to 1967."

37. For more information on Will Dockery and his plantation, see *Biographical and Historical Memoirs of Mississippi* (Chicago: Goodspeed, 1891), Vol. 1, 652–53; and Marie M. Hemphill, *Fevers, Floods and Faith: A History of Sunflower County, Mississippi, 1844–1976* (Indianola, MS: Marie M. Hemphill, 1980), 403–5.

38. Tom Cannon pronounced Miller's first name as Lugene (*sic*).

39. Evans, *Big Road Blues*, 182, 190–93.

40. Calt and Wardlow, 254.

41. On Charley's application for a marriage license to Gertrude Lewis in Cleveland, Mississippi, on September 12, 1908, he made his mark (X) by his name recorded by the court clerk. Tom Cannon states that Charley must have been "pulling somebody's leg." Probably the clerk, a Chas. Christmas, simply wrote Patton's name on the form and asked him to add his mark, assuming that he was illiterate. Charley's military draft registration from 1917 contains a signature, which appears to be genuine and is written in good handwriting. These are the only two pieces of evidence that attest directly to his degree of literacy.

42. This song is probably an adaptation of C. D. and W. S. Martin's well known hymn of the same title, published in 1905.

43. Bessie Turner perhaps meant Renova, where her brother recalled Charley preaching in a church located on land owned by the family. Tom Cannon stated that Charley did most of his preaching in parts of the hill country where he was not well known as a blues singer.

44. Charters, 37.

45. Henry Balfour, "Ritual and Secular Uses of Vibrating Membranophones as Voice-Disguisers," *Journal of the Royal Anthropological Institute of Great Britain and Ireland* 78 (1948), 45–69.

46. The 1940 US Census for Bolivar County, Mississippi, lists a Millie Toy [*sic*, Torry], age 50, living in a household with West Barnes, age 80. This man was very likely her father.

47. William F. Gray, *Imperial Bolivar* (Cleveland, MS: *Bolivar Commercial*, 1923), 18–19.

48. Gray, 14.

49. This phase of his career must have been brief, as he cannot be clearly identified in Memphis city directories during the years 1924–34.

50. Welding, 135.

51. O'Neal, 36.

52. Charters, 56.

53. Charters, 54.

54. "Good Morning, School Girl" was recorded by John Lee "Sonny Boy" Williamson in 1937, three years after Patton's death. Bessie Turner must have confused this song with another one by Patton with a similar theme.

55. Palmer.

56. Reverend Rubin Lacy, interviewed by David Evans, John Fahey, and Alan Wilson, Ridgecrest, California, March 19, 1966.

57. Perls, 59.

58. Klatzko.

59. Lacy.

60. On this point see Evans, *Big Road Blues*, 188.

61. Perls, 59.

62. Perls, 59.

63. Klatzko.

64. Lacy.

65. Palmer, 70.

66. Klatzko.

67. Calt and Wardlow, 83–84; van der Tuuk, 259.

68. Klatzko.

69. Klatzko.

70. Klatzko; Calt and Wardlow, 149–50.

71. Klatzko; Calt and Wardlow, 150.

72. Perls, 61.

73. Charters, 56.

74. Perls, 60.

75. Patton's death is discussed in detail, and his death certificate is printed, in Wardlow and Roche.

76. Charters, 54.

77. Charters, 56.

78. For a discussion of the workings of this folk-blues tradition, see Evans, *Big Road Blues*, and David Evans, "Formulaic Composition in the Blues: A View from the Field," *Journal of American Folklore* 120 (2007): 482–99.

79. Stefan Grossman, *Delta Blues Guitar* (New York: Oak, 1969), 45. The discussion in this paragraph is revised and adapted from Evans, *Big Road Blues*, 239–41.

80. See, for example, Evans, *Big Road Blues*, 146–50; David Evans, "Structure and Meaning in the Folk Blues," in Jan Harold Brunvand, *The Study of American Folklore: An Introduction*, 3rd ed. (New York: W. W. Norton, 1986), 563–93.

81. On symmetry in folk blues texts see Evans, *Big Road Blues*, 68–69; David Evans, "Traditional Blues Lyrics and Myths: Some Correspondences," in *The Lyrics in African American Popular Music*, ed. Robert Springer (Bern: Peter Lang, 2001), 17–40; and Evans, "Formulaic Composition in the Blues."

82. For a somewhat different treatment of the symmetry of this text, see Evans, "Traditional Blues Lyrics and Myths," 32–33.

83. For a more detailed interpretation of the text of this song, see Evans, *Big Road Blues*, 146–49.

84. Hemphill, 403–4.

85. O'Neal, 38.

86. For an interesting account of life in Merigold at a slightly later period, see Jimmy Smith, *Merry Memories of Merigold, Mississippi* (Memphis: JRS Productions, 1982). For further discussion of Patton's "Tom Rushen Blues," see David Evans, "Ramblin'," *Blues Revue Quarterly* 6 (Fall 1992): 10–12.

87. For a detailed discussion of "Alabama Bound"/"Elder Green" and related songs, see Luigi Monge and David Evans, "New Songs of Blind Lemon Jefferson," *Journal of Texas Music History* 3, no. 2 (Fall 2003): 8–28.

88. For more detailed descriptions of the flood and its effects, see Pete Daniel, *Deep'n As It Come: The 1927 Mississippi River Flood* (Fayetteville: University of Arkansas Press, 1996); and John Barry, *Rising Tide: The Great Mississippi Flood of 1927 and How It Changed America* (New York: Simon and Schuster, 1997).

89. For a study of all of the blues and gospel recordings on this flood, see David Evans, "High Water Everywhere: Blues and Gospel Commentary on the 1927 Mississippi River Flood," in *Nobody Knows Where the Blues Come From: Lyrics and History*, ed. Robert Springer (Jackson: University Press of Mississippi, 2006), 3–75. At the time of publication it was still generally believed that Patton recorded his two-part blues in October 1929. Although I expressed some uncertainty that his Part II was actually about the 1927 flood, I was not able to relate it to the flooding that occurred in January 1930. More recent accurate dating of Patton's recording session now makes this identification possible. For the most current research on the dates of Patton's second and third recording sessions, see Guido van Rijn and Alex van der Tuuk, *New York Recording Laboratories Matrix Series, Volume One: The L Matrix Series (1929–1932)*, rev. ed. (Overveen, NL: Agram Blues Books, 2015), 5–7, 29–31.

90. Calt and Wardlow, 200.

91. On Mattie Delaney and her recording, see Evans, "High Water Everywhere," 20, 71.

92. For newspaper accounts of the flooding in Northeast Arkansas, see "Cold Halts Floods After Levees Fail," *New York Times*, January 17, 1930, 25; "Flood Menace Shifts to Mississippi Area," *Commercial Appeal* (Memphis), January 23, 1930, 1, 3; "Ice Blocking Rescue of Flood Sufferers," *Commercial Appeal*, January 24, 1930, 1, 2; "Workers Rescue 150 from Big Lake Area," *Commercial Appeal*, **January 25, 1930?**, 1, 3; "Suffering in Flood Section Is Passing," *Commercial Appeal*, January 26, 1930, 1, 2.

93. This strike is discussed in Colin J. Davis, *Power at Odds: The 1922 National Railroad Shopmen's Strike* (Urbana: University of Illinois Press, 1997). All of the facts presented here about this strike are drawn from this source.

94. For an analysis of "Son" House's song, see Luigi Monge, "Preachin' the Blues: A Textual Linguistic Analysis of Son House's 'Dry Spell Blues,'" in David Evans, ed., *Ramblin' on My Mind: New Perspectives on the Blues* (Urbana: University of Illinois Press, 2008), 222–57. For historical background on the drought, see Nan Elizabeth Woodruff, *As Rare as Rain: Federal Relief in the Great Southern Drought of 1930–31* (Urbana: University of Illinois Press, 1985).

95. Big Joe Williams, "Big Joe Talking," *Piney Woods Blues*, Delmark DL-602, LP (1958). Williams's statement contained the first published information about Patton's life. Reverend Booker Miller, interviewed by Gayle Dean Wardlow, gives a brief description of this incident in disc 7, tracks 2 and 11, of *Screamin' and Hollerin' the Blues: The Worlds of Charley Patton*, Revenant 212, 7-CD box set (2002).

96. Fahey, *Charley Patton*, 110.

97. Palmer, 87.

98. For further discussion of "High Sheriff Blues," see David Evans, "Ramblin'," *Blues Revue Quarterly* 7 (Winter 1993): 14–15.

99. For a more detailed description of this event, see David Evans, "Ramblin'," *Blues Revue Quarterly* 2 (October 1991): 6.

Elementary Blues and Tonal Scale in Charley Patton's Recordings

—Daniel Droixhe

The problems of classification in traditional blues lead us to distinguish, among more or less "canonical" forms, some differing interpretations, of which two types will be considered here. Their difference lies in the structure of interpretation or seems to be essentially accidental.[1]

We will consider these differences in a limited body of material: the songs reissued on the double album devoted to Charley Patton (*Charley Patton: Founder of the Delta Blues*, Yazoo LP-1020). More precisely, we would like to examine the relationship between the tonal scale, as it has been defined by John Fahey in his nice work on Patton, and what we shall call here the bluesman's "elementary blues."[2] In this category belong pieces whose harmonic material is more reduced than in the most widespread classical blues formula, namely the three-chord pattern (3C) with two textual verses (2V). In order to become familiar with the type of notation that we shall use, let us keep in mind that the 3C2V pattern produces various canonical forms:

The twelve-bar blues is constructed on the I, IV, and V chords with a musical stanza form in AAB. It is well known that the v_1 (also designated by A) is sung on the root chord (C_1), which is used for more or less four measures. The same verse is then repeated on the subdominant chord before returning to the root chord. Another verse, v_2 or B, appears with the dominant chord, at the ninth measure, after which the singer/player goes back to the root chord. Using a formalization that will appear somewhat pedantic but which will show its utility, we shall synthesize this well-known formula like this:

$$3C(CHORDS) \times 2V(VERSES): C1V1 + C2V1 + C3V2$$

This system of notation is of course rudimentary, since it does not take into account the notion of measure and the overlap of a verse on different chords. It also simplifies the extension of V2 on the dominant and subdominant chords when it only mentions the dominant one.

Combining three chords with two verses allows other formulas. Let us limit ourselves to two of them.

The "Rollin' and Tumblin'" type has a double climbing to the subdominant chord, each one being followed by a short instrumental sequence; the ninth measure introduces, as above, the dominant chord and the second verse. In the classic Hambone Willie Newbern version of this blues type "Roll and Tumble Blues" (1929),[3] the progress is more melodic than harmonic. The type finds its achievement in Robert Johnson's "Traveling Riverside Blues." Thus, the structure may be written like this:

$$3C \times 2V: C2V1 + C5 + C2V1 + C1 + C3V2$$

We have not found any song completely constructed like this in Patton's recordings. The introductory stanza of three songs, however, has this pattern: in chronological order, "Heart Like Railroad Steel" (February 1930), "Mean Black Moan" (February 1930), and "Jersey Bull Blues" (1934), where the climbing to subdominant at the beginning of the second sung stanza is more clear. The rest of the song quits this pattern and belongs to the first family of songs distinguished by Fahey, the "High Water Everywhere" family. The latter shows a classical pattern in $3C \times 2V$ and is characterized by a right-hand syncopated strike—the typical "puh chang," with a possible descending bass, which is a Mississippi trait.

Another canonical pattern is known under the name of "Slidin' Delta," and has been popularized by Big Bill Broonzy under the title of "Key to the Highway." Patton recorded it as "Jim Lee." One may find in Fahey's book the features of the piece, which probably belongs to an old body of traditional titles and may be considered as an "elementary blues" by the second, third, and ninth stanzas of the song's Part 2. The latter are textually rudimentary, as they display the repetition of the one and only verse that covers the whole musical stanza. It may even be supposed that this verse retains a survival of the song as it was transmitted earlier by tradition; in the other stanzas, there is no textual repeat, unlike what can be found in the "Rollin' and Tumblin'" AAB.

To transcribe the "Slidin' Delta" pattern, the measure being recorded by a figure between parentheses, it would be represented as"

3 C: (1)C1 + (2)C3 + (3–4)C2 + (5)C1 + (6)C3 + (7)C1 + (8)C1–3

It is now time to consider the blues of elementary pattern, which has perhaps something to do with the genesis of the musical genre, from a logical if not chronological point of view.

The simplest form is illustrated by "Mississippi Bo Weavil Blues," the first song recorded by Patton, in Richmond, Indiana, on June 14, 1929. "Mississippi Bo Weavil Blues" is a narrative threnody on one chord without any textual repetition, that is to say without any organized textual form. The annotators of the Yazoo album think that it was recorded in open E tuning. Fahey thought that it was made, like more than half of the recorded production by Patton, in open G tuning. All of Patton's religious songs seem to have been played this way also, with bottleneck or knife. The guitar was probably held flat on the knees, which allows the player to reach the highest notes. The elementary character of the song also appears in the tonal mode, Fahey's mode I (48). Fahey considers two main modes, on the basis of a statistical examination of the most frequently used tones, in a study undertaken with Alan Wilson. The tonal scale combines the tones as follows:

$$C—D—E\flat—E—F—G—A—B\flat—C$$

Fahey notes W. C. Handy's assertion, according to which blues fundamentally was pentatonic *like the slave songs in the past*, omitting the F and the B. Fahey disputes this idea, objecting that, in Patton, the B is not only present, but is used more often than the D. Thus, the tonal scale would mix the Dorian and Mixolydian modes. But we have to consider whether Handy's statement is not confirmed by "Mississippi Bo Weavil Blues." The song is ranked in the category of the "Gapped blues mode I," characterized by a non-use of the total underlying tonal scale—the tonal "deep structure." Missing are the 2nd, 4th, and 6th tones, according Fahey's transcription. That is to say: lacking any D or F, and practically no A (one occurrence). So, there remain:

$$C \; E\flat \; E \; G \; B\flat$$

Another elementary pattern is illustrated by "Hammer Blues," where *hammer* must be understood as *hammock*. The Yazoo album commentary stresses that the vocal character is here more important than the instrumental one, as the guitar part follows the voice. The song is also limited to one chord, but a progression is obtained by the repetition of a first verse, which finds its complement in a second verse closing what is now a stanza-unity. "Mississippi Bo

Weavil Blues" displays a continuous succession, a sort of rosary of relatively independent verses. Here, the stanza is appearing. This is the same pattern used by Son House[4] or Robert Johnson in "Preachin' Blues," or by Blind Joe Reynolds in "Outside Woman Blues."[5] The Yazoo commentary stresses how "loosely structured" the song is.

A new step in Patton's recordings is constituted by a second grouping defined by Fahey as the "Minglewood blues family." There is no song in Patton's discography with the title "Minglewood Blues"; Fahey explains that the word was chosen because several songs were derived from "Minglewood Blues," recorded by Cannon's Jug Stompers in 1928.[6] In one of those versions, Patton even reproduces the refrain of the original: "You ever go down to Memphis, stop by Minglewood," etc.

Chronologically, the first song of the group is "Banty Rooster Blues," whose words were borrowed from a Walter Rhodes recording, "The Crowing Rooster" (1927). Everybody knows that it led to Howlin' Wolf's "Little Red Rooster." "Banty Rooster Blues" is one of the first songs recorded by Patton, the fifth during the June 14, 1929, session.

Just after this, he recorded "It Won't Be Long," which also has the verse mentioning Minglewood. Fahey adds "Down the Dirt Road Blues" and "34 Blues" to this family. It seems, however, that those last two songs could form a separate category that could be called "Down the Dirt Road Blues" or "Overseas Blues," because this last title perhaps gives Patton's original, traditional one. The register of recordings mentions "Over the Sea Blues" as the song's alternate titles and the expression "overseas blues" is repeated in the two verses of the fourth stanza. Those songs are constructed upon three chords and thus pertain to a later harmonic stage.

"Banty Rooster Blues" and "It Won't Be Long" introduce a two-chord system, even if the second one is only suggested. In fact, it is reduced to the basic tone, but the intent to break with a single chord is perceptible. The first eight measures, with the repetition of the first verse, keep the same harmonic ground, but the relative break provided by the second verse, at the ninth measure, is sustained by a passing to the dominant. If the song is played in E, we stay in that tone until the second verse, for which there is a passing to B, with an effect of change announcing the closing of the stanza on itself. It is the scheme illustrated by Skip James in "Cherry Ball Blues," "Cypress Grove Blues," etc. Thus, the "It Won't Be Long" and "Banty Rooster Blues" structure may be read:

$$2C \times 2V: C1V1 + C1V1 + C3V2$$

"High Sheriff Blues" also belongs to the category of blues of two chords and two verses. But the way of distributing them is absolutely different, because the song offers another answer to the question of the progression and of the interior dynamics of each stanza. "High Sheriff Blues" is one of the first songs recorded by Patton in 1934 after four years between recording sessions. Was he getting back, like he did for the June 1929 session, to what he had kept as the most typical part of the traditional heritage? However, we arrive here at a superior degree of elaboration.

The beginning of the song is identical to what we have in the standard "modern blues": verse 1 is repeated on two chords, the basic and subdominant tones being perceptible without being harmonically clear. But while one waits for a dominant at verse 2, the song simply goes back to the basic first chord. The effect of an "overtaking" or outcome, after the opposition of the two chords, is obtained by an elementary combination of the first chord and a different verse. So, we find here a real progression in three parts realized with the simplest means, with a minimum of elements, just by mixing text and music in an original way. Logical purity becomes aesthetics. It is also a very suggestive form, from the point of view of the blues deep structure, as it shows "in genesis" a sort of fundamental Hegelian triad.

Let us compare, to summarize, the two last patterns described.

"It Won't Be Long": C1V1 + C1V1 + C3V2
"High Sheriff Blues": C1V1 + C2V1 + C1V2

We have no tonal scale, in Fahey, for "High Sheriff Blues." But we get one for "Pea Vine Blues," which gives another resolution, with the same material of two chords and two verses. Again, the chords are suggested rather than completely carried out. The second, fourth, and sixth stanzas are constructed on this principle: when verse 1 is repeated, an effect of change is created by the climbing to the dominant, and a new effect of change or outcome is produced not by a harmonic break but on the level of text by verse 2. So, we have:

C1V1 + C3V1 + C3V2

The pattern is less satisfactory than in "High Sheriff Blues," for we feel that the song falls into some harmonic deadlock, as if a third chord was missing, when the second verse appears at the ninth measure.

We still have to stress the fact that some of Patton's recordings mix more or less two types of blues—a combination that the listener may receive as an effect of free improvisation or variety, and which eventually goes back to the elementary forms of the genre. Thus, the Yazoo annotators of "Pony Blues" were right when they wrote that its strength mainly lies in the rhythmic contrast established between the guitar and the voice. The holding of the vocal note that starts on the fourth beat of the measure gives, in fact, the sensation of "a measure of 3 followed by a measure of 5, in the sung part," a division in contrast "with the two measures of 4 beats of the instrumental part." "Pony Blues" and the related "Stone Pony Blues" mix stanzas in which the three ordinary chords are sufficiently marked by the fundamental notes, with other stanzas of a rougher harmony, accentuating the feature of simplicity. Those versions begin with a stanza where the A and B chords are perceptible. So, we have here an ordinary type in:

$$3 \ CV2: C1V1 + C2V2 + C3V2$$

But after this, when the voice begins the second stanza of "Pony Blues," at the moment when the initial verses are repeated the guitar simply follows the sung melody, without any real harmonic change. This is announced by a syncopated playing in c1v1. On the contrary, when this second part is ending, the instrument enters the second part and provides the contrast, with a firm subdominant chord. Thus is avoided (in those two versions of "Pony Blues" that take place between the II and III formulas) the monotony of a too-regular rhythm, aligning singing to music, as well as the banality of a mechanical repetition of the three chords (so often heard in modern blues).

In the same way, we may appreciate how formula II is converted by the dialogue between voice and guitar in "When Your Way Gets Dark." The response of the instrument is full of independence and so tasteful, when it lingers over several measures before the joint resolution of a second chord and a different verse. In the introduction, it is the singing that answers. In other blues by Patton, the alternation becomes rather harmonic, and one can distinguish, for example, the influence of "Rollin' and Tumblin'" in "Down the Dirt Road Blues" or "Green River Blues." The search for the various ways explored—more or less consciously—by a great artist to express himself may be an essential part of the pleasure of the *amateur*.

Notes

1. Prof. Droixhe thanks Miss M. Collart for the translation of the 1984 paper. He is a member of the Belgian Academy of French Language and Literature and of the Walloon Society for Eighteenth-Century Studies.

2. *Charley Patton*, Studio Vista, London, 1970.

3. *Mississippi Blues*, volume 3, Origin Jazz Library OJL 17.

4. *Son House: Complete Recordings, Volume 1*, Wolf WSE 116; Biograph BLP 12040; Origin OJL 5, etc. The same type is used by House in "Dry Spell Blues," recorded at Grafton, Wisconsin, in 1930.

5. *Roots of Rock*, Yazoo L-1063; *Delta Blues Heavy Hitters 1927–1931 (William Harris, Blind Joe Reynolds, Skip James*, Herwin LP 214.

6. *Cannon's Jug Stompers: Complete Recordings*, Herwin H 208.

PART 2

Charley Patton, Mississippi Delta Blues:
Comparison with Other Regional Styles and Mutual Influences

Louisiana Country Blues: A Comparison with the Delta Country Style of Charley Patton and Followers: Mutual Influences

—John Broven

In my book *South to Louisiana* (1983), I noted: "while blacks in states like Mississippi, Texas, Georgia, and the Carolinas developed identifiable rural blues styles, there was no parallel development in Louisiana.... The one-man-and-his-guitar back-porch sounds were confined principally to the small farming communities around Shreveport and Baton Rouge."

With a scattered black population, poor communications, and unique cultural areas like cosmopolitan New Orleans and Cajun South Louisiana, it is not surprising there was a lack of a unified early Louisiana country blues sound. The coterie of bluesmen from Shreveport were influenced, naturally, by the nearby Texas blues played by Blind Lemon Jefferson, then by Lightnin' Hopkins, but fall outside the scope of this chapter. Nevertheless, I'd like to give name checks to local post–World War II bluesmen Country Jim, "Stick Horse" Hammond, Jesse Thomas, prewar artist Oscar Woods, and of course Shreveport's most famous son, Lead Belly.

Still, I do hope to be able to show the influence the Charley Patton school of Delta bluesmen[1] had in particular on those musicians living in the Baton Rouge area. At this stage, I must say that I have found it hard to detect "mutual influences" on the Mississippi blues by Louisiana artists.

The most famous rural Louisiana bluesman, I believe, was Robert Pete Williams, a man who did not have the charismatic qualities of Patton or indeed Blind Lemon Jefferson. As if to emphasize the fragmented nature of the Louisiana blues scene, Williams did not start to assert himself until the blues revival years of the 1960s. Like Patton and Blind Lemon, he did have an individualistic style, as can be heard on his classic recording of "Prisoner's Talking Blues."

Robert Pete, as he is generally known, was first recorded by Harry Oster while incarcerated in Angola prison in 1959. Williams was an intensely personal artist, an introvert lost in his own music. He was not the sort of man to influence young contemporaries, as Patton did in Mississippi.

Charley Patton was a first-generation bluesman, but also performed ragtime tunes, popular blues, hillbilly music, folk songs, and spirituals. His blues vocals, full of moans and asides, embraced poignant basic lyrics, while his guitar playing—with occasional bottleneck—was heavily rhythmic. He was, as his records cannot show, a great showman and entertainer, qualities that were vital factors in his popularity.

Patton's main area of activity was central and northwest Mississippi, around the Yazoo River Basin, and also east Arkansas. So, how did he come to influence the aspiring bluesmen of neighboring Louisiana? There were no personal appearances, though he was said to have been in Kentwood and New Orleans, and it was hard to buy or hear his records. I feel the greatest influence was exerted in hand-me-down tradition by way of other Mississippi artists who came under Patton's spell. The line stretches from pre–World War II down-home bluesmen Tommy Johnson, Son House, Willie Brown, and Robert Johnson to the postwar Big Joe Williams, Roebuck Staples, Muddy Waters, Elmore James, John Lee Hooker, and Howlin' Wolf. This Patton link is illustrated by Clarence Edwards, one of the best Baton Rouge bluesmen, on his version of the famous Wolf number, "Smokestack Lightnin'," here called "Smokes Like Lightning."

Edwards was born in Lindsay, Louisiana, in 1933, a late date for a down-home bluesman. He learned to play the blues by listening to his grandmother's old records by John Lee "Sonny Boy" Williamson, Kokomo Arnold—and Charley Patton. Like Robert Pete Williams, Edwards was first recorded by Harry Oster, who at the turn of the 1960s was a professor at Louisiana State University, Baton Rouge, and was working for Folk-Lyric Records under the auspices of the Louisiana Folklore Society. These recordings have been acquired by Chris Strachwitz's Arhoolie label. Incredibly, this was the first time that the old-time rural Baton Rouge bluesmen had been captured on record.

One of the most primitive bluesmen, stylistically, was Butch Cage, who was described by Oster in his liner notes to the *Country Negro Jam Session* album as "a great representative of the now virtually extinct 19th century Negro fiddle tradition."[2] Cage had a raw sound similar to that of Henry "Son" Sims, who accompanied Patton on record. Just listen to Butch Cage performing another Mississippi blues popularized by Howlin' Wolf: "44 Blues."

Butch Cage was born in Mississippi in Franklin County in 1894, and took the songs of his youth with him when he moved to Louisiana in 1927. The trip was relatively easy thanks to Highway 61 connecting Memphis to New Orleans via Vicksburg and Baton Rouge. Other modes of travel were by the Illinois Central Railroad, which ran from Chicago via the Delta to New Orleans, and Mississippi River steamboats. The migratory path out of Mississippi was not only northward.

Another old-style Mississippian who left the oppression of his home state—and let us never forget the appalling social conditions and racial atrocities that are at the heart of any discussion on the blues—was Robert Brown, better known as Smoky Babe. He came from Itta Bena, just fifty miles from the Delta blues capital of Clarksdale. Eventually, he settled in Scotlandville, near Baton Rouge, and brought the Mississippi blues with him, as he shows in "Too Many Women."

The song itself is reminiscent of Robert Petway's "Catfish Blues" and Muddy Waters's "Rollin' Stone." Interestingly, Smoky Babe's performance brings to mind the big Louisiana swamp-blues artist of the time, Lightnin' Slim, an impression enhanced by the presence of Slim's harmonica player, Lazy Lester, under the pseudonym of Henry Thomas; at the time Lester was contracted to Excello Records of Nashville, Tennessee.

The Baton Rouge swamp-blues tradition took root within a fifty-mile radius of the state capital in small farming communities like Rosedale, Zachary, Maringouin, and Port Hudson—all relatively near Highway 61, the railroad, and the river. Musicians were in demand at house parties, small dives, bars, juke joints, picnics, and suppers. A man not unfamiliar with such a way of life is Roosevelt Holts. His style has been directly influenced by Tommy Johnson, an immediate Patton disciple, as can be heard on "Packing Up Her Trunk to Leave." Originally from Tylertown, Mississippi, Holts was a friend of Johnson. So, too, was the part-time New Orleans bluesman, Boogie Bill Webb.

Up to this point, all the records discussed have been deep blues. As I have already observed, Charley Patton was not merely a bluesman, he was a songster whose all-around repertoire included spiritual songs. Remember, Saturday night was for entertaining, Sunday was for the Lord. The Patton gospel link is readily evident in the work of Roebuck Staples (with the Staple Singers), who in turn influenced one of the most uncompromising Louisiana preachers, the Reverend Charlie Jackson, from Baton Rouge. The wild gospel-blues record "Testimony of Rev. Jackson" was made for the Booker label of New Orleans. The testimony is in praise of Jackson's recovery from a severe stroke. In his playing it is possible to detect the influence of Mississippi-born John Lee Hooker as well as Roebuck Staples.

All of the primitive blues I have cited so far were recorded in the 1950s and later. In a way the recordings are relics of a former era, which sadly went unrecorded in rural Louisiana. However, during the 1950s, mostly younger bluesmen from Baton Rouge began to be impacted by the contemporary popular records of postwar blues stars such as Muddy Waters, Howlin' Wolf, Bo Diddley, and especially Jimmy Reed—all from Mississippi and subsequently domiciled in Chicago; other highly influential artists with Chicago connections were Little Walter and Chuck Berry. The Texas legacy, in the capable hands of Lightnin' Hopkins, was another important factor. These records would have been heard over the airwaves through Radio WLAC in Nashville, Tennessee, where disc jockeys Gene Nobles, John R., and Hoss Allen reigned supreme; the jukebox was another crucial medium for dispensing the sounds of the time. All of a sudden, Baton Rouge artists such as Lightnin' Slim, Slim Harpo, Lazy Lester, and Silas Hogan were forging a new regional style: the *swamp blues*. The essence of this style was lazy, unhurried vocals over wallowing walking rhythms, much in the vein of Jimmy Reed's recordings. A vivid example of a local artist in thrall of Reed was Jimmy Anderson.

A crucial factor in the growth and development of this swamp-blues style was the presence and accessibility of J. D. "Jay" Miller's recording studio in Crowley, less than 100 miles from Baton Rouge along Highway 90. As it happened, Lightnin' Slim had a regional hit with his first record, "Bad Luck," for Miller's Feature label in 1954, thus convincing the record man there was a market for down-home blues records. Until then, Miller had specialized in Cajun and hillbilly recordings. With Lightnin' Slim as his major act, Miller soon landed a finished-product distribution deal with Excello Records of Nashville. The Mississippi blues influence can be found in certain Slim recordings, especially "I'm Leavin' You Baby."

Lightnin' Slim was born Otis Hicks in Good Pine, Louisiana, in 1913. As fellow Louisiana bluesman Boogie Jake once remarked, "Lightnin' Slim was the king of the blues in Louisiana; he influenced everybody."[3] Yet at the start of his recording career, Slim was primarily a Lightnin' Hopkins devotee.

Another important Baton Rouge swamp bluesman was Slim Harpo. From Lobdell, he recorded three notable songs between 1957 and 1966: "I'm A King Bee," "Rainin' in My Heart," and "Baby Scratch My Back." Somewhat underrated as a harmonica player, he possessed a voice that at times had the dark tones of the best Mississippi bluesmen, as evidenced by "Blues Hang-Over."

As a matter of interest, Lonesome Sundown, another leading Excello swamp bluesman recorded by Miller, was based in the Opelousas area, as were Guitar Gable and Leroy Washington. Other bluesmen such as Charles Sheffield and Clarence Garlow came from the Louisiana-Texas border area. Indeed, these latter artists headed for Eddie Shuler's Goldband Records studio in Lake Charles. It wasn't all Baton Rouge.

Just when an identifiable Louisiana swamp-blues sound was evolving, the bottom dropped out of the southern blues market in the wake of the civil rights movement. Negroes were now black and proud, and wanted soul music. Matters were not helped when Miller and Excello Records, under new management, parted company acrimoniously in 1966 after the Nashville label's hierarchy signed Slim Harpo directly to Excello.

As the black audience disappeared, so another sector was already taking its place: the young and enthusiastic white college crowd. In 1970 Arhoolie and Excello both spotted this trend by holding "revival" recording sessions in Baton Rouge. Among the artists recorded was Whispering Smith, whose style is exemplified on a slightly funky "Coal Black Mare." This theme, derived from a recording by Mississippi-born Arthur "Big Boy" Crudup, had been used by Patton on "Pony Blues" and Howlin' Wolf on "Saddle My Pony." As with some of the artists discussed earlier, Moses "Whispering" Smith was born in Mississippi, in Jefferson County, in 1932. He came to Baton Rouge in 1957, where he found work during the daytime and jobs in the clubs and bars at night. He, too, recorded for Excello under Miller. His declamatory vocal style—the "whispering" part was an ironic synonym—readily recalls that of Howlin' Wolf, and Wolf's mentor, Charley Patton.

At the Excello "revival" sessions, guitarist Arthur "Guitar" Kelley was recorded, and also Patton-Wolf stylist Clarence Edwards: "I Want Somebody."

Throughout the 1970s into the 1980s, Louisiana blues artists performed regularly at the New Orleans Jazz & Heritage and Baton Rouge Blues festivals. A great proponent of the local blues culture has been Ernest "Tabby" Thomas, only a moderate musician himself but a good hustler. His club, Tabby's Blues Box & Heritage Hall, provided a vital outlet for the swamp bluesmen, old and young. One of the club's regular artists was Henry Gray. Originally from Kenner, Louisiana, he enjoyed a long stint as pianist with Howlin' Wolf in Chicago before returning in 1968 to Alsen, just outside Baton Rouge. Gray's style is a mix of Louisiana and Chicago blues, as he showed on a single recorded for Sunland Records in 1983: "Don't Start That Stuff."

By this time many of the older bluesmen had passed away, including Robert Pete Williams, Lightnin' Slim, Slim Harpo, and Whispering Smith. Understandably the Michael Jackson and hip-hop–sated generation did not have the same empathy for the blues that their predecessors had. Young exceptions were the Neal Brothers band and Chris Thomas, each with bluesmen fathers, Raful Neal and Tabby Thomas. I would like to finish by citing a recent single by the Neal Brothers band with father Raful for Fantastic Records: "Down Home Blues."

Yes, the down-home blues. Although the Mississippi blues connection is rather tenuous, the song was recorded originally by Z.Z. Hill for Malaco

Records, of Jackson, Mississippi in 1982, and has become a standard in every southern bluesman's repertoire.

Fast forward some thirty years to 2015: Pioneering swamp-bluesmen Lazy Lester and Henry Gray are still performing regularly and, as I write, a complete Slim Harpo CD box set is about to be released by Bear Family Records of Germany under the aegis of Martin Hawkins. In fact, the Baton Rouge blues scene has been well served by CD reissues, particularly by Arhoolie of California and Ace of London. Hawkins is finalizing a biography on Harpo, who, being more in tune with the changing times of the 1960s, is recognized today as the standout Baton Rouge bluesman of his generation in place of Lightnin' Slim. Younger black artists throughout South Louisiana now seem to be consumed by zydeco and hip hop.

In conclusion, I consider it difficult to discern a definitive Louisiana country-blues style, although the state's swamp-blues idiom did acquire an identity—centered on Baton Rouge—through the Excello recordings produced by J.D. Miller. As I believe I have shown, the musical influence of neighboring Mississippi has been all-pervasive, especially through Tommy Johnson, Muddy Waters, Howlin' Wolf, and Jimmy Reed. But when you say "Mississippi blues," you cannot exclude the spiritual influence of its founding father, Charley Patton.

Discography

"Prisoner's Talking Blues," Robert Pete Williams, from *Angola Prisoners' Blues*, various artists, Arhoolie LP 2011, CD 419.

"Smokes Like Lightning," Clarence Edwards, and "44 Blues," Butch Cage, from *Country Negro Jam Session*, various artists, Arhoolie LP 2018.

"Too Many Women," Smoky Babe, *Hot Blues*, Arhoolie LP 2019 (part of *Louisiana Country Blues* with Herman E. Johnson, CD 440).

"Packing Up Her Trunk to Leave," *Roosevelt Holts and His Friends*, Arhoolie LP 1057.

"Testimony of Rev. Jackson," Rev. Charlie Jackson, *Testimony of Rev. Charlie Jackson*, Booker EP 806.

"I'm Leavin' You Baby," Lightnin' Slim, *I'm Leavin' You Baby*, Excello 2150.

"Blues Hang-Over," Slim Harpo, *Blues Hang-Over*, Excello 2184.

"Coal Black Mare," Whispering Smith, and "I Want Somebody," Clarence Edwards, from *Swamp Blues*, various artists including Henry Gray and Silas Hogan, Excello LP 8015/6.

"Don't Start That Stuff," Henry Gray and the Mighty House Rockers, *Don't Start That Stuff*, Sun Land 103.

"Down Home Blues," Raful Neal with the Neal Brothers, *Down Home Blues*, Fantastic 103.

Notes

1. Charley Patton, *Founder of the Delta Blues*, Yazoo LP L-1020.
2. *Country Negro Jam Session*, various artists including Clarence Edwards and Butch Cage, Arhoolie LP 2018.
3. Mazzolini, Tom. "Boogie Jake," *Living Blues* 31 (March/April 1977).

Bibliography

Broven, John. *South to Louisiana: The Music of the Cajun Bayous*. Gretna, LA: Pelican, 1983.

Broven, John. *Walking to New Orleans: The Story of New Orleans Rhythm & Blues*. Bexhill-on-Sea, UK: Blues Unlimited, 1974. Republished as *Rhythm & Blues in New Orleans, Revised and Updated*, Gretna, LA: Pelican, 2016.

———. *Record Makers and Breakers: Voices of the Independent Rock 'n' Roll Pioneers*. Urbana & Chicago: University of Illinois Press, 2009.

Eagle, Bob, and Eric S. LeBlanc. *Blues: A Regional Experience*. Westport, CT: Greenwood, 2013.

Fahey, John. *Charley Patton*. London: Studio Vista, 1970.

Harris, Sheldon, *Blues Who's Who*. New York: Arlington Houser, 1979.

Oliver, Paul. *The Story of the Blues*. London: Barrie and Rockcliff, 1969.

Palmer, Robert. *Deep Blues*. New York: Viking, 1981.

The Influence of the Mississippi Delta Style on Chicago's Postwar Blues

—Mike Rowe

I'm going to write about the influence of the Mississippi Delta blues on post-war Chicago blues style. And I'm going to be citing a lot of Muddy Waters records. I make no apology for this because when talking about the influence of the Delta on Chicago in postwar years, we are really talking about the rise and the success of Muddy Waters.

When Otis Spann, Muddy's piano player, said: "Chicago is the greatest blues area there is—it's built from the Mississippi blues," this is interesting from two points of view. First, it's interesting that the singers themselves recognized regional styles of the blues and the differences between them and that it isn't a convenient fiction of blues writers but it actually true that there were differences in blues in different areas. And it's also interesting because it was so obviously true at the time, for Otis was talking about 1952, 1953, etc.

But prior to the 1940s there had been no Mississippi influence whatsoever on the blues, or certainly not recorded blues, in Chicago before the war. The early singers, the popular ones like Blind Lemon Jefferson and Texas Alexander, came from Texas; Blind Blake and Tampa Red came from Florida; Leroy Carr from Indianapolis; and in the beginning Chicago's black population was drawn pretty evenly from most of the southern states. There was heavier migration from the border states, Kentucky and Tennessee, but there was little migration from the Deep South.

By the time the great Delta blues artists appeared on record the Depression was on, and no matter how magnificent the music is to us today, the artists really had very little impact. They had poor sales (not that anyone was selling records anyway) and very little discernible effect on the prevailing musical style. But after the Depression, when recording picked up again a recognizable style had developed in Chicago. The early country bluesmen had died or disappeared, and by the late 1930s there was an urban blues style that was smoother and more regular, which it had to be because the instrumentation had changed as piano players were added to the solo guitarists. Double bass players were also added, as were drummers, and the result had to be a much more uniform kind of blues style. Top artists were Big Bill Broonzy, Bumble Bee Slim, Tampa Red, and Memphis Minnie, and they all played in a more or less urban blues style. Toward the late 1930s the bands were further augmented by brass and reeds as trumpets, clarinets, and saxophones were added, and this produced a lively and sophisticated form of blues, much more jazzy but not very much like the country blues as we know it. The music was typified by the output of Lester Melrose, the A&R man whose artists supplied most of the music of the RCA Bluebird and Columbia catalogues.

There were still Delta bluesmen recording in the 1940s, but they had very little effect on the sound of the day. Booker (Bukka) White had recorded quite early in 1930 and up to 1940; Tommy McClennan and Robert Petway, another two artists from Mississippi, recorded in the early 1940s, as did Robert Lockwood Jr., whose attachment to the Delta blues was particularly intimate as he was Robert Johnson's stepson. Robert Lockwood Jr. recorded in 1941 and made four classic Delta blues, which again made no impact whatsoever on the prevailing market.

Musical Example 1: Robert Lockwood Jr., "Little Boy Blue"

Unfortunately, the time wasn't right for Lockwood in 1941. But there was gradually a change taking place, and by 1945 for instance, Big Boy Crudup (from Forrest, Mississippi) could get a couple of Top Ten R&B hits in Chicago with "Keep Your Arms Around Me" and "Rock Me Mama." But the prevailing sound was still that of the city—the bigger bands and the more sophisticated city style of blues, the kind of thing that Roosevelt Sykes had a hit with in 1946.

Musical Example 2: Roosevelt Sykes, "Sunny Road"

However the major companies—RCA, Columbia, Decca—for the first time were now beginning to face competition from all the new, independent record labels, often one-man operations set up by local businessmen or hustlers in the black areas who divined that there was a need or a chance to make money out of providing black music for black people. And while the major companies had by then grown conservative and set in their ways, the new independents, through inexperience and naivety, were quite happy to record anything and anybody.

In Chicago the Chess brothers ran a nightclub, the Macomba, and Leonard and Phil Chess with one lady partner Evelyn Aron started up the Aristocrat label and began to record everything from polkas to spirituals, from jazz to city blues. Then Muddy Waters was taken along to Aristocrat to record with Sunnyland Slim. Muddy had been in Chicago four years (he had had one unissued session for Columbia in 1946 and had even appeared on one bizarre session for 20th Century, but not under his own name), serving his apprenticeship in the city playing house-parties and bars. But again the sound at the time was that of, as he called it, the "sweet blues." He was playing with Eddie Boyd and Boyd hated Muddy's playing. As Muddy said, "He couldn't stand my playing because he wanted me to play like Johnny Moore, which I wasn't able to play the guitar like. He wanted it to be a kind of 'sweet blues.'" Anyway, when Muddy cut his first issued Aristocrat record with Sunnyland Slim, it was not exactly a sweet blues but was rather more in keeping with the Bluebird sound of the day.

Musical Example 3: Muddy Waters, "Gypsy Woman"

There is nothing very much wrong with this record, but it did not sell and Len Chess was not very excited with his new discovery. It was hard to know what would sell. Muddy also said, "I sing deep Down South blues straight out of the bottom." The Chess brothers had not heard any, but Muddy had recorded in 1941 for John Work and Alan Lomax of the Library of Congress on Stovall's Plantation near Clarksdale, Mississippi. Playing in his natural Delta style, one of the songs he cut was "I Be's Troubled."

Musical Example 4: Muddy Waters, "I Be's Troubled"

For his second Aristocrat session he tried to record this song. He told me later what happened. He started to play and Chess looked up in amazement, "What's he singing? I can't understand it. Stop it." After arguments, Evelyn and Sammy Goldstein, the Aristocrat talent scout, eventually got together and persuaded Leonard to let Muddy record the song, with the fortunate result that it was later to be described as "the big hit of 1948." This was Muddy with "I Can't Be Satisfied."

Musical Example 5: Muddy Waters, "I Can't Be Satisfied"

This was the turning point for the postwar Chicago blues. It's interesting to ask, Why did it happen in 1948? Why didn't it happen in 1941 with Lockwood or any of the other Delta blues stylists?

It happened because the audience had changed dramatically. During the war there was massive migration, from the farms to the cities, of blacks searching for work for the war effort. There were jobs in munitions plants, factories, and steel mills, and the wages were much higher than on the Southern farms. So blacks left the Deep South for the northern cities and the shipyards of California. Migration to New York was straight up the Eastern Seaboard from the Carolinas; to California it was from Texas, Oklahoma, and western Louisiana, but the huge migration was to Chicago from Mississippi, Arkansas, and central Louisiana. When one of the early independent record men, George Leaner, said, "The Illinois Central brought the blues to Chicago," it was a vivid if slight oversimplification, but there was a lot of truth to it. The I.C. Railroad ran through all the heavy blues country of the Mississippi Delta and though the eastern hill country of Jackson, and in the decade 1940–50 Chicago's black population increased by 55 percent through migration. That's in only ten years, and 40 percent of that increase came from Mississippi alone. So there was this huge change in Chicago's demography in a very short space of time. It had two effects. Of course, one was a new compact city-based audience with cash in their pockets for the Mississippi blues. And the other was that there were in town a lot of new artists from Mississippi with this Delta tradition behind them.

This was not lost on Len Chess, who was beginning to learn his blues by now; but he did not want to change a winning team, so Muddy was always recorded solo at first with Big Crawford on double bass. Chess realized the selling point was this tremendously exciting amplified slide guitar, and he wanted more Delta blues like it. So Muddy introduced to him the veteran Bluebird artist Robert Nighthawk, again with the happy result that Aristocrat had another blues hit in 1949 with Robert's "Annie Lee Blues."

Musical Example 6: Robert Nighthawk, "Annie Lee Blues"

Reflecting on those early years, Muddy Waters said, "We kept that Mississippi sound—we didn't do it exactly like the older fellas with no beat to it. We put the beat with it—put a little drive to it." And the next year, 1950, they had another hit with "Rollin' Stone." But there were changes taking place again. Chess was recording Muddy solo, but Muddy was playing with a band in the clubs and had always worked in a band since arriving in Chicago—and if Len Chess did not want to record the whole band, then other people did. So the Leaner brothers recorded the group under Baby Face Leroy, the drummer's name, for Parkway. And this was the wild result.

Musical Example 7: Baby Face Leroy, "Rollin' and Tumblin' (Pt. 1)"

The label said Baby Face Leroy, but the slide was unmistakably Muddy's, and along with Muddy was Leroy on drums and, significantly, Little Walter on harmonica. Len Chess was furious, and he insisted that Muddy cut "Rollin' and Tumblin'" again, this time with just Big Crawford, to kill the Parkway record—with the predictable result that both records were killed!

Anyway, enter Little Walter. Chess was learning slowly, and he finally decided to let Walter accompany Muddy on record for the first time. And once again he was rewarded with another hit. This was "Louisiana Blues" from 1951.

Musical Example 8: Muddy Waters, "Louisiana Blues"

With the addition of Little Walter on harp, the group was getting bigger on record as it was in the clubs. There were other influences shaping the Chicago blues. Along with the amplified guitar there was the amplified harmonica contributing to this new classic Chicago sound. The Delta rhythms were still there and there was still the impassioned vocal, but the Delta influence was becoming weaker. For instance, there were other Delta artists who failed to make any impression at this time. Muddy could have hits with a string of Delta songs but nobody else did apart from Robert Nighthawk. The Delta influence came from Patton, from Son House, but especially from Robert Johnson, and it was Johnson's playing that influenced most of his contemporaries. Johnny Shines, who ran with Johnson for many years, said, "Some of the things Robert did with the guitar affected the way everybody played. He'd have that boogie beat strumming on the bass strings while he played, and nobody was doing that."

Musical Example 9: Johnny Shines's "Ramblin'"

Shines came closer to Johnson than any of the postwar Chicago artists, and he cut for Joe Brown of JOB Records. "Ramblin'," a version of Johnson's "Walking Blues," although an extraordinary Delta blues performance, was not successful. One could argue that Shines was unsuccessful because he was recording for Joe Brown, but something more than JOB's erratic distribution was the reason, because the year previously JOB had had a big record with Floyd Jones, whose "Dark Road" was an echo of the other Johnson, Tommy, and was a big seller in 1951.

Musical Example 10: Floyd Jones, "Dark Road"

What was happening was the rise of the harmonica-led groups. Little Walter was becoming more popular than his leader Muddy Waters, and the harmonica was becoming the most popular blues instrument. The seeds of this had been sown back in the early 1940s, when Big Joe Williams recorded "Break 'Em on Down" in 1941 with Sonny Boy Williamson accompanying on harp.

Musical Example 11: Big Joe Williams, "Break 'Em On Down"

John Lee "Sonny Boy" Williamson from Jackson, Tennessee, was the other great influence on the sound of the Chicago blues. He had been recording since 1937 and since the success of his first record, "Good Morning School Girl," was always very popular. At the same time that Muddy dug deep into his Delta roots for "I Can't Be Satisfied," Sonny Boy had a hit with "Better Cut That Out."

Musical Example 12: Sonny Boy Williamson, "Better Cut That Out"

All the new young harmonica players in Chicago were copying Sonny Boy, and Little Walter was no exception. Walter probably was only in the city a couple of years before Sonny Boy was murdered in 1948, but Walter learned quickly and added so much more to the harmonica sound and extended the role of the harmonica in Chicago blues. And after Little Walter cut "Juke" with Muddy's band, the Delta slide guitar was just going to be an adjunct to the driving harmonica-led blues groups.

Musical Example 13: Little Walter, "Juke"

After the deserved success of this 1952 recording, Little Walter left Muddy to form his own band and in fact took over the role of Chicago's blues king from Muddy for the next few years, with hit after hit from 1952 to 1954. But if we are looking for any Delta blues influence in Walter's records of the time, we'd probably find that Little Walter had more in common with Charlie Parker than Charley Patton! And it was only the two newcomers to Chicago, Howlin' Wolf and Elmore James, who could hold their own with their particular brand of Delta blues. Elmore's influence again was Robert Johnson, and he made a couple of hit versions of "Dust My Broom" (after Johnson), but Robert Lockwood was denied any kind of success with his version of Johnson's "Sweet Home Chicago." Somehow Lockwood missed the boat again. In 1955 he recorded "Aw Aw Baby."

Musical Example 14: Robert Lockwood Jr., "Aw Aw Baby"

The last great successful Chicago bluesman was Jimmy Reed, again from the heart of the Mississippi Delta, but if there was any Delta influence in his music, it was not obvious. Reed's trademarks were the whining vocal and piercing harp, and probably the only concession to the Delta was the rolling boogie bass of Eddie Taylor.

His partner Taylor never forsook his Delta roots and on record was often paying homage to his background. From one session in 1956 there were lyrics from Patton, "heart like piece of railroad steel," and the year before there were themes from Mississippi too. In 1956 again he recorded "Ride 'Em On Down," the old Robert Petway song itself derived from an earlier hit by Mississippian Bukka White.

Musical Example 15: Eddie Taylor, "Ride 'Em On Down"

By now the Delta influences were dying out. The real successes were Little Walter and Jimmy Reed, but the Delta had done its bit: it had sparked off this amazing period of creativity from the late 1940s through the early 1950s and had pointed the Chicago blues in a whole new direction. But once again the audience was changing. Those migrants who moved to Chicago in the 1940s were confirmed city dwellers by the late 1950s and 1960s and had undergone great social and environmental changes. The Delta no longer held the kind of sway that it had. But Mississippi was not losing its grip on the Chicago blues; there was a new generation of young Mississippi artists who would develop a new city style on Chicago's West Side. Among these were Magic Sam and Otis Rush, and while ostensibly owing little to the Delta apart from the anguished vocals, one could imagine there was a lot more of Mississippi and the Delta and Patton's influence in the songs even though they sounded so very different and so very modern. Otis Rush especially had all the qualities to forge a new style of blues; was he going to be the Patton or Robert Johnson of the 1950s?

Musical Example 16: Otis Rush, "Groaning the Blues"

Otis Rush brings us to the end of my old-fashioned survey of the early postwar Chicago blues, which will be brought up to date when Jim O'Neal discusses later developments in Chicago.

Discography

1. Robert Lockwood, "Little Boy Blue" (Bluebird B8820); *Mississippi Blues Vol 4: Delta Blues Goin' North 1935–1935*, Document DOCD 5682
2. Roosevelt Sykes, "Sunny Road" (RCA Vic 20–1906); *Roosevelt Sykes Vol 8 1945–1947*, Document BDCD 6048
3. Muddy Waters, "Gypsy Woman" (Aristocrat 1302); *The Complete Aristocrat & Chess Singles 1947–1962*, Acrobat ACQCD 7072; *Rollin' Stone: The Golden Anniversary Collection*, MCA/Chess 088 112 301
4. Muddy Waters, "I Be's Troubled" (LC AAFS 18); *The Complete Plantation Recordings*, MCA CD 9344
5. Muddy Waters, "I Can't Be Satisfied" (Aristocrat 1305); *His Best 1947–1955*, Chess MCD09370/ MCA 1125472; *The Complete Aristocrat & Chess Singles 1947–1962*, Acrobat ACQCD 7072
6. Robert Nighthawk, "Annie Lee Blues" (Aristocrat 2301); *Prowling With the Nighthawk (1937–1952)*, Document DOCD 32-20-06
7. Baby Face Leroy, "Rollin' and Tumblin' Pt 1" (Parkway 501); *The Blues World of Little Walter*, Delmark DD 648
8. Muddy Waters, "Louisiana Blues" (Chess 1441); *His Best*, Chess MCD09370/ MCA 1125472; *The Complete Aristocrat & Chess Singles 1947–1962*, Acrobat ACQCD 7072
9. Johnny Shines, "Ramblin'" (JOB 116); *Evening Shuffle: The Complete JOB Recordings 1952–53*, Westside WESM 635
10. Floyd Jones, "Dark Road" (JOB 1001); *The Chronological Floyd Jones 1948–1953*, Classics 5130
11. Big Joe Williams, "Break 'Em On Down" (Bluebird B8969); *Big Joe Willlums Vol 1 1935–1941*, Document BDCD6003
12. Sonny Boy Williamson, "Better Cut That Out" (RCA Vic 20–3218); *Sonny Boy Williamson Vol 5 1945–1947*, Document DOCD 5059
13. Little Walter, "Juke" (Checker 758); *Chess 50th Anniversary Collection: His Best*, Chess CHD 9384
14. Robert Lockwood Jr., "Aw Aw Baby" (JOB 1107); Sunnyland Slim & Friends, *"Sunnyland Special": The Cobra & JOB Recordings 1949–56*, Westside WESA 910
15. Eddie Taylor, "Ride 'Em On Down" (VJ 185); *Bad Boy*, Charly CD BM35
16. Otis Rush, "Groaning the Blues" (Cobra 5010); *Good 'Uns: The Classic Cobra Recordings 1956–1958*, Westside WESA 858; *The Essential Otis Rush: The Classic Cobra Recordings 1956–1958*, True North TND 224

Memories of Chester "Howlin' Wolf" Burnett and Willie Johnson

—Dick Shurman

Part 1: Memories of Howlin' Wolf

It would be easy to draw a detailed historical and musical link between Charley Patton and one of his musical protégés, Chester Burnett, the Howlin' Wolf. Of course, Wolf was a product of the Mississippi Delta blues tradition, with personal contact with Patton and a strong Tommy Johnson influence. Wolf recorded Patton's "Pony Blues" as "Saddle My Pony,"[1] and later did a classic version of "Spoonful"[2] more related through vocal style than lyrics.[3] Other Wolf songs, including "Smoke Stack Lightning"[4] and "Down in the Bottom,"[5] contain Patton rhythms and lyrics. It's easy to hear Patton's growl in Wolf's vocals, and some of Patton's clowning obviously left a strong impression on young Chester. But rather than giving a dry analysis of an exciting blues artist, I prefer to take this occasion to celebrate and remember Howlin' Wolf as first and foremost a unique personality and an individual.

To me, one of the basic themes in the blues is the triumph of the individual over often oppressive and adverse conditions. Blues is a music whose power comes from self-expression. Even if the performer is interpreting another composer's song, the feeling must be there for the performance to be convincing. The great blues artists, especially those from the deprived background of the Delta, received little or no formal music instruction, so while their styles were built to some extent on external influences, they were also very personal and idiosyncratic. Often sheer force of personality was the greatest asset a person like Wolf or the young Muddy Waters could summon to rise above a life of sharecropping and poverty.

In Wolf's case, he was a particularly unforgettable individual. Johnny Shines told Peter Guralnick, "I first saw Wolf, I was afraid of Wolf. Just like you would be of some kind of beast or something . . . at that time Wolf had the most beautiful skin anybody ever seen in your life, look like you can just

Chester "Howlin' Wolf" Burnett, late sixties. (Photographs by Georges Adins. Collection of Robert Sacré)

blow on it and it'd riffle . . . well, it wasn't his size. I mean, what he was doing, the way he was doing, I mean the sound that he was giving off."[6] Sam Phillips's description of Wolf to Guralnick is just as striking: "Ah, Chester—the vitality of that man was something else. Just to see that man in the studio—God, what I would give to see him as he was in my studio, to see the fervor in his face, to hear the pure instinctive quality of that man's voice."[7] And Phillips, who considered Wolf to be the most powerful and distinctive artist he ever recorded (which included the likes of Elvis Presley, Jerry Lee Lewis, B.B. King, and too many other outstanding blues artists to list here), told Robert Palmer, "When I heard Howlin' Wolf, I said 'this is it for me. This is where the soul of man never dies' . . . I tell you, the greatest show you could see to this day would be Chester Burnett doing one of those sessions in my studio."[8] Wolf's life and music are well documented,[9] although I wish the owners of the Chess masters would do a second volume and complete the digital release of that catalog. What I want to cover is his personality, as I recall it through some treasured experiences with Wolf fifteen years ago.

As I was growing up in Seattle, Washington, two thousand miles from Chicago, in the mid-1960s, my first exposure to Wolf came through records. His fierce and totally unique sound came through to me especially strongly on the Memphis and early Chicago recordings then available on the Chess *Moanin' in the Moonlight*[10] and *More Real Folk Blues*[11] albums, and on the Memphis album then issued on Crown, Kent, and United,[12] which has since been released in the UK by Ace with much better sound and extra tracks.[13] Wolf's music and band radiated an unforgettable atmosphere, with Wolf's vocals and harmonica matched in impact by Willie Johnson's ferocious guitar, piano, and rudimentary pounding rhythms. The sound was urgent, immediate, incredibly ambient, and compelling.

When I moved to Chicago in 1968, I heard many stories about Wolf, including his physical brutality and his alleged hostility toward whites. I was awed and slow to approach him, but finally, after I started booking blues shows at the University of Chicago, I gave him a call. (He and Muddy Waters remained listed in the Chicago phone book under their real names as long as they were residents.) He was very friendly and invited me over for dinner, then drove me to his job.

Seeing Wolf at home that winter of 1969 was quite a shock to my preconceptions. He lived in a neat, well-kept South Side bungalow at 829 E. 88th Street, with his Pontiac station wagon parked in front. The living room trappings included plastic covering over the white fabric upholstery and a picture on the wall with lights that lit up. He had to listen to blues records in his basement; his wife and stepdaughters banned them from upstairs in favor of more contemporary music like the Jackson Five. His wife Lillie was a head secretary at a large office. His college-age (two days older than me) stepdaughter Barbra was taking time off from school to "find herself" and working at a financial/real estate firm in the Loop. By then Wolf had been noticeably slowed by physical problems; he needed help getting his sweater on, and his personality was undoubtedly toned down, too.

When we got to the club, the Key Largo at 1959 West Roosevelt Road, it too was far more sedate than Wolf's legend. The music was in the back room, where white tablecloths adorned all the tables. Wolf had a liquor interest in the club, as he did at Sylvio's. He owned a small p.a. system for his vocals and harp, which any self-respecting white teenage band would have laughed at, but it was a rare luxury in a blues world where artists like Otis Rush or Magic Sam were singing through their small guitar amplifiers, which too often didn't even belong to them.

Despite what I'd heard, Wolf was more than just polite or courteous to me early in our acquaintance. He seemed to think that I was a young man who could benefit from fatherly advice, which he was quick to volunteer. I'd take a cab to the Burnett home. Sometimes Lillie would cook up a gourmet meal, then Wolf would drive me to and from the club where I'd make a tape. On the way, he loved to give me morality lectures on how to live right, and how other people were living wrong. (I later came to understand retrospectively that telling people how to live was near the top of his favorite pastimes.) Some of his malapropisms were amusing, to say the least. In the middle of a lecture about safe driving, a motorist cut into our lane abruptly. Wolf said "See that guy there? He nearly made me have an occlusion!" I ended up taping three full evenings of the band in 1969 and 1970. I'm still gratefully amazed at the trust and generosity that allowed those tapings. At the same time he was telling interviewers about how all the young white blues bands and record companies everywhere were cheating him, he responded to a reassurance from me that I was just making my tapes because I had all of his records and still couldn't get enough of his music by telling me "That's too bad. I was hoping you'd sell 'em and make yourself some money!" I never have, although a breach of trust resulted in some appearing on Wolfgang's Vault.

Peter Guralnick had done a lengthy review in *Crawdaddy* of Buddy Guy's first Vanguard album[14] and lamented in passing about how commercial considerations stopped projects like Chess recording Wolf's Patton repertoire. I'm not sure how much of it there still was, but Wolf gladly agreed to the idea of doing it for me in his basement. Unfortunately, I left Chicago temporarily, and it just never happened.

Wolf was seemingly a very basic and elemental person and musician, but he was full of contradictions and complexities. Just when an observer would be sure he was in the grips of auto-hypnosis and totally inside the song he was doing, he would leer in a way that introduced a layer of detachment impossible to overlook. Possessor of a name that suggested an untamed menace, Wolf spent his last years living in one of the most middle-class settings of any blues artist I knew. When he saw an acquaintance, sometimes he would be warm and friendly; the next time he might look right through the same person. The phrase "brooding majesty" applied strongly.

Wolf was also very authoritarian. He once told me, "My daddy was a plantation foreman, and he raised me right." Some of the band members he physically, mentally, and financially abused might not agree about the rightness, but he ran the group and bandstand with an iron hand.

Pride was another essential element in Wolf's character. He savored his accomplishments and his place in the blues community, for which he worked so hard and gave so much. I remember him during a 1970 performance of "The Hucklebuck," giving a little sermon about "I am the man of the day" and how he'd triumphed over all the obstacles in his path. Along with the pride went determination. There is no better testimonial to its strength than the way he lived his final decade, literally performing until he couldn't perform any longer. Wolf came as close to dying on the bandstand as he could, making his music his way.

Finally, despite the bizarre and vulgar showmanship that ranged from clowning with the microphone to crawling around the floor using his handkerchief as a tail or climbing the curtains, there was a dignity that could not be missed. When Chester Burnett took the name of Howlin' Wolf, he took a persona and an image and spent his life living up to them.

Wolf performed many songs, doing long and very spontaneous versions so that he could work in his raps and routines. He told me that he made the band learn two new songs every week, so that no imitators could keep pace. "Big House" and "Highway 49" were staples, along with many of his popular recordings. If he was in the mood, he'd play the same song every set or even more often. Though he couldn't be an acrobat any longer, he'd tip way forward in his chair, stare, glare, stab his finger toward the sky in a gesture picked up by Yardbirds singer Keith Relf, and do all sorts of nasty things with the microphone. He saved his real showmanship for special occasions like the 1969 Ann Arbor Blues Festival, when he came out on stage on a motorbike with a baseball cap on sideways and made motor noises. His first words to the crowd were "You like it? Get one too!"

Wolf usually alternated sets on harp and guitar, when he played guitar at all. The harp was much more satisfying. He still blew fiercely, and often used up a harp in one night. After a heart attack, doctors had told him to stop the harp playing, but he wouldn't or couldn't. The guitar work I witnessed (never including any Delta slide) was cumbersome, though he went to music school and had instructors like Reggie Boyd. He was clumsy, his big fingers got in the way, and he didn't know or care much about the fine points of music theory. He supposedly once waved a thousand-dollar bill at Reggie Boyd and said angrily, "I can't make this kind of money playing that progressive shit!" One night in 1969, I saw him plod proudly through a minor scale with band accompaniment. Later in the night he said, "We have a special request to do that one again!" and repeated the scale. He was insecure and jealous of other guitarists like Hubert Sumlin, whom he'd lecture on the bandstand about his playing: "You're tryin' to play lead and chords at the same time!" Once I heard him tell an audience, "These boys think they know music, but they don't know life!"

By the time I started seeing him, due to the demands of his performances, some of his most entertaining moments weren't the songs themselves. They were his little gimmicks. He'd imitate a telephone, philosophize, or brag: "I am the king of all snakes, and if I happen to bite you, you ain't never gonna get well no more."

Wolf's sickness resulted in both heroism and sadness. He had at least one heart attack, a bad auto wreck, and needed kidney dialysis. But nothing could stop him from playing until two months before the end. Off the bandstand, Wolf was just an uneducated and defensive man trying to make his way in a threatening and confusing world that he could best meet and master through sheer force, cunning, or avoidance if possible. When he sang and played the blues, he was The Mighty Wolf. Long after Muddy Waters stopped playing ghetto clubs, Wolf was a fixture who could be heard almost every weekend when he was in town on the West Side, and sometimes in between at places like Pepper's. Despite occasional North Side jobs at places like Alice's Revisited where he recorded his live album,[15] his club work the last few years was mostly in joints on West Roosevelt Road or West Madison Street, like Key Largo, Big Duke's, Big Duke's Flamingo, and finally his own 1815 Club later run by bandleader Eddie Shaw.

Like most artists and cultural spokesmen, Wolf spoke most loudly to his peers. His crowd was mostly older, middle-class blacks dotted with whites making the pilgrimage to see a living legend. I used to be struck by the sight of the older people with their heads down, actually sleeping through a late or weak set by a man who, in his prime, may have been the most powerful blues artist. But just as often, the electricity would return, the eyes would flash, and that iron will would drive the band to play as a unit tailored to the sound of its undisputed leader.

Jim O'Neal and I were lucky enough to catch Wolf's last two nights of performance, as far as I know. In November 1975, disc jockey and promoter Pervis Spann put Wolf on a big package show at Chicago's International Amphitheater. He gave a truly inspired show, summoning all of his power, stalking around, and rocking the house with dynamic guitar by Hubert Sumlin and then staying to hear his old friend B.B. King close the evening. The next night the show went to Memphis, but Wolf stayed in town and played his regular gig at the 1815 Club. It was the birthday of Steve Tomashefsky of Delmark Records, so we all went over to hear Wolf and party. Wolf was obviously drained from the previous night, but amid the festive occasion, none of us thought it would be our last encounter. Soon afterward, Wolf checked into the Veterans Hospital. After some ups and downs, his condition weakened considerably, and as 1976 arrived, everyone knew he was dying. On a cold winter Sunday, I was running some errands and stopped by Johnny Littlejohn's garage near Big Duke's on Madison, and got the bad news from Johnny. On January 10, 1976, Wolf died, at the age of 65. He had a big funeral with distinguished pallbearers. True to his many contradictions, the crowd was a curious mix of blues people and associates from the American Legion, a relic of Wolf's World War II military service.

There are still many Wolf imitators in Chicago. Highway Man (William Holland), Tail Dragger (James Yancey Jones), Little Wolf (J.J. Sanders), and another Little Wolf (Lee Solomon) lead the parade. Drummer Willie Williams tries to assume Wolf's personality, with laughable results. There's even a white sax player on the streets who calls himself "Little Howlin' Wolf." But the act of taking Wolf's name and mannerisms so totally eliminates these people as worthy successors. As Johnny Littlejohn told me, Wolf had said upon being introduced to one of his would-be clones, "Hell, he ain't no Wolf; he ain't even a little cub!" Chester Burnett didn't choose to live as Little Charley Patton. He was his own man all the way, Texan J.T. Smith (who also appropriated the same nickname prior to Chester) notwithstanding. And while he was a great individual and a great blues man, he was more than a man—he was The Wolf.

Part 2: Willie Johnson

Willie Johnson was one of Howlin' Wolf's best-known associates in the South and Chicago, and one of the most electrifying and exciting guitarists of the 1950s. Blasting out a flashy, distorted mix of swing chords, fluid bop solos, and Delta blues patterns, Willie made Wolf's early recordings doubly amazing. He can also be heard on many other recordings by the likes of Willie Nix,[16] Sammy Lewis,[17] and Tot Randolph.[18] One of the most remarkable Willie–Wolf collaborations is Wolf's "House Rockin' Boogie,"[19] where Wolf exhorts him to "Play that guitar, Willie Johnson, till it smokes!" The way Willie played, the whole studio must have melted.

Willie followed Wolf to Chicago after Wolf's winter 1954 relocation there, but eventually went his own way. Wolf told me once that they were always fighting and "I didn't mind the fighting, but he wouldn't let me get no rest!" Willie made a few recordings as a sideman in Chicago during the 1950s and 1960s with people like Wolf, Bobo Jenkins,[20] and Harmonica George,[21] and was on some other Atomic H sessions.[22] But he was far from the limelight that reflected upon him when he was at Wolf's side, and was generally considered too unreliable, elusive or quarrelsome. Billy Boy Arnold remembered his shock when Willie actually showed up to go with him on a southern tour, where both recalled gleefully in 1970 how Willie had outplayed Johnny "Guitar" Watson. While Hubert Sumlin developed a very personal style that became a trademark on Wolf's records just as Willie's had once been, Willie mostly worked small clubs in obscurity. As alcohol and neglect eroded his skills, those jobs, too, faded through the 1970s. Today Willie still talks about playing again and making a trip to Europe, but while such a tour would show dimensions such as his singing and slide playing that aren't readily apparent from his recordings, he's just in no shape musically to do justice to his legacy.

Willie was one of my first real blues heroes. I must not be alone, because Robert Palmer makes a somewhat tenuous case in his book *Deep Blues*[23] for Willie as the father of most of the rockabilly and British blues-rock guitar styles. When I was hanging around Wolf in Chicago beginning in 1969, I never encountered Willie. But in early 1970 *Blues Unlimited* mentioned that he was making a comeback in Chicago at the Upstairs Lounge. (As it turned out, he'd never stopped playing.) So as soon as school was over that June, I got a ride from Seattle, where I lived, to Chicago and traveled two thousand miles in the back seat of a small car with a fifty-pound tape recorder on my lap. When I went by the Flamingo to hear and tape Wolf, bassist Calvin Jones told me where Willie was playing, at the Washburne Lounge (a.k.a. the Upstairs Lounge) at Washburne and Hoyne on the West Side. Jones had a dubious opinion of Willie's band ("When I heard 'em, they weren't ready"), but the next night I drove over with Billy Boy and Louis Myers. We got there during intermission on a hot June night, and everyone was on the street. Billy Boy yelled "Willie Johnson!" and a somewhat grizzled, wild-eyed man who looked to be in his fifties jerked around defensively. He recognized Billy Boy with relief, and we went inside.

That club was a definitive blues experience. It was tiny and it was in an awful neighborhood, even for a blues club. Dirt-colored alley cats ran under the tables and out the door too quickly to touch. The bandstand was so small that the drum kit was on a platform overhead, about eight feet off the ground. The guitar amplifier was atop a phone booth next to the platform. The ladies' washroom was right behind where Willie stood, next to the phone booth. The washroom was so small that the oink was on the outside, on the wall between Willie and the bassist's amplifier. Women who needed to use the washroom were definitely on public display! Beyond the bass amp, there was just enough room for the bassist to stand in front of the door to the alley. It was definitely a blues club and crowd. The few people indoors and on the sidewalks included musicians, prostitutes, and pimps, and all had pistols.

The next week Johnny Littlejohn drove across town to take me back to the club for an evening of taping, and sat in on drums to try to help the music. I taped two nights of Willie in June and July, and Willie and bassist-vocalist Roosevelt Broomfield (Magic Sam's brother-in-law) stopped by the 1815 Club and sat in while I was taping Mighty Joe Young. Most of the music at the Washburne Lounge was flashy and sloppy jazz-tinged instrumentals, with occasional vocals by Broomfield, club owner Roosevelt Jones, or guests. But Willie showed he could sing, too, ranging from his Sun recordings to Charles Brown stylings. He also responded to a set by Elmore James clone Joe Carter by playing some wild slide. Though he was sloppy, the sound was still there, and he was a very impressive gutbucket guitarist. I finally coaxed him into an interview at his apartment and sent it to *Blues Unlimited*.[24] However, Willie didn't do much for his credibility when shortly after the interview, he told me he was also known as "Little Willie Kedzie" [pronounced like "cat's-eye"]. "Kedzie" was actually Willie Kizart, a totally different man who played with Ike Turner on "Rocket 88"[25] and is now in St. Louis. Like Wolf, however, Willie contradicted his image by being generous and trusting to me, allowing me to tape him, inviting me into his home when he had a reputation for being very evasive at all times, and even going by the 1815 for me.

I didn't see Willie again for a few years. He continued to play small clubs on and off, and also worked occasionally with Sunnyland Slim in the early 1970s. I know of at least a couple tapes of that band, also including Broomfield, at Alice's. Willie also went by the 1815 Club in 1975 and sat in with Wolf for the last time. In 1978 Cilla Huggins, then of *Blues Unlimited*, fulfilled a dream and came to Chicago to meet Willie and do the definitive interview, to be published in *Blues Unlimited*.[26] We had an evening none of us will forget. There are just too many stories to tell here, but Cilla and her husband seemed as stunned by Willie and his wife's drunken antics as Willie must have been when his Friday afternoon party with the upstairs neighbors was interrupted by two foreigners who presented him with so many recordings and names from another generation. Unfortunately, it was obvious that drinking and lack of application had robbed him of much of his guitar ability, and he was no longer an active musician. He did sit in with Kansas City Red, but the results were chaotic at best. He did more work with Red around that time, and also sat in at John Brim's Broadway Nite Club and at B.L.U.E.S. During most of this time, he worked days in the near western Chicago suburb of Maywood, making mag wheels for automobiles. The last time we saw each other, at B.L.U.E.S. in 1982, he looked sharp in a suit and his hair was white. He sat in for a slide guitar duel with Big Smokey Smothers, but again, the result was mostly nostalgia for his past prowess.

In 1984 Willie was still living on Chicago's South Side, after spending many years on the West Side.[27] I want to salute a nice guy, and a terrific musician who made a major contribution to Howlin' Wolf's career. Willie also made a lasting contribution to the recorded history of electric blues, and the way he played the blues made the music especially accessible to young whites who tuned in to his high-volume, high-energy attack. He was truly what he told us his nickname used to be in his younger days: "The Monster of the Guitar."

Notes

1. Chess 1515.

2. Chess 1762 and subsequent reissues.

3. Otis Rush told Jim O'Neal that composer Willie Dixon offered him the song before Wolf recorded it.

4. Chess 1618 and subsequent releases, also recorded earlier as "Crying at Daybreak," RPM 340 and subsequent releases.

5. Chess 1793 and subsequent reissues.

6. Peter Guralnick, *Feel Like Going Home*, New York, Outerbridge & Dienstfrey, 1971, 77.

7. Guralnick, *Lost Highway*, Boston, Godine, 1979, 331.

8. Robert Palmer, *Deep Blues*, New York, Viking, 1981.

9. The vast preponderance of his studio catalog is available through reissues on Ace, Bear Family, P-Vine, and Universal Music Group. His biography by James Segrest and Mark Hoffman, *Moanin' at Midnight: The Life and Times of Howlin' Wolf*, New York, Da Capo, 2005, and the 2003 video documentary *The Howlin' Wolf Story: The Secret History of Rock & Roll* (Bluebird) are good supplements.

10. Chess LP 1434.

11. Chess LP 1512.

12. Crown LP 5240 and subsequent reissues.

13. *Howling Wolf Sings the Blues*, Ace CDCHD 1013.

14. Guralnick, "Buddy Guy," *Crawdaddy* 16 (June 1968): 41–45.

15. *Live and Cooking at Alice's Revisited*, Chess LP 50015.

16. RPM 327, Checker 756 and subsequent reissues.

17. Sun 218 and subsequent reissues.

18. *Blues Train*, Bear Family (G) BCD17310, *The Sun Blues Box*.

19. Crown LP 5240 and subsequent reissues.

20. Boxer 202/Duchess 101.

21. Delmark DE- 624, *Chicago Ain't Nothin' But a Blues Band*.

22. He is reputedly on at least one session by Little Mac Simmons.

23. Palmer, 235–36.

24. *Blues Unlimited* 93 (July 1972): 4, 5, 7.

25. Chess 1458 and subsequent reissues.

26. It remains unpublished.

27. Willie died in Chicago on February 26, 1995.

"I Was Born in Arkansas and Raised Up in Chicago"

—Luther Allison

Arkansas

First of all, I would like to say "thank you all for letting me be here." [1] I'll tell you who my influences were. My basis was Otis Rush, but Willie Johnson, he told me I would be somebody someday. He said, "you'll get a chance, but you'll get to fight!" An' you know, today, I heard a lot of information about the beautiful people you mentioned, like Howlin' Wolf, Muddy Waters, Jimmy Reed, Little Walter . . . I worked with these people! I spent a lot of hours, a lot of time at Muddy's home; Calvin Jones—Muddy's bassist—is the main reason why I'm on stage today. Calvin said, "you won't chase women, you won't drink, you won't do a damn thing, so you should play music . . ." So I play music, this is what I had to do! But you want to know how I started . . . I'll tell you. Now look, they tell me, I celebrate two birthdays, and my birth certificate says August 17th, 1939, but my sister and my mother say August 18th, so I am caught in between, but I do know I was born around midnight. My real name is Luther Sylvester Allison, and I was born in Mayflower, Arkansas, and my father and mother were farmers. They was the greatest ballad singers you wanted to hear, gospel field; my father passed away in 1960, I think it was. He wasn't much of a church person; my mother was more of a church person than my daddy was, you know. They raised eleven boys on a farm. I have ten brothers, one whole sister, and two half-sisters. It's not easy to say "I'm Mr. True Blue," you know; you gotta hustle, but good, good father. I didn't see a lot of father the way, you know, a youngster would have to deal with his dad, but as a family, we were very close and we are still very close.

Well, my first musical inspiration was back when I was about five to ten years old down there in Arkansas. I remember the Grand Ole Opry, I remember the King Biscuit Boys, WDIA radio, Joe Hill Louis the one-man band, I can remember this even at the age of five and six years old. Then I don't even know where I got the idea of taking a broom wire and a brick and a bottle. It weren't showed to me, it was just something that say, well, I gotta come up with this sound. I'm hearing these guitars, and then drums and stuff, you know. Say "How do I do this?" I tried tin cans, you know; I'd tie a bunch of cans together and take a stick and just rattle them around—Pet Milk cans— that's what they fed the babies on down there—the mothers had to be in the fields, right? There's gotta be a way, so I was doing something, trying to make a cart with Pet Milk cans for wheels, and one of the wires got caught on something and made a sound like a bass sound, you know. I said, "Hey yeah, this sounds good," but the wire was thick like hay baling wire. Say, "Now this is too heavy for me—The higher you twisted the, uh, more tension . . . the higher you're supposed to get it, but that hay baling wire wouldn't go high. So I said, "I'm gonna tear up this broom, I'm gonna tear it," and my old man come home and found that broom all tore up, and get that wire off and tacked up against the wall, with a brick to tighten up each end. So I tried it just once more . . . OK, Robert Nighthawk, you know, the slide, something that gives these pitches. Go in the house and get a glass, take it up and the higher it goes, just another pitch. Yes, I heard Robert Nighthawk over the radio, you know, and the Grand Ole Opry with all of the banjo and all that stuff. You're not conscious of it, but you like what you hear—it's music, and living in the country, you hear the crickets at night and the mosquitoes singing, and my dad and my mother would come home and sit out till dark just singing hymns, you know. I'm way down there, I'm next to the baby, right, and my brothers would sing and they'd be practicing the gospel, the church thing, you know, like they have in church box suppers, where the girls would bring the dinners and the guys would draw names. So I always wanted to follow them, 'cause it looked like they was just having so much fun. Their group was called the Southern Travelers. They were pretty popular, and they had two other members that weren't with the family. There was six or seven of them, but I remember that well. They had a good group, and as a matter of fact I talked to the Mighty Clouds of Joy in Europe, and they remembered them. I did three or four gigs with the Mighty Clouds of Joy over here, and it was fantastic singing that gospel with Marie Knight, right, who I've heard since I was this tall; and like I said, I came through the gospel field and I was taught that respect, to the gospel. That's why I can't really understand why I'm in blues today, except the fact I know blues now and gospel and jazz is from the same family.

The only people I saw was in church, that was the local gospel groups. Like B.B. King, my seventh brother Ollie—he died in 1977—they used to run together before B.B. went in service, and B.B. asked Ollie to join him after he came out of the service, and my brother said, "Hey, look, you gotta do your thing, I gotta do my thing," 'cause Ollie, he was just one of those kind of guys who would go into anything, you know; he would carry electrician, barber, and he didn't know what he wanted to do until he got to Chicago. Even down there, my dad bought him his first guitar, down South. He could play the darn thing, but it wasn't nothing that really interested him until the early '50s, and then I think that's when he got his band together called the Rolling Stones, and they used to call him Little Muddy, Little Muddy Waters, you know. So he preferred "the Rolling Stones." That name? Just came, you know, I guess. It has a lot to do with the South, the Rolling Stones were down south, you know, stones, and sticks and stones, break my bones. That's a gospel movement, and Ollie had to come up with it.

Down south, in school you only go up to about seventh grade in grammar school, and I was in Madison, Arkansas. I went to grammar school, that was just one of the schools I went to, and then the high school took you from the eighth or ninth grade right on through. So I had to change and go to high school, which is in Forrest City. And my brother was with me as well. Grant, you know, came on into the high school, now from there, go to Chicago.

Chicago Here I Come

My oldest brother went to Detroit after the Marines; working for Ford, and everybody else kind of moved, uh, to Chicago, except, you know, I'm speaking in terms of not Ollie, but M.C., he was the first one went in the service behind my oldest brother. And as a matter of fact, they was the only two went in the service out of eleven boys. It was only two brothers moved to Chicago and my half-sister. We lived in an apartment, my baby brother, my mother, my father, and Ollie—his family lived in the back.

When I got to Chicago, I was afraid, excited but afraid. Chicago was a whole 'nother scene, and I couldn't relate to the kids that was on the outside. What would happen, I fell into a thing, it's called a hotel where you have to stay for a year or so, but I became 14, 15 years old. And in the hotel there was a shoe repair shop, and there was a preacher, and he gave me a job, teach me how to repair shoes and how to shine shoes and all that. That's the South Side, 29th and Vernon, and that kept me out of that growing-up street movement until I moved to the West Side.

But Ollie's group, the Rolling Stones, they were practicing. Every day I come out of school they'd be practicing—I wasn't even aware of it. I'll only just be outside riding a bike, but my nephew left his guitar there on the bed, and I mean I would just kinda hit it and kept going. But I was on my way to school that morning, and the sound kept ringing in my ear, man—I came back and they was practicing. Say, when they got through practicing, "Would you show me something on what you're doing?" As a matter of fact, I even called what I want to do, boogie woogie things. He said "Sure, I'll show it to you."

When I got to the high school, Muddy Waters's son was going to the same high school, which was Hyde Park High School, and we got to know each other some kind of way—in gym or something. And I found out that Muddy Waters was living only about seven or eight blocks from where I was, and I would stop at his house and he'd be doing the same trip as my brother was doing, the rehearsal thing, which I got interested in then. Then I had to drop out of school during my senior year to get a job and support, because my baby brother was only like 6 or 7 years old and my parents were old. I wasn't learning anything after I got that far 'cause I got interested in music. I worked in car washes, factories. Car washes was like 75 cents—50 to 75 cents an hour, and washing dishes the same. And most of the time just dealing with myself, out there, went up and down the streets trying to just play the guitar after all of this. If I didn't go to school, be staying at my brother here, or staying at my friend's there. Then I'd go back, you know, so it got to the point where I was learning more on the streets than I were in school, 'cause I lived in the streets, I knew everybody out there. . . .

But when I moved to the West Side, when I had to deal with—I'm 16 or 17 years old now I got to deal with gangs and . . . 'cause I'm big, you know. Every gang wants me, and I've been taught not to be in that trouble thing, and I could see it myself as trouble. So what I did, I saw a guitar in a pawn shop, a little before I move from the South Side to the West Side. Was on the West Side for about six-eight months before I was able to pay that twenty dollars and get that guitar out of the pawn shop . . . and then, plus another twenty bucks to get an electric pickup to put on, and then, of course, another twenty bucks to put the little old raggedy amplifier, about a foot wide either way. I was too young to be getting into the clubs. I was only 17, and then Ray Charles came out with "What'd I Say." That was the first in public I recall, and "Sweet Sixteen" by B.B. King was the second as far as the public was concerned. On a higher scale, of course, Jimmy Reed was also there after I moved to the West Side, and then I could see Magic Sam, who was two years older than me, and Freddie King was about two or three years older than me, so I got interested, very interested. After, I met Jimmy Dawkins. See, Jimmy Dawkins came on the South Side, who was living in the West Side, but I was living like, what, six blocks from where he played, and he liked what I was doing. And I cared, I didn't drink, I didn't smoke, I don't care nothing about girls, I'm just totally into blues, into the musical thing, and that's all you could hear at the time except for groups like the Cadillacs or the Platters, and that was too much like gospel, you know, the harmony!

B.B. King, Jimmy Reed, Muddy Waters, Little Walter, Jimmy Rogers, everybody had records out in those days. On the radio, that's where you heard it. And that's what really killed me in the last part of me deciding what I wanted to make this a profession now. . . . I stuck with it, it kept me out of the gang scene, see what I mean? So I just walked the streets and played guitar, and I would create my own tune, you know.

The first club I played in, think it's called the Democrat Club, and I was with Ollie. That's on 47th street, near the 708 Club in Chicago. And then I was playing guitar, bass guitar, right. And the second club I picked was on 43rd Street, and the third was called the Sundown Lounge. That's when I got with Jimmy Dawkins. That was on 39th Street, on the South Side, and then we moved to the West Side. In Ollie's group I can only remember three of the names, that was Ollie, harmonica player was James, and the bass guitar player was George Conner, and the drummer was named Oliver something; he was really good. But hey, where do you go from there? You know, all of them had families and stuff, and you couldn't sit down and say, "I'll write this and I'll do that," because writing just came in recently for us. We just got in and everybody else's material, just like everybody's doing everybody's material now, just the way it was then, you know. Yeah, like Muddy Waters was, like B.B. King, in those days all the same. The Rolling Stones were in those days, where they played the major clubs, the big clubs where everybody's in there. There's Muddy Waters, Little Walter, Howlin' Wolf, B.B. King, of course, just gonna be at these places sooner or later, you know. . . . Elmore James, oh, I worked right on the stage with Elmore. He the one that told me, said like, "you got something and I'm not telling you what to do, but if I were you I would continue." I was playing lead guitar. I was just getting into "Sweet Sixteen," and, uh, Elmore, Homesick James, J.T. Brown playing at a place called Thelma's Lounge on Carson Avenue on the West Side. And "Sweet Sixteen," I was the only somebody, the only blues artist was singing "Sweet Sixteen" other than B.B. King 'cause my voice was five times higher than it is now. I had some lungs on me, so I started smoking, 'cause my voice was too light. I wanted to have a heavy voice like Brook Benton, you know, not having a little crazy little thing.

And Willie Johnson, he was a man who really, just really cared for me. Sometimes the guitar player, when I was coming up, would tell you things to make you just stop, just to get you off the way, but it weren't like that with Willie Johnson now, believe me. He told me I would be somebody someday. At that age I hadn't studied no music, I hadn't listened to a lot of people, but he had something . . . I could relate to what he was saying. So he would come and would be able to go to the pool room. I didn't drink, not then, and we could talk about—I would look up to him, see, by the family that I come from, he were not telling me nothing wrong. And then I'd go to this place, there's Otis Rush playing left-handed. Now that really got to me. I'm watching the guy. I'm right handed, I can't do this, and I always heard that a left-handed person can do things a bit better than a right-handed person, for some reason. Otis has just been super in my life, to help . . . that whole trip after I moved to the West Side, he used to play right around the corner from my house. So I'd say "hey wow—you're afraid to ask these people doing their thing," you know, and I would take that home with me and learn a little bit on it, be a really nice song. 'Cause Otis, in fact, played upside down, he doesn't cover the strings I'm interested in, like a right-handed guitar player would smother the bottom strings, a left-handed guy would just, I don't know . . . doing that "Violent Love," you know, or "I Can't Quit You Baby" and all that stuff. I'd say, "Yeah, this is my thing." Then B.B. King did "Please Love Me," "Whole Lot of Lovin'," and stuff. I said "I wanna be fast like that."

And all of a sudden, Chuck Berry comes here in my life, a whole other thing. Now, if I could, "I'm gonna do this, I'm gonna do it." So Willie James Lyons, on the West Side, and I play a lot at Ma Bea's now and a lot of clubs, we came up together. We were so close, we called ourselves brothers. We were just that close. And he had me playing like five years before I even thought about it. But we was in that media then, we had to deal with things that was going on which was blues. And we were sitting in the room all night, and just, he'd trade licks with me, I trade. He played bass, but we'd take one guitar, he'd play the bass part of it, and like I say, I'm behind the guy. I'd play the lead part of it, and so therefore if I had become a full-time bass player, I would know exactly what the lead player, and if I'd become a full-time lead player, I'd know exactly what to expect from the bass. 'Cause like they have to teach the whole beat, you know, you listen to the real thing—Jimmy Reed had it and Eddie Taylor had it—perfect beat. I'm just building 'round, you know, "Don't You Know That I Love You, Honest I Do." That was the tune, you know. As a matter of fact, before I heard it, we was doing that same tune. That's what we tell everybody, these changes right here, Willie James and I really put that together, yeah.

Oh, Magic Sam was hot in those days. He was very, very, very accepted. Young. And didn't really have no sense of the fact that he wanted to be professional, because of he was young, and I would sit in with Sam after that point, after I got old enough to go to these places. And Sam was so glad to see me some, 'cause he could give me the guitar—he was just not serious about what he was doing, so to speak. And he would give me the guitar and take off and go home and stay and watch TV the rest of the night, 'cause he knew I was doing basically what he was doing. And we'd see each other the next day, say,

"You turkey, why did you leave me? It was your show." "You know, I was tired."
He was always jiving. He was phenomenal, you know.

We did everybody's thing. It wasn't so much of a structure of what you did.
I mean, I guess everybody was based on Jimmy Reed and Muddy Waters and
Jimmy Rogers and Howlin' Wolf, etc. . . . When I stopped singing "Sweet Sixteen," I remember very well it was a hot summer night, club was smokey, no
air conditioner plant, and they raised the window and I got hoarse. And the
next time my voice just wouldn't do it. And I was doing it three octaves higher
than B.B. King. It was just amazing, you know. Something'd happen. We got
a show, you know. I'm no singer anyway, and a lot of time you'd get singers,
man, but they might leave you stranded on the job going chasing women, you
know. So only reason I started singing, the singers took off chasing ladies or
something, you know. Somebody had to carry it.

Muddy Waters and Little Walter, those folks were on the South Side, and
Jimmy Rogers and Howlin' Wolf were so to speak on the West Side. So that's
what brought it all together. And you can move from the West Side to the
South Side—it's like going from Chicago to New York to a gig, you know.
So they would have a battle of the blues. Now battle of the guitarists and the
drummers. That's when Little Walter used to wipe out all those horn players
with the harp. They have them standing in line and do that stuff—pow! pow!
pow!—Just . . . battles—disaster, man And these guys, like even J.T. Brown who
was heavy, but J.T., even guys like him wouldn't stand close to Walter. . . . Big
rivalry, oh yes, but it was all music.

Then you know in the church they'd have battle of groups like the Soul Stir-
rers, the Five Blind Boys, the Mighty Clouds of Joy, the Dixie Hummingbirds,
everybody coming in there, and there's big blowout in church, and they'd have
blues musicians that's gospel oriented. . . .

Freddie King, well, yes, the big trip was we was raised up together, yeah,
a bunch of jam sessions, Blue Monday parties, Sunday cocktail parties. . . .
Freddy was hot like, he used three pieces. Freddie King, you know, played the
bass guitar, the basic stuff, you know. And Big Mojo Elem was the first somebody to, so to speak, take the guitar and wound the strings down and play
bass from there. When I took over Freddie King's band at Walton's Corner in
1963, Freddie was playing and Bobby King was playing—three, no more than
four nights a week. I played five. I don't even know what we was called at that
point. It wasn't Luther Allison, I forgot what it was called. But after that I got
my own thing with my brother called the Four Jivers. So that took us to the
Three Jets, which was back to T.J. McNulty and Mojo Elem, after we had broke
up and stuff, without Freddie, you know. I didn't have the problems that Freddie had. I weren't singing, so to speak, so it was just one of those kinda movements. Then after Freddie King made "Hideaway," nobody could take his spot

'cept me. And then we used to steal three pieces. And that's where Walton's Corner came in—I made my move right there.

We Got to Make a Record

You hear about all these other people on the radio, you know, getting on the radio somehow—"We got to make a record; how do you make a record?" Oh hell, we heard Muddy Waters do this tune—"Let's do this tune and go somewhere and get it recorded in a studio." . . . So, my first recording, '67, but there was one before that. We made a demo on CBS that was never issued. In '67, the One-Der-Ful session,[2] I didn't have no contract; it was just a matter of me using the One-Der-Ful studios. Delmark bought the tapes or whatever. And I was involved with Shakey Jake, who was involved with Delmark, that whole trip. I had people at One-Der-Ful interested, like Harold Burrage. I went to Chess, I went to King Records, Vee Jay Records, and One-Der-Ful Records to try to get something recorded, and that's why I wrote "Gotta Move on Up" and "My Luck Don't Ever Change." That's what I wanted to do with One-Der-Ful Records. . . . But at the same time, people believed in me, all of these people I got to meet really believed in me. They knew I had a lot to learn, but they didn't even bother about telling me I got a lot to learn. They say "You got something, don't stop." Because I was a quiet person with a whole bunch of respect when you tell me something, you know. I must have been 25 years old before I say I'm cursed with—drink some Scotch or smoke a cigarette, you know. I was just raised that way, tightly—do unto others as I want them to do unto me, you know.

I moved to Peoria in July 1967. I got a job at Keystone Steel and Wire Company. and Caterpillar Tractor Company, Kitchen Maid Pies, and still drove back to Chicago after I got off work, which I had the second shift, and I had all three jobs, drove back to Chicago to the 1815 Club, after eleven-thirty. I would get back about one o'clock. They don't close until four, five, and Jimmy Dawkins would sit in for me until I got there. Oh oh, long miles, 165, 170 miles from Peoria to Chicago, but I could stay the whole weekend . . . except when the job asked me to be there Saturday and I had to do that too. I'd get off at 4 o'clock and be back at Peoria to go to work at three in the evening and get off again eleven thirty and drive back to Chicago . . . I did it!

Shakey Jake sent for me from California. See I put together a group in California called Lou Allison & the Blue Nebulae,[3] and we recorded under Luther Allison. So many people said, I like Luther; that's your name, use it. We stayed in California one year. We played in Los Angeles, the Ash Grove, the Back Door in Ventura . . . At one time we made fifteen dollars a night per person. I would eat breakfast and send the other part of it home, which was about eleven dollars, that's all . . . If I didn't work, I didn't eat. Hard times!

You know, it freaked me out when I played the Black Door and I got on that acid trip. Had a headache and asked somebody in the audience did they have an aspirin for me, so this chick say, "No, I don't have an aspirin. I have something better; just take this little bit . . ." You know, I'm green. I'm not hip, because I believe in people. Anyway, Shakey Jake was going through some family problems, and he just kinda throws up, and I called back home to a couple of my brothers and said, "Send me a plane ticket so I can get back," and so I finally got enough to get back to Peoria.

The Motown Experiment

Well, I played the place, you know, Detroit, called the Checkmate, and Joe Peraino came down. He sat in and asked me who I was recording, which I wasn't, recording with anyone, because I had this big argument with Bob Koester from Delmark prior to that. "So work for Motown."—We finally got into the studio, got signed up about eight, six or eight months later after that day. Well, you know, for me at that point, man,—"Wow, I'm going with Motown Records"—my break lay there, and realizing that I would be the only blues artist, because I didn't care about who didn't like blues, or blues wasn't selling anymore, and that stuff, it didn't bother me, so we signed up, and my manager at the time was an attorney and was signing the contract, it was that simple. And Motown was glad to have something like this, you know. We recorded three albums. I just had a *Guitar Player* review, you know, just had a *Rolling Stone* review. How much can you get and the company don't catching on you—like Ann Arbor, I'm the only artist played every blues festival. I mean, what can you do? I played the Berkeley Jazz Festival, the Philadelphia Folk Festival, I played Montreal . . . I mean what else can you do? And your record company don't catch their eyes on this. I'm playing to the mass of people. They could have done a whole heck of a lot better, but you know, "Why spend all this money on the blues? The blues is a dying cause"—right?—as far as they are concerned. So they haven't done too much for me. . . . Now I know not to sign those stupid contracts . . .

Luther Allison Today

My point now is to prove to them I'm still struggling for what I started with, yeah, maybe someday. Actually I'd rather not be called Luther Allison & His

Blues Band. I'd rather be called just me, because this way it doesn't put me in a rut. 'Cause if I go in a rut, I'm gonna be lost, just like a whole bunch of good blues, jazz artists back in Chicago or wherever, because they tried to be one thing, no way; B.B. King isn't one thing, Muddy Waters isn't one thing, Chuck Berry isn't one thing.

No, I had no musical training. I made the chords from musicians that you hear. I say "A" and you get that "A" in your ear. I hear pretty good, you know. Don't tell me nothing about reading, no. It's not for real. It's good to read if you're gonna structure your own music, but how do you do that after all these hundreds of years of music? It's no way. Like what discotheque doing now? What is soul music doing now? Sanctified church put together gospel and Baptist church music put together. What is jazz doing now? Same thing it was doing when it started....

As they say, "The blues will never die," but it's not gonna ever sell a big mass-million seller, but it'll always sell. Put together ten years of blues and ten years of rock and roll, the blues gonna outweigh it. That's why these record companies really holding on to tapes and stuff, you know. Since the late '70s I have a nice following here in Europe; I made the festivals, Nice, Montreux, Den Haag, etc.... Many people attended my concerts and I made records for Black & Blue, Rumble, Black Silver, Free Bird, and others, and I live in Paris, France; I'm feeling great since I'm with PARIS-ALBUM Records (ENCORE) and Jean-Philippe Martin-Payre, because this was the first time I had the opportunity to do exactly what I wanted to do. The *Time* album, for instance, this was the first one that I've written completely with the opportunity to go in and do what I wanted to do. The title cut is far from blues, as far as blues listeners say, this is not a blues song because of the beat. What it is really doing is putting down the disco thing! And just listen to my new album, *Life Is a Bitch* ... We got to reach the mass that's been out there. I can't keep on being B.B. King, or Muddy Waters, or ... I gotta be Luther Allison. It's hard on, me but I gotta do it ...

I'm feeling that a lot of young people in America and in Europe is catching a message from what Luther Allison is trying to say.... You might say, "That's not blues, Luther." Luther says, "You don't know ... Who are you to say I'm not playing blues, simply because I'm not just where Robert Johnson, or Charley Patton left?" Anyway, I'm a part of them all, without Charley Patton, Robert Johnson, Robert Jr. Lockwood, and Muddy Waters, and others, I could not be standing here in a blues situation ... and be quiet, I'll still be playing the blues. But I'll play Luther's blues. That's the way it is.

Thank you folks!

Discography (updated by Robert Sacré)

1969 *Love Me Mama*, Delmark CD 625

1973 *Bad News Is Coming*, Motown/Gordy 964

1974 *Luther's Blues*, Motown/Gordy 967

1975 *Night Life*, Motown/Gordy 974

1976 *Sweet Home Chicago*, anthology, Delmark LP 618 (1967); Charly Records (UK), collection Charly Blues Masterworks, vol. 37, recorded live in Chicago

1977 *Love Me Papa*, Black & Blue (F) 334524, reissued as Estudio Eldorado 524 (Brazil) and Evidence 26015

       Standing at the Crossroads, Night and Day, collection Blues Reference, recorded 1977, mostly made with titles from *Love Me Papa*

1979 *Gonna Be a Live One in Here Tonight*, Rumble 100, reissued as Red Lightnin (UK) 0036; *South Side Safari*, 1984 (and M.I.L. Multimedia 1983)

1979 *Power Wire Blues*, Rumble 1004, Charly (UK) 1105

1979 *Live in Paris*, Paris Album/Buda (F) 2–28501, Platinum 16154, Ruf Records (D) 1354, Free Bird (F) 209/Flyright (UK) FLY06, Plane 88295.

1979 *Live*, Blue Silver 3001/332

1980 *Time*, Paris Album/Buda 2–28505 (F)

1980 *Let's Have a Natural Ball*, JSP (UK) 1077

1984 *Life Is a Bitch*, Encore!/Melodie 131 (F); Blind Pig 2287 (retitled *Serious*) 1987

1985 *Here I Come*, Encore!/Melodie 133 (F)

1987 *Rich Man*, Ruf Records (D) 8001, also RFR 1005, Charly CRB 1227

1989 *More from Berlin*, Live 1989, East West LACD 1991–2

1992 *Hand Me Down My Moonshine*, Inak/Ruf 1047; also Acoustic

1994 *Soul Fixin' Man*, Alligator 4820; also in Europe as *Bad Love*, Ruf 1021

1995 *Blue Streak*, Alligator 4834; Ruf Records 7712 in Europe

1996 *Live '89, Let's Try It Again*, Ruf Records 1028

1996 *Live in Montreux: Where Have You Been*, recorded 1976–94, Ruf Records 1008 (D) 1996

1997 *Reckless*, Alligator 4849; Ruf Records 1012 in Europe, 1997

1999 *Live in Chicago*, Alligator 4869; Ruf Records 1042 in Europe

2001 *Live in Paradise*, DVD, Ruf Records

2002 *Pay It Forward*, Ruf Records 1060

2007 *Underground*, Ruf 1132 (recorded 1968)

2009 *Songs from the Road: Live in Montréal, 4 July 1997*, Ruf 1157, with a DVD of the show

2017 *A Legend Never Dies: Essential Recordings, 1976–1997* [1,500 limited and numbered sets], Ruf Records, deluxe box set consisting of 7 CDs; 4 DVDs, featuring a 1987 show in East Berlin, a 1991 concert where Allison plays alongside his son Bernard, and live performances from 1997; and an 88-page coffee table book by Art Tipaldi, featuring Allison's story, comments from his friends and associates, and rare and private photographs to mark the twentieth anniversary of the passing of Luther Allison

Filmography

1986   *Otis Rush & Friends live à Montreux* with Eric Clapton & Luther Allison (Eagle
       EREDV554) DVD
2001   *Live in Paradise*, DVD, Ruf Records 2001

Notes

1. This group interview with Luther Allison took place at the 1984 symposium and included Cilla Huggins, Marcel Vos, Jim O'Neal, Dick Shurman, Mike Rowe, John Broven, Robert Sacré. A similar interview was conducted in 1980 by Cilla Huggins and Bill Greensmith for the magazine *Blues Unlimited* in the UK (issue 139, Autumn 1980).

2. The whole session is on a *Sweet Home Chicago* anthology—Delmark LP/CD 618, recorded March 1967.

3. Delmark LP/CD 625 *Love Me Mama*, Luther Allison & the Blue Nebulae (recorded late 1968)

Modern Chicago Blues: Delta Retentions

—Jim O' Neal

Mike Rowe and Dick Shurman have discussed the relationships between Charley Patton, the Delta blues, and postwar Chicago blues. What I'd like to do now is to bring the Delta-Chicago blues story up to date and examine the retentions of the Delta in modern Chicago blues today and the new status of Mississippi vs. Chicago in the blues world.

As we have seen, the blues of the Delta was a major influence on the way blues developed in Chicago in the 1940s and 1950s. Many of the great blues artists of that period—Muddy Waters, Howlin' Wolf, Elmore James, Sonny Boy Williamson, Jimmy Reed, and others—were either born in the Delta or were performing there before they came to Chicago. The songs of these men are still carried on in the repertoires of almost every blues band working in Chicago today. Among the leading Chicago blues artists now, including Junior Wells, James Cotton, Sunnyland Slim, Jimmy Rogers, Koko Taylor, Son Seals, Little Milton, Syl Johnson, Jimmy Johnson, Jimmy Dawkins, Luther Allison, Fenton Robinson, and Magic Slim, most also came from the Delta or nearby towns in Mississippi, Arkansas, and Tennessee.

As black musicians continued to leave the Delta throughout the 1940s and 1950s, Chicago became the primary center for the continuation and modernization of the Delta blues traditions. One will probably still hear more traditional Delta blues influence in the music played by Chicago bands than by bands in other cities, and in some cases more than by the modern bands I have heard that are still playing in the Delta itself.

But Chicago blues has changed over the years as it has incorporated other musical trends. Whereas Delta blues was at one time the primary basis of Chicago blues, it is now just one of several elements that make up the modern Chicago sound.

Other elements have come from popular soul, R&B and funk music, and from the contemporary blues of B.B. King, Albert King, Bobby Bland, and Little Milton. It is probably fair to say that B.B. and Albert King have played the greatest role in influencing Chicago in the past twenty years. The blues they play is not usually called Delta blues, but we should remember that B.B., Albert, and Little Milton came from the Delta, too, and Bland was born just across the state line in Tennessee.

So, either directly or indirectly, there are still strong retentions of the Delta in Chicago. I am not speaking only of the music, because the music came to Chicago with the people of the Delta, and much of the lifestyle of the black Delta community was also transplanted to Chicago. This includes churches, social functions, neighborhood gatherings, music, food, and language. There is still a strong sense of loyalty to the Delta, or to some other region of the native South, among the black population of Chicago. Often families and friends would move to Chicago from the Delta together, and one can still find apartment buildings where all the parents and older relatives may be from Greenville or Clarksdale, Mississippi, and the children were all born in Chicago. Some of the popular social events during the year are reunions of people from certain towns or states, held at a nightclub or dance hall on the South or West Side, and of course some blues artists from that home town usually provide the entertainment.

Another Delta style social and musical gathering place in Chicago is the Delta Fish Market. This is one of the most active and visible continuing links between Chicago and the Delta. The Fish Market is in a black West Side neighborhood and is owned by a slide guitar player named Oliver Davis, who idolizes Elmore James and whose father was a bandleader in Greenville, Mississippi. This is reportedly the largest retail outlet for selling fish in Chicago, and it is also the biggest outdoor jam session for blues artists in the city. There is a bandstand on the parking lot, and with the bands playing and people partying and eating fried catfish, it is like a downhome southern picnic every Friday and Saturday.

Even the catfish comes from the Delta—a truck goes down to Mississippi every week to bring back fresh fish and the truck driver is always one of the local blues musicians.

There is also still some back-and-forth movement of blues musicians between Chicago and Mississippi, although we do not have the large black migrations of the early postwar years anymore. But it is not unusual for a band of Chicago musicians to get together and go back home to play in the juke joints around the Delta for a week or two. Singers like Little Milton still play the "chitlin circuit" in Mississippi regularly and make pretty good money doing it. Occasionally new Mississippi blues musicians show up in Chicago, and sometimes Chicago musicians move back to Mississippi. Sam Myers, a harmonica player from Jackson, Mississippi, learned to play in what is essentially a Delta-influenced Chicago blues style by spending his summers in Chicago, learning from James Cotton, and listening to Chicago blues records.

The thought of moving back is a common theme with people from Mississippi in Chicago. The way they often put it, they may be staying in Chicago and working there, but Mississippi is still home. For economic reasons, most of them continue to stay in Chicago. But the recent reemergence of a successful blues recording industry in Jackson, Mississippi, has created economic reasons for a couple of soul-blues singers, Bobby Rush and McKinley Mitchell,[1] and Johnny Littlejohn to record in Jackson in recent years. The Malaco record company in Jackson has had some enormous commercial hits by Z.Z. Hill, and they are now recording Little Milton, Denise LaSalle, and Latimore. Bobby Rush records for another Jackson label, LaJam, and he also has had some big hits on the R&B charts. This is something that no Chicago record company has been able to do lately, and it has to do with the fact that Malaco and LaJam have been successful in marketing a contemporary commercial style of blues to a young and middle-aged black audience that is much larger than the predominantly white blues audience that today's Chicago labels are selling to.

Obviously, the situation has changed a lot since the 1950s, when Muddy Waters was having hit records from Chicago on the black R&B charts, but times have changed and the older style of Delta blues does not seem as relevant to young black record buyers today.

Now I would like to get back to the theme of our conference in Liège and check if there are examples of the retentions of Charley Patton's music in modern Chicago blues. Charley Patton is not a familiar name to most Chicago musicians today. There are probably none of his songs that are played intact by any of the modern bands. Only a few of the older Chicago bluesmen remember Charley Patton or his records. Some of them, like Honeyboy Edwards and Blind Jim Brewer, have recorded Patton's songs recently, but they have been in a traditional solo country blues style. Among the younger blues bands, the influence Charley Patton has had has come primarily by way of the late Howlin' Wolf, who used a number of Patton's themes in his songs.

Wolf's version of "Smokestack Lightning" has a verse similar to one found in "Moon Going Down" by Patton. Some lines by Charley Patton from "Down the Dirt Road Blues" also appeared in a song called "Can't Stay Here" from the last album ever recorded by Howlin' Wolf. Authorship of the song was credited to Wolf's bass player, Andrew "Blueblood" McMahon, who also recorded it on one of his own albums (as "I Can't Stay Here"). Homesick James Williamson recalls that he and McMahon wrote the song one day at Homesick's apartment in Chicago. This song has also been recorded by Chicago guitarist Johnny Littlejohn under the title "Chips Flying Everywhere"—with composer credits either to McMahon and record producer Al Smith, or to Littlejohn himself—and has also been performed in the clubs by a few other Chicago bluesmen, such as Lefty Dizz.

A lot of Patton's verses have been reworked on a couple of recordings I have done just during the past year.[2] For instance, the "smokestack lightning" theme from Charley Patton's "Moon Going Down" appears in a new version of "Smokestack Lightning" by a new young Chicago singer, Valerie Wellington.

What is interesting is that the particular line I am talking about is based on the old Charley Patton record and not on Howlin' Wolf, although the rest of the song is done much the way Wolf did it.

Charley Patton, "Moon Going Down"[3]
Lord, the smokestack is black and the bell it shine like, bell it shine like, bell it shine like gold. Aw the smokestack is black and the bell it shine like gold. Lord, I ain't gonna walk this levee 'round no more.

Valerie Wellington, "Smokestack Lightning"[4]
Well, the smokestack is lightnin', and it shines like, yeah, and it shines like gold.

For comparison, note the way Howlin' Wolf[5] sings it: "Oh, smokestack lightning, shinin' just like gold." Valerie Wellington's phrasing comes from the Patton version, not Wolf's, on this line.

Now here are a few verses from "Down the Dirt Road Blues" by Charley Patton,[6] and the corresponding lines the way they are used by Johnny Littlejohn. Johnny Littlejohn is in his fifties and to my knowledge has never heard the Charley Patton record, unless someone has played it for him recently. Note that the meaning of the lyrics, as discussed earlier by David Evans, has also been changed in the context of this song.

Charley Patton, "Down the Dirt Road Blues"
I feel like choppin', chips flyin' everywhere.
I feel like choppin', chips flyin' everywhere.
I been to the Nation, Lord, but I couldn't stay there.

Some people say them oversea blues ain't bad.
Some people say them oversea blues ain't bad.
It must not a-been them oversea blues I had.

Every day seem like murder here.
Every day seem like murder here.
I'm gonna leave tomorrow, I know you don't bit more care.

Johnny Littlejohn, "Chips Flyin' Everywhere"[7]
Well, I feel like choppin', chips flyin' everywhere. [2x]
Well, I can't make a nickel, oh boy, but I can't stay here.

Well, now every day seem like murder here. [2x]
Well, I can't make a nickel, oh boy, but I can't stay here.

So, while Charley Patton's songs have not entered into the Chicago blues legacy the way Robert Johnson's did, at least it's still possible to hear some retentions fifty years after his death.

What may happen in the future is that we'll hear more, not less, of the Charley Patton legacy and of other traditional Delta blues, in the music of new Chicago blues bands because of the interest some of the young black performers are showing in their blues heritage. There is a whole new generation of blues artists who were born in Chicago and who probably have had no contact with the Delta except through their parents, if at all. There are now many Chicago bluesmen who have sons who are playing blues on the local scene. Willie Dixon has three sons performing. Carey Bell has five—plus a few cousins. Eddie Taylor has two, and Lonnie Brooks, Luther Allison, Eddie Shaw, Little Howlin' Wolf (Jessie Sanders), Otis Rush, Bobby Davis, Lefty Dizz, and others all have musical children who have grown up with the blues. There are other young artists who didn't grow up in a blues household and may have played soul, rock, or rhythm and blues before they found the blues, like Billy Branch, Valerie Wellington, and Sugar Blue, but they are just as dedicated to perpetuating the blues, and they all have a strong appreciation for the roots of the music.

In closing, I would like to quote one more new recording by a band from the Chicago area that shows that the Delta blues is still alive in Chicago, or in this case, Gary, Indiana, a steel mill town just outside the city. The artist is Big Daddy Kinsey, the band features his three sons, the song is about Gary, Indiana, and the roots are obviously in Muddy Waters and the Delta.

Big Daddy Kinsey, "Gary, Indiana"[8]
I was born in the Mississippi Delta, but I was raised in a Indiana
ghetto town.
Born in the Mississippi Delta, and I was raised in the Indiana ghetto town.
Well, I never shall forget, people, the morning I left my home sweet home.

The town I'm singin' about, people, is just thirty miles east of the Windy City.
Yeah, the town I'm singin' about, people, is just thirty miles east of the
Windy City.
Well, you know, it produced some of the greatest people that the world has
ever known.
Michael Jackson! William Marshall!
(I'm talkin' about the Steel City, y'all.)
So this is my story, people, about G-A-R-Y.
Oh, this is my story, people, about G-A-R-Y.
Well, you know it's been good to me, though some people try to put it down.
(My home town, y'all.)
(I'm talkin' about Gary, Indiana, yeah!)
(My good friend, the Great Baby Boy, a great harmonica player,
and of course my right arm, the great Nathaniel Armstrong, yeah!)
(All right, Pinetop!)
(Yeah, I remember Deniece Williams. Fred Williamson. Albert King.
Jimmy Reed.
And of course, yours truly, Big Daddy Kinsey.)
(Yeah, ladies and gentlemen, we all got our start in Gary, Indiana.
That's why I say it's been good to me, yeah.)

Postscript: Chicago to Mississippi (2017)

Living Blues magazine was in transition at the time of the Charley Patton conference in Liège in 1984. Amy van Singel and I transferred publication rights to the University of Mississippi in 1983, after we and our editorial staff, including Bruce Iglauer and Paul Garon, had published *LB* in Chicago since 1970. In 1986 I moved to Oxford, Mississippi, to be able to work more closely with the new publication staff.

The move brought me in closer touch than ever with blues in the Delta, and in 1987 I moved to the Delta (Merigold and then Clarksdale, both towns once frequented by Patton) and I spent the next eleven years there. I continued to make trips to Chicago for recording sessions, blues clubbing, research, and the Chicago Blues Festival, which started in 1984 when we were still in Chicago to serve on the founding committee. One result of the move to Mississippi was a strengthening of the Mississippi/Chicago blues connection. I and others brought Mississippi-born Chicago blues artists back to their home state perform, sometimes for the first time in their professional careers, and we also coordinated bookings of Mississippi-based blues artists at the Chicago Blues

Festival and in various nightspots. The state of Mississippi and the city of Jackson have regularly sponsored stages at the festival in recent years.

Over the years, of course, the Chicago blues scene changed, with more of the well-known acts performing at white North Side clubs and at downtown venues frequented by tourists and visiting businessmen. With the success of the Chicago Blues Festival and growing publicity for the music, the City of Chicago officially embraced and promoted the blues as a tourism draw. "Sweet Home Chicago," a song only occasionally heard in the clubs in earlier years, became the ubiquitous theme song of the city.

Of the list of Chicago performers I cited in 1984, only a few are still alive. A new generation of blues, much of it funk- and rock-influenced, has emerged. At the same time, there is a greater awareness and appreciation of the blues heritage in the twenty-first century. Almost everyone knows about Robert Johnson thanks to the way the legends, myths, and controversies surrounding his songs, his life and death, and his alleged deal with the devil entered mainstream consciousness through the *Crossroads* movie of 1986, the phenomenal sales of the 1990 box set of his 1936–37 recordings,[9] countless cover versions of his works, and news stories about movie scripts, inheritance battles, and assorted Johnson minutiae. Musicians today know about Charley Patton, too, though he never caught the public's fancy as Johnson did. A key to Robert Johnson's appeal, aside from the fascination with the facts and fables, was his synthesis of the blues into a format ready-made for other musicians, including electric blues bands and rock groups, to follow. Patton's music, on the other hand, was all but inimitable.

I had recognized Patton's importance when I was in Chicago, but I never appreciated his magnificence until I delved deep into his music and his life story after I moved to the Delta. I focused on documenting, recording, and promoting the blues artists who were still playing in the Delta, but I also began gathering more and more historical information. In 1990 I accepted an offer to write a chapter on Patton for a book of essays edited by Pete Welding and Toby Byron called *Bluesland*. I embarked upon a new Patton quest, gathering recollections from older Delta residents, family members (Tom Cannon, Big Amos Patton, and Rosetta Patton Brown) and others who recalled Patton from their youth, while compiling more data from county courthouses, marriage license applications, and census entries. I had already met Tom Rushing (of Patton's *Tom Rushen* [sic] *Blues*)[10] in Merigold, and I later interviewed "Rooster" Holloway, whose father, a local bootlegger, was also immortalized by Patton in the song. [See the "Tom Rushen Blues" section that follows for some previously unpublished research and an example of the reminiscences I was able to record.] A thread that ran through many of the comments I heard was that Patton was someone these informants—who were mostly teenagers and young adults when they knew him—was someone they looked up to, not the contentious squabbler that some of Patton's contemporaries—who were often also his rivals—depicted in various published accounts I had read.

Stephen Calt and Gayle Wardlow's book, *King of the Delta Blues: The Life and Music of Charlie Patton*, was published in 1988 when I was in Clarksdale.[11] Despite its editorial biases and factual errors (including names of people and places that were becoming familiar to me in Mississippi by then), it provided a valuable framework for more research, along with David Evans's essay in the original 1987 Belgian edition of *Voice of the Delta*, John Fahey's 1970 book,[12] Bernard Klatzko's OJL LP liner note booklet,[13] and various Wardlow interviews. As it turned out, my proposed Patton chapter was so long that there was no room for it in *Bluesland* (full title: *Bluesland: Portraits of Twelve Major American Blues Masters*; with my chapter it would have been *Thirteen*),[14] but I did get a shorter version of it published as a liner note booklet to a Japanese 2-CD Patton compilation.[15] For that CD set I also spent a month listening to Patton's songs with headphones to do the best I could to transcribe his lyrics, not an easy task. I doubt any of us will ever decipher some of the words, although earlier transcriptions helped and I realized that Patton's pronunciation and accent were familiar to me on some level because he grew up in Hinds County, adjacent to Simpson County, in the same part of Mississippi where my mother's family had lived since the 1800s and where I once spent a lot of time with older relatives. My grandmother, Ione Turner Burns, even remembered black fiddle players who played on her parents' farm (the sweetest music she ever heard, she told me).

Through Clarksdale fireman and blues buff Robert Birdsong I met Patton's daughter Rosetta Patton Brown, and was later honored to deliver her substantial royalty checks from the reissue of her father's music by P-Vine Special Records in Japan. (She used a little of the money to buy her first CD player so she could hear her daddy's songs again.) I assisted Skip Henderson of the Mt. Zion Memorial Fund in placing a headstone for Patton in 1991 in Holly Ridge and wrote the inscription for the stone. Rosetta and Pops Staples attended the headstone dedication, as did Creedence Clearwater Revival icon John Fogerty, a primary donor to the fund; Fogerty said he likened the importance of Patton's work to the Dead Sea Scrolls.

I left Clarksdale in 1998 to relocate to Kansas City, but my fact-finding mission on Mississippi blues has continued all along, especially through my work co-writing texts with former *Living Blues* editor Scott Barretta for the

Mississippi Blues Trail historical marker project. The first marker on the trail was placed on December 11, 2006, at the Holly Ridge cemetery where Patton is buried. Patton's life and music have also been discussed on later markers at Dockery, Lula and others sites.[16]

The Mississippi Blues Trail research led to clues on Patton's probable birthplace and birth date. The date had been widely accepted as April 1891 based on the 1900 census and on the age cited on Patton's death certificate. But one day, looking at that census entry again for the umpteenth time, I noticed that the census enumerator had listed the Patton family in chronological order by birthdate, yet something was amiss. Charley's sister Viola had told David Evans that Charley was her older brother, born in 1887 (the date often cited in accounts of Patton's life prior to the release of the 1900 census data). But in the census entries, Viola's birthdate was cited as June 1887 while Charley's was April 1891. The most logical explanation, based on similar confusion I had seen in other entries, was that the enumerator must have transposed the entries on Charley and his next sibling Viola, having written Viola's name before Charley's. The 1887 birthdate is also closer to July 12, 1885, the date cited on Patton's World War I registration from September 12, 1918 (another piece of evidence that had not been uncovered in early Patton research). However, even the entry on the registration must be questioned: Charley's age is given as 34, which would place his birth year as 1884. Documentation on African Americans is notoriously inconsistent in such early records.[17] (See David Evans's chapter for more discussion of the family history.)

With help from Hinds County historian Ed Payne, I was able to determine that the Patton birthplace cited in the Calt and Wardlow book as "Heron's Place" was the plantation of Samuel L. Herring between the towns of Bolton and Raymond, and that location on Sam Herring Road—surprisingly not identified or sought out by the myriad of blues pilgrims searching for Robert Johnson's grave, the crossroads, and other sites of blues lore—became the site of a Mississippi Blues Trail marker in 2014.

The most surprising and most visible public recognition of Charley Patton was soon to follow. Unaware of some of the promotional efforts the Mississippi Blues Trail had undertaken, I was taken aback while driving through Southaven, Mississippi, just south of Memphis on Interstate Highway 55. Beside the highway, clearly visible at the top of a huge lighted display sign for the Tanger Outlets shopping mall, was the image of the first Charley Patton marker. More Mississippi Blues Trail markers were depicted in the mall. The display was still there the last time I was at the mall in 2016. Charley Patton's name is up in lights.

Tom Rushen Blues

David Evans's essay includes a good discussion of "Tom Rushen Blues" and the recollections of Tom Rushing himself. Here is more on the song, Charley Patton, the Rushing family, and events in the Delta, written in 1991, intended for the book *Bluesland* but never published:

It was long taken for granted by blues scholars that Patton was put in jail for drunkenness by "Tom Rushen" and that "Holloway," whoever he was, had also been caught with whiskey by "Mister Day." On a brief field research trip in 1963, Bernard Klatzko and Gayle Dean Wardlow came to a house on a dirt road near Merigold. In his liner notes to the first Patton reissue album (*The Immortal Charlie Patton* on OJL Records), Klatzko recounted:

I noticed the mail box read: Mr. Halloway [sic]. The words to Patton's *Tom Rushen Blues* flashed in my mind . . . Could it really be THE Halloway. That would be fantastic! . . . A tall, dark, heavy but rather young looking man greeted us. '"Where can we find Mr. Halloway?" I asked. "I'm Mr. Halloway."

"Did you know that Charley Patton sang about a Mr. Halloway in one of his songs?" I asked hopefully.

"Sure, but he was singing about my father. My father's dead. He used to make whiskey in those days." Halloway answered with a big grin—his only reaction to a rather startling question.

"Who was Tom Rushen," I pursued further.

"Tom Rushen was the sheriff of Merigold. Mr. Day was the sheriff before him." Halloway explained, anticipating a question about Mr. Day. Mr. Day's losing his position would explain another verse in Tom Rushen.

Klatzko's account provided a basis of research for years to come. Wardlow and Stephen Calt later learned that "Tom Rushen" was Paramount Records' misspelling of Tom Rushing. In *King of the Delta Blues* they wrote:

An apparent arrest for drunkenness led him to concoct a sedate blues that smacks of an attempt to curry favor with the recently-installed high sheriff of Merigold, O.T. Rushing . . . Patton's Merigold crony Willie (Have Mercy) Young recalled Rushing as a "right young law" . . . Like his brother, who worked as the bookkeeper of Dockery's plantation, he was renowned for his athletic prowess, which he turned to good account on his job. "He was a law who wouldn't shoot you for nothin,'" Young said appreciatively. ". . . I don't care what you done: if you outrun him, he let you go." . . . Instead of elaborating on his own confinement, Patton devoted three couplets to the doings of Rushing's deputy, a man named

Days, who had arrested one of his friends for bootlegging and apparently aspired to become sheriff.

David Evans took the search a step further by actually interviewing O. T. "Tom" Rushing in 1985. Rushing was living on the family land near Merigold, where, ironically, his grandson Sam was operating the Winery Rushing, Mississippi's first legal winery since Prohibition (when it was Tom's job to prohibit the manufacture and sale of alcohol). Tom Rushing explained that he had been a deputy sheriff in Bolivar County when Tom Day was the marshal of Merigold and Joe Smith was county sheriff. He remembered Patton's record well, saying Patton had even given him a copy. He also remembered Holloway as a sharecropper who "had a little still out east of Merigold," but could recall no details of Holloway's arrest. He was, Evans wrote, "emphatic that he did not arrest Patton."

Evans's continuing research on Patton brought him back to the Winery Rushing in 1989 in search of clues that might lead to a rumored brood of Pattons in the countryside near Merigold. Patty Johnson and I joined the junket, and though no Patton relatives turned up, we did find people who had stories to tell about Charley Patton. I later returned to visit one of them, Willie "Sugar Boy" Lewis, and his reminiscences led to more revelations both about Charley Patton and the story of "Tom Rushen Blues," as well as to clarification of a few obscure bits of Patton history. For one thing, Lewis's wife Minnie confirmed that a guitarist named Sam Riley used to play with Patton. Riley, who was mentioned in Bernard Klatzko's OJL notes but in none of the three subsequent books on Patton, was married to Minnie Lewis's sister. Sugar Boy was living on the old Zumbro plantation on the Sunflower River, where he said Patton had also stayed: "He used to live in around here on Zumbro, and up there on a place they call White Track, Spidlins [Stribling's], and Smith & Wiggins, and J.C. Hallman, and all them places—well, he just lived all over. In other words, he was just a roundabout fellow . . . On up in the years he'd come right up there at that store there, and play music out there and pass the hat around and folks'd give him money. At Zumbro store right up there. This is Zumbro Planting Company now but it was Zumbro Plantation then. That was old man Joe Smith."

Plantation owner Joseph L. Smith was evidently someone who figured prominently in Charley Patton's life. He was the same Bolivar County Sheriff Joe Smith who employed Tom Rushing as a deputy; he was in all likelihood also the J. L. Smith who put in the order at the Bolivar County courthouse for "Chas Patton" and Roxie Morrow to obtain a marriage license on November 12, 1918. (Most of Sugar Boy Lewis's memories of Patton date from at least a

decade later, when Patton was apparently still circulating in the same area.)
Tom Cannon also recalled hearing that Patton had preached at a church "out
from Merigold there, over on the Smith place." Zumbro, "the Smith place," may
have been one of Patton's rotating home bases in the same sense as Dockery Farms. Will Dockery was noted as a humanitarian and philanthropist; a
local paper praised Smith as a "benefactor to countless thousands of people."
A photo of Smith appears in Linton Weeks's *Cleveland: A Bicentennial History*
performing a marriage ceremony for some of his black tenants. In the photo
with Smith are eight black people; unfortunately, Charley Patton is not among
them. Weeks's book notes that Smith was also a brother of Clarence Richard
Smith—the C. R. Smith on whose plantation Patton's alleged mentor Earl Harris may have lived, according to Calt and Wardlow. Histories that were written separately but that evolved side by side in the Delta—of the prominent
planters and of their blues-singing tenants—have interfaced to bring a larger
picture into view, a feat inspired in no small part by the art of Charley Patton.

Sugar Boy Lewis recalled a number of musicians from the local plantations
who played with Patton.

> Buddy Johnson, he used to blow a harp. All these Saturday night breakdowns,
> Buddy would go around and carry his harp with him, and he would play with
> Charley Patton. . . . Tony Stewart was a preacher and he was playin' with him.
> Tony Stewart playin' a mandolin and Charley Patton was playin' a guitar and
> Will Stewart was playin' the fiddle. And they had the washboard, I don't know
> who that sucker was, but man, he could cut up with that washboard and them
> two spoons! Every Saturday night and Sunday, man, shoot, they'd go all over the
> country, all out on Six Mile Lake and all down to Boyle, Shaw, and Mound Bayou,
> Merigold—they just goin' everywhere. It wasn't no telephones or nothin'. They'd
> come and ask him to come and play for 'em if they're gonna give some kind of
> party or a weddin' or ever what. Anything, it didn't make no difference what it
> was, he'd play. They'd give him four or five dollars, eight or ten. Go along with the
> hat and take up collection.

Lewis's version of the events immortalized in "Tom Rushen Blues" finally
led to another source even closer to Charley Patton. "Mr. Day and Mr. Tom
Rushing was the laws in Merigold," Lewis explained. "And he [Patton] was
playin' at a Saturday night supper out there that night, and the fellow named
Holloway was runnin' it. And, well, he was a terrible fellow. He'd make whiskey
and give them Saturday night breakdowns, and had a house full of chillun. I
remember when they caught him selling whiskey. Mr. Tom Rushing and Mr.
Day come out there and raided the place for whiskey. The county caught him

[Holloway] and he wouldn't pay his fine. And they carried him to jail.... Holloway got a son in Cleveland. Rooster Holloway ... He can tell you anything about Charley Patton you want to know, near 'bout."

Osborn "Rooster" Holloway was sitting on his front porch, probably pretty much as he'd done every day since he retired from his job, when I found his house in Cleveland the next day. "I don't do nothin'," he mused. "I gets tired of settin' down. I been settin' up here eleven years, gettin' lonesome." The chance to talk about his father and Charley Patton provided a welcome break from the monotony, and his spirits perked up as the story of "Tom Rushen Blues" and the exploits of Charley Patton and his friends came to life. A son of "the Halloway [sic]" of "Tom Rushen Blues," Rooster was also a brother of the man Wardlow and Klatzko had met in 1963 whose name they reported as Halloway, a spelling perpetuated in writings on Patton ever since. Rooster was able to provide an intimate perspective on Charley Patton, because Patton once lived in the Holloway household, and Rooster regarded him almost like a big brother or an uncle.

His father, Rooster explained, was

Seab Holloway. Now that's the man that Charley Patton stayed with so long.... Them old men stayed together a long time. Since I could remember, Charley, my daddy used to bring him to the house before he started to stayin' with him. And he got to be such a good friend, my daddy told him, "They ain't no expenses on you. You might's well just go on and stay with me. Have plenty of whiskey. You can work if you want, if you don't you can sleep," and Charley said, "That's what I want." So he'd play that guitar and stay in bed all day and get up and play at night and come back in the bed and sleep all the next day. He didn't work. Um-um. No. He didn't do nothin' but play that guitar and drink that corn whiskey. And he could drink it too! Now him and my daddy could drink more corn whiskey than anybody I ever seed in my life. I see them take a pint fruit jar, fill it up. In a few minutes it's gone ... He'd just lay that guitar across his lap, and he had a piece of bottleneck what he'd talk with, I reckon—I say he'd make it talk. He'd just drag that bottleneck over them strings. You could name any kind of song you wanted to hear. If he knowed that song, he'd play it, that guitar, it'd tell you just exactly what he was singin'. I never seed a man play a guitar like Charley. It's just a gift, I imagine. But he was bad with that guitar. Ooh!

One Saturday night, it was in '28, him and a woman was his old lady, he had that guitar around his neck, she would do the singin', but he'd do the playin'. My daddy was makin' corn whiskey. We had a great big house. It was ten of us chillun. We lived seven miles from Merigold. They come in there and started to playin', and somebody went to town and told 'em, said Charley Patton was in town: "He out to Old Man Holloway's playin'." And, man, the whole town come out there. The man they call Tom Rushing, he come out there too. He was the sheriff; 'course he was buyin' more whiskey than any of the rest of 'em from my daddy! And, man, they played there till day the next mornin'. My mother cooked a lot of fish, and oh, man, they eat and drank. Daylight the next mornin' the house was still full. Charley Patton, then he commenced to stayin' with us.

He'd play every night somewhere and sleep all day. 'Cause wouldn't nobody be at home but him. We'd be in the field choppin' and plowin' them mules, and Charley'd be layin' there asleep, and when night come he'd get up in there and eat and go on to playin' guitar somewhere. His wife would go with him sometimes. The average time he'd leave her there where he stayed at, at my daddy's house. We had a house with twelve rooms in it. And he had him a room there and she'd just stay there and lay up in the bed and read a book all the time. Till night come, and they'd be up, they dress up and go out.... He'd make seven or eight dollars a night. That was big money way back in there. Yeah, old Charley had a sack of money. And couldn't drive a car. He'd pay somebody to carry him anywhere he wanted to go. Me and my brother, all of us had cars. Bully—that was his name he was callin' on the record. My daddy or my older brother, one, would carry him where he wanted to play, and then before they'd go to work the next mornin', they'd go pick him up and bring him back home. And whoever he gon' play for, if they had a car, they would come pick him up.

We had a great big old mule barn and we had that still settin' up in that mule barn. That's where this record was about. Tom Day— he say he got it "from under his head." He didn't get it from under his head. He [Charley] made that to make his record. He got it out of that barn. That's where he got that whiskey from. Man, there was some whiskey just rolled off all around side the wall, and steady makin'. Peoples was comin' from Drew, Rosedale, everywhere. Gettin' it by the five gallon. Wasn't sellin' it but for three dollars a gallon. And we couldn't keep enough. My daddy never did do no work to amount to nothin'. He just stayed in that barn and made whiskey most of the time. Make us work! Whilst he make whiskey.

Somebody told on him. Told where he was makin' that whiskey and everything.... When Mr. Day arrested him, he turned it over to the federal people and they took him from Cleveland. They carried him to Clarksdale and he spent right at two months up there in Clarksdale jail. And they never did arrest him no more.

The Holloways, Rooster said, did not know that Patton intended to immortalize the incident in song: "He didn't tell us. I don't know how, he studied it up and wrote it out and made that record, and when we heared the record, we were surprised. How did he think of all that? But my daddy said, 'Well, that's all right. I'm glad for the people to know I was thought of that much to have a record made about me. It wasn't nothin' for me to say.'" The Holloways figured that Charley had even put Seab's son Bully in the song as Patton's chauffeur, interpreting one of the lines Patton borrowed from Ma Rainey as "It takes Bully to carry me through."

Holloway shared the opinions Patton apparently held of Tom Rushing as a friendly lawman and of Tom Day as more of an adversary. Rushing, he said, never arrested his father, "'cause every night he'd come there and get him a big old jar of whiskey....He'd tell my daddy, 'I'll keep 'em off you. Don't you worry. You just give me the whiskey when I come.'" Patton, to Holloway's knowledge, was never arrested by either Rushing or Day, but did have his run-ins with Day. He recalled when Charley and Son Patton used to play in Merigold:

It was a man called One Armed Cleve. He had a great big barbershop there in Merigold, and Charley would play there every Saturday. And all of them fellows wanted hair trims, it wasn't but twenty cents, and they give them hair trims, he'd give Charley two, three dollars. Wouldn't nobody be buyin' nothin' in them stores, listenin' to Charley play at that barbershop. Tom Day, he was the law then. He didn't like him. Mr. Day told him he couldn't play there no more. Somebody'd get runned over, all in the road and everywhere. They'd be out there dancin' in the road. He run 'em away from there ... police stopped him from playin' there, and he quit playin' there. He'd go on out in the country where nobody wouldn't bother him....Now that's when it was a cousin of his'n played with him. Him and his buddy, they'd play with him sometime there in town. But they never did go with Charley to these different places through the country. His cousin say he wasn't gonna play in no country.

(Will "Son" Patton was Charley's brother, but Holloway recalled, "He just always would say 'That's my cousin.'")

"Tom Rushen Blues" was, for obvious reasons, the most famous Charley Patton record to Rooster Holloway, who recalled little about Patton's other recordings. The Holloways didn't own a phonograph, and the nearest neighbor who had one lived a two- or three-mile mule ride away, he said. Close-up memories of Patton the person stayed with him through the years, though: "Every once in a while when we all come in out of the field, he'd set up and talk with us a while. That house had four fireplaces to it. We sat 'round the big log fire at night and he'd crack jokes and play with us boys around there awhile ... talkin' 'bout where he had been in his lifetime and all that.... Then he'd get ready and get out from there. When he would come in the next mornin', we'd be in that field.

"He dressed nice. He wore nice suits of clothes. Yeah, he'd go dressed up, had all kinda diamonds on his hand. But he wore his pants up along here all the time," Holloway explained, gesturing a few inches above his ankles.

He wouldn't let his pants down for nothin' in the world. I said, "Mr. Charley, how come you won't let your pants down?" "Catchin' air, boy! Go on back in the house. You don't need to know why I got my pants up," and all such a foolishness as that. My daddy asked him one time, said, "Is you kin to a Chinaman?" Chinamen wear their pantses short, you know. He said, "Hell, I don't know. I'm here, that's all I know." Now he wouldn't talk about it much. My daddy just quit, you know, sayin' anything. And he told us, "Don't y'all ever say nothin' to him about his color or nothin' like his hair or nothin'. Don't say anything about it, 'cause he don't like it." And we just wouldn't say nothin' about it. "Hey, I don't know nothin' 'bout that. I'm here and that's all I care about." That's the way he turned him off.

But he was a nice fella as far as I knowed of. I never did know him to bother nobody, or nothin'. He didn't carry a gun. He had a little old bitty knife, had a chain on it. And he'd keep it in his watchpocket all the time.... I never heared him cuss. He drank whiskey, I never did know him to gamble. He drank whiskey and play that guitar, that's all—now he was bad at women, though. Yeah, he was bad at women. But I never knowed nothin' else of him. I never known him even to have a fight with nobody.

The testimony of Rooster Holloway, Sugar Boy Lewis, and others has already effected amendments to the book on Charley Patton and "Tom Rushen Blues." But the epilogue is still unfolding after a bizarre series of events involving the Rushing family.

Sam Rushing and his wife Diane built the Winery Rushing into a popular Delta landmark, famed for its muscadine wine, tea room, and Southern hospitality, as well as for its blues connections. Until recently, callers might even find Tom Rushing himself outside picking strawberries or inside charming a visitor with his conversation. Someone literally pulled the plug on the Rushings one spring weekend in 1990: not only was the winery burglarized and vandalized, but 8,000 gallons of wine were emptied into the Sunflower River. A disgruntled former employee suspected of turning the spigots was charged with the burglary. Before the case came to trial, Sam could joke about the incident ("All the people fishing on the bank were using aspirin for bait for about three weeks, those fish had such a bad head"), while to the blues enthusiast of course the line that came to mind was "goin' where the water tastes like wine." Given "the blues" by this incident and also inspired by the growing international interest in Patton/Rushing blues lore, Sam Rushing had a friend design a label for a new brand of Mississippi Delta Muscadine White wine, "Dedicated to the Mississippi Delta Blues." The label quoted lyrics from "Tom Rushen Blues" and bore an inscription from Sam: "This song was written about my granddaddy, 'Big Tom' Rushing, who was Deputy Sheriff of Bolivar County during this time. Charlie Patton was one of the earliest Delta blues musicians and lived for a time around Merigold, playing at tonks and parties. He died under mysterious circumstances and is believed to be buried around Holly Ridge. I dedicate this vintage in remembrance of the Delta Blues, and all of us who sing them from time to time." Neither Tom Rushing nor the public ever got to sample the new blues wine, though. Tom Rushing died on September 2, 1990, at the age of 92, at a nursing home in Cleveland. In December the burglary trial ended in acquittal, and Sam and Diane, who had already received threats, found their dog dead. Before any more serious reprisals could be mounted, the Rushings put the winery up for sale and moved to Colorado. Were Charley Patton still alive, it would be hard to imagine him not composing a song about the Rushings' ordeal.

Notes

1. McKinley Mitchell died in Chicago on January 18, 1986; see obituary in *Living Blues* 69 (1986): 41–42.

2. 1983.

3. Charley Patton, "Moon Going Down," Paramount 13014, OJL-1, Yazoo L-1020, recorded 1930.

4. Valerie Wellington, "Smokestack Lightning," Rooster Blues R2619, recorded 1983.

5. Howlin' Wolf, "Smoke Stack [Smokestack] Lightning," Chess 1618, LP 1434, 1P 1544, CH 60016, 2ACMB 201, CH-9107, Argo LP 4026, Festival FR 1008 (US issues only listed). Recorded 1956.

6. Charley Patton, "Down the Dirt Road Blues" ("Over the Sea Blues"), Paramount 12854, OJL-7, Yazoo L-1020, recorded 1929.

7. Howlin' Wolf, "Can't Stay Here," Chess CH50045, recorded 1973.

Andrew "Blueblood" McMahon, "I Can't Stay Here," Dharma DB4401, recorded 1973.

Johnny Littlejohn, "Chips Flyin' Everywhere," ABC Bluesway BLS-6069, recorded 1973.

Johnny Littlejohn, "I Can't Stay Here," MCM 900300, recorded 1976.

Johnny Littlejohn, "Chips Flyin' Everywhere," Full Scope 8200, recorded 1980.

Johnny Littlejohn, "Chips Flyin' Everywhere," Rooster Blues R2621, recorded 1984.

8. Big Daddy Kinsey & the Kinsey Report, "Gary, Indiana," Rooster Blues R2620, recorded 1984.

9. Robert Johnson, *The Complete Recordings*, Columbia 46222, 1990.

10. Charley Patton, "Tom Rushen Blues," Paramount 12877, OJL-7, Yazoo L-1020, and many CD reissues, recorded 1929.

11. Stephen Calt and Gayle Wardlow, *King of the Delta Blues: The Life and Music of Charlie Patton*. Newton, NJ: Rock Chapel, 1988.

12. John Fahey, *Charley Patton*. London: Studio Vista, 1970.

13. Bernard Klatzko and Gayle Dean Wardlow, *The Immortal Charlie Patton, 1887–1934. Number 2: 1929–34*. Origin Jazz Library OJL-7, 1964.

14. Pete Welding and Toby Byron, editors, *Bluesland: Portraits of Twelve Major American Blues Masters*. New York: Dutton, 1991.

15. *The Complete Recorded Works of Charley Patton*, P-Vine Special PCD-2255/6/7, 1992 (Japan).

16. Mississippi Blues Trail website: www.msbluestrail.org.

17. Census and military records retrieved from www.ancestry.com.

For updates on Charley Patton research, see the Charley Patton page at www.bluesoterica.com.

CONCLUSION

Mississippi Blues Today and Its Future

—David Evans

New Preface, 2015

Beyond the correction of a few minor errors of fact, I have not changed or updated this article from the text that was originally published in 1987. Looking back over almost thirty years, I think it gives a good account of the state of blues in Mississippi in the mid-1980s. At that time the Chicago style of small-combo electric blues, with a prominent lead guitar sound, was the favored style among American and overseas white fans of the music, while soul blues remained popular with the music's black listeners. Some writers at the time were declaring that the Mississippi blues tradition was dead or moribund, but from Memphis, just across the Mississippi state line, and from several years of involvement in research and recording of Mississippi blues, I found the tradition to be still healthy and with a seemingly bright future. I classified the Mississippi blues artists into three categories of traditional, neo-traditional, and contemporary, recognizing that some of them shared traits of more than one category. Traditional artists performed in older styles of folk blues or commercial styles of an earlier era, often solo and with acoustic instruments. Neo-traditional artists drew upon traditional styles and repertoire but had shaped individual styles and added modern elements, often performing with electric instruments and sometimes in small combos, thereby managing to retain some popularity with audiences in their communities. Contemporary artists performed in modern styles of either Chicago or soul blues and still had a fan base of black listeners. My assessment of the health of Mississippi blues proved to be accurate, and by the 1990s and first decade of the twenty-first century popular attention shifted to neo-traditional Mississippi artists such as R. L. Burnside and Junior Kimbrough and some new discoveries from the state such as Robert Belfour (resident in Memphis but originally from Mississippi), James "Super Chikan" Johnson, Paul "Wine" Jones, and

T-Model Ford. Today in 2015 most of these artists and the others that I mentioned in my original essay are deceased or inactive. They have been replaced largely by blues artists in a new category, namely *revivalists*. The blues revival, characterized by an interest in and support for the music by people outside the traditional black community, was certainly a factor in Mississippi blues already in the mid-1980s in respect to research, recording, and the sponsorship of festivals and other performance venues, but at that time the revival more or less took artists as they had been performing in Mississippi black communities and presented them in new settings for new audiences. Now, thirty years later, there are many blues artists, both black and white, who have begun their performing careers with an orientation toward the blues revival audience. Another new factor that was only hinted at in my original essay is the appearance of blues families, that is, blues artists whose parents or grandparents were also blues artists. There are now several descendants of Junior Kimbrough and R. L. Burnside, as well as other blues artists, active in Mississippi blues, a situation paralleled on a national level by blues-performing descendants of ex-Mississippians Muddy Waters, John Lee Hooker, Elmore James, Jimmy Rogers, Eddie Taylor, and others. These performers draw their styles and repertoires at least partly from their family traditions, but they perform mostly for revival audiences. Mississippi has a rich blues heritage, and there is still a lot of blues in the state. It will be interesting to revisit and assess its blues scene in another thirty years. My original essay from 1987 follows.

◆ ◆ ◆

The state of Mississippi has always been a hub of blues activity. Some of the best and most detailed early reports of this folk music come from Mississippi, such as W. C. Handy's observations of blues around 1903 in the Delta towns of Tutwiler, Cleveland, and Clarksdale, and Professor Howard W. Odum's discussion of blues that he collected in Lafayette County between 1905 and 1908.

It is not difficult to see why Mississippi has been such a stronghold of blues. The music has always been most associated with black people of rural origin. Mississippi is one of the nation's most rural states, with no large industrial cities. It also has a higher percentage of black population than any other state in America. This percentage is particularly high in the Delta region in the northwestern part of the state, reaching as high as ninety percent in some counties. The Delta's rich soil served as a huge vortex, drawing black farm workers from the hill country on its east and south and sending many of them back to the hills or on to the cities of Memphis, St. Louis, and Chicago. A great many of the famed "Delta" bluesmen were actually born or grew up in the hill country. Among these were Charley Patton, Tommy Johnson, Bukka White, Big Joe Williams, Howlin' Wolf. No doubt they brought musical ideas with them to the Delta from the hills. The Mississippi River and the railroads that intersected the Delta also brought new musical ideas to this region and served as arteries for entry, internal movement, and escape. The Delta, then, despite its rural and overwhelmingly black character, was far from an isolated region and was relatively more prosperous than the surrounding hill country. The highly intensified plantation and sharecropping system made the region somewhat like a rural factory, sharing to a certain degree some of the characteristics of an urban environment. Like many American cities with their immigrant communities, the Delta served as a center of innovation, opportunity, and cross-fertilization of ideas as well as for the retention of old ways and patterns uprooted from their former homes.

Mississippi, and the Delta in particular, served as a center of blues development and innovation, while older styles of black folk music that predated the blues also thrived in the state. A type of homemade one-stringed instrument of African origin is particularly well represented in the Delta and the adjacent hill country. Fife and drum music is played at picnics in the hills just east of the Delta and was until recently also played near Natchez. Black string bands, such as those led by Son Sims and Sid Hemphill as well as the famed Mississippi Sheiks, were also once prominent in the state. The one-stringed instrument, fife and drum music, and banjo and fiddle tunes, all coexisting with the blues for many years in Mississippi, are no doubt largely responsible for the prevalence of repeated riffs—short, repeated melodic/rhythmic phrases— that are found in many of the blues from this state and which serve as basic compositional building blocks in the creation of new songs. This riff style occurs in a number of the blues of artists like Charley Patton, Bukka White, Big Joe Williams, Howlin' Wolf, and especially Fred McDowell, to name just a few. It is one of the factors that make Mississippi blues so exciting and unpredictable, removing it from the twelve-bar rut that characterizes so many blues from other areas.

Mississippi blues artists combined great variety and creativity with a strong sense of tradition. These qualities can be easily detected in the work of artists who recorded in the period between 1927 and 1931, such as Charley Patton, Willie Brown, Tommy Johnson, Ishmon Bracey, Rube Lacy, Skip James, Louise Johnson, and Garfield Akers, and they are also readily apparent in the work of artists from the mid-1930s like Bo Carter, Johnnie Temple, Robert Johnson, and Big Joe Williams. The same qualities were present in unparalleled abundance in the work of Mississippi blues artists who recorded commercially in the early 1940s, such as Bukka White, Tommy McClennan, and Arthur "Big

Boy" Crudup, as well as ones who made field recordings at this time like Son
House, David Edwards, and McKinley Morganfield (Muddy Waters).

The 1940s and 1950s, however, ushered in rapid social changes in Mississippi, and these resulted in equally serious changes in the blues tradition. World War II and the Korean conflict brought to the black community
unprecedented opportunities for travel, world experience, new aspirations,
and a heightened sense of belonging to American society. At the same time,
agriculture was rapidly becoming mechanized and the sharecropping system
went into serious decline. These factors caused an increase of activity in the
civil rights movement, which enjoyed its greatest victory in the 1954 Supreme
Court decision outlawing racial segregation in the nation's public schools.
While the plantations of the South had less need for black sharecroppers
every year, it was a time of increased prosperity in the industrial North. During and after the wars there was a massive migration of blacks from Mississippi and other southern states to the North and the West Coast. Among these
migrants were many of the best and most innovative of the blues musicians,
particularly those of the younger generation.

The migration of musicians caused great disruption in the Mississippi
blues scene. Another factor that brought about enormous change was the
electrification of instruments, particularly the guitar. The electric guitar,
which was readily adopted by Mississippi blues artists, had much greater volume, power, and sustaining quality than the acoustic guitar. It enabled the
guitar to compete with other instruments and for the first time to become a
lead instrument in a large band with drums. Beginning with artists like B.B.
King and Little Milton, Mississippi has produced a steady stream of outstanding electric lead guitarists in the blues. The more intricate and delicate older
styles of blues guitar picking exemplified by artists like Mississippi John Hurt,
Bo Carter, and Tommy Johnson did not make a successful transition to the
electric guitar. On the other hand, the tradition of Son House and Robert
Johnson, which emphasized sparer figures, more driving rhythms, bottleneck
style, boogie bass lines, and riff patterns, found expression in the postwar
electric guitar work of Muddy Waters and a host of others. Perhaps the ultimate postwar expression of the riff style and boogie figures is found in the
work of Mississippi-born guitarist John Lee Hooker. It is highly doubtful that
Waters and Hooker would have achieved such great commercial success if
they had played their music in an earlier era on acoustic guitars. While many
of the Mississippi blues artists who had grown up playing acoustic guitars
found themselves without an audience in the postwar years, those others who
could adapt their styles to electricity began increasingly to play in small combinations of two, three, or four pieces. This combo sound could be heard in

Mississippi juke joints and is exemplified by artists like Charley Booker and Houston Boines and in some of the Trumpet recordings of Elmore James, Willie Love, and Sonny Boy Williamson (Rice Miller). Typical combinations were guitar and harmonica, guitar-piano-drums, and later guitar-bass-drums. One important big band even emerged from Mississippi, led by Ike Turner from Clarksdale.

There was a brief flurry of commercial recording of Mississippi blues artists in the first half of the 1950s, most notably on the Trumpet and Delta labels based in Jackson. Sam Phillips of Memphis recorded a number of Mississippi artists at this time, at first selling the masters to Modern Records of Los Angeles and Chess Records of Chicago and later releasing blues on his own Sun label. The Bihari Brothers of Los Angeles made field trips through Mississippi with Ike Turner acting as talent scout and soon set up the Meteor label based in Memphis. Other Mississippi bluesmen, such as Papa Lightfoot from Natchez and Guitar Slim from Hollandale, recorded in New Orleans. But by 1955 most of this commercial recording activity was over. Johnny Vincent's Ace Records, based in Jackson, was a highly successful company for a few years and was certainly in a position to record Mississippi blues artists, but most of the label's top talent was drawn from New Orleans.

From 1955 through the end of the 1970s there have been only a few scattered commercial releases (i.e., designed for sale mainly to black customers) by Mississippi-based blues artists, such as Sammy Myers, Frank Frost, Woodrow Adams, and Junior Kimbrough. This rather sparse pattern of commercial recording activity, however, was supplemented by considerable recording of former Mississippi artists based in Memphis, the northern cities, and the West Coast. There is no doubt that we hear strong reflections of the Mississippi blues sound in the records of artists like Jimmy Reed, Muddy Waters, Howlin' Wolf, Jimmy Rogers, Robert Nighthawk, Elmore James, and Big Lucky, even though the downhome characteristics are sometimes fused with an urban musical sophistication. While it would be a mistake to consider these artists' records to be pure Mississippi blues, we can still hear strong southern elements in them, and it is these elements that often give the records their power and charm.

Just at the time when commercial recording of blues in Mississippi was slowing to a trickle, serious researchers began to make field recordings in the state. Even in the late 1930s and early 1940s John A. Lomax and his son Alan Lomax had documented Mississippi blues artists for the Library of Congress. Many of these artists had made or would make commercial recordings, and others were certainly as good as the best of the commercial recording artists of the period. In the mid-1950s jazz historian Frederic Ramsey Jr. made some fine recordings in the southwestern part of the state that appeared on the Folkways label. In 1959 Alan Lomax returned to Mississippi and discovered the great Fred McDowell in Como along with some other fine artists whose recordings appeared on the Atlantic and Prestige record labels. British researcher Paul Oliver briefly visited Clarksdale in 1960 and made the first recordings of Wade Walton and Robert Curtis Smith. Meanwhile, Samuel Charters and others began piecing together the early history of blues in the state and calling attention to the work of the great pioneer recording artists of the 1920s and 1930s. As some of the great recordings of this early period began to be reissued in the early 1960s, a series of "rediscoveries" took place. Mississippi John Hurt, Son House, Skip James, and Bukka White were found and brought out of musical retirement for successful appearances in coffeehouses, concerts, and festivals. From the mid-1960s through the mid-1970s field recording continued, carried on by George Mitchell, William Ferris, and myself, resulting in several books and record albums. In the late 1970s and early 1980s European researchers Gianni Marcucci and Axel Küstner made more field recordings in Mississippi, which appeared on Italian and German record labels. All of these researchers in the postwar years were searching mainly for older styles of folk blues played on acoustic instruments. Although they made some fine recordings, many of the artists had retired from active music making in their communities or had become reduced to performing at home for small gatherings of friends and family. Rarely did the researchers record electric blues in the juke joints. Only a handful of recordings from 1967 of small combos led by Houston Stackhouse, Woodrow Adams, and Son Thomas reflect this more contemporary community blues tradition. Furthermore, much of the research and fieldwork had little impact in Mississippi itself. The artists who were discovered and recorded did not find their local careers greatly enhanced, and their recordings were generally unavailable to the public in Mississippi. The rediscovered artists performed mainly outside the state, and some even moved to the North.

By 1982 most of the great Mississippi folk blues discoveries had died or permanently retired from performing. The list included Mississippi John Hurt, Skip James, Bukka White, Son House (still living but long retired), Fred McDowell, Sam Chatmon, Joe Callicott, and Big Joe Williams. Even many of the giants who had moved north from Mississippi in the 1940s and 1950s were now gone, including Jimmy Reed, Muddy Waters, and Howlin' Wolf. The deaths of so many great artists, the earlier massive loss of talent to the northern cities, the scarcity of commercial blues recording of Mississippi-based artists after 1955, and the heavy emphasis of blues researchers on documenting older acoustic styles of folk blues all served by the early 1980s to give the impression that the Mississippi blues tradition was virtually dead. It is my purpose here to try to dispel this unfortunate notion and to point out what remains of the old traditions in Mississippi as well as some exciting new developments that have been taking place there in recent years. This brief survey should indicate that Mississippi blues are alive and well in the mid-1980s and that they have the potential to enjoy a creative development at least through the end of the twentieth century.

There are still many fine traditional blues artists active in Mississippi. Eugene Powell in Greenville and Jack Owens in Bentonia represent the best in folk styles that were current in the 1920s. Powell, who recorded in 1936 under the pseudonym Sonny Boy Nelson, is a superb guitarist in the tradition of Bo Carter, Sam Chatmon, and "Hacksaw" Harney. Owens performs powerful haunting blues in the tradition of Skip James with his younger blind harmonica partner Bud Spires. Powell and Owens are both magnificent players who still entertain small groups of friends, but they are prevented from touring and gaining wider exposure by the need to care for seriously ill wives. Another fine artist of the same generation is Monroe Guy Jackson of Holly Springs, who performs in a style somewhat reminiscent of Fred McDowell, featuring insistent riff patterns. Jackson plays for friends and has performed at festivals in Holly Springs and Memphis as well as a brief tour in New York. Another slightly younger artist in the same stylistic tradition is Ranie Burnette of Senatobia, who still performs at house parties in the country and has made a few tours and festival appearances. Both Jackson and Burnette play electric guitars. Other artists who perform a synthesis of traditional and commercial sounds more or less from the 1940s are Wade Walton of Clarksdale and blind Wilbert Lee Reliford of Holly Springs, both of whom are adept on harmonica and guitar and still entertain groups of friends. Johnny Woods is a fine harmonica player from Olive Branch, who plays for his drinking buddies on country store porches and sits in with bands at house parties and juke joints. Son Thomas from Leland is perhaps the state's best-known active traditional bluesman. He performs versions of many songs that were recorded by downhome blues artists in the 1950s but also plays a number of traditional pieces that represent an older layer of Mississippi blues. Thomas has played at many festivals and toured throughout America and in Europe a number of times. Another artist with a similar repertoire and considerable potential is Elmore Williams of Natchez. Both Thomas and Williams perform locally at juke joints and house parties. Several artists lead small combos that perform the type of blues that could be heard at juke joints in the 1950s and 1960s. Among them are Roosevelt Barnes of Greenville, Raymond Hill of Clarksdale, and Frank Frost of Greenville. Each of these artists is adept at more than one instrument and can be heard with a band at local clubs on most weekends.

Some of the most interesting blues in Mississippi today are performed by artists that I would call "neo-traditional." That is to say, they are firmly rooted in the Mississippi stylistic tradition, but they have forged a sound that is distinctive and personal, not based on any particular style of the past. The youngest of these artists is Lonnie Pitchford of Lexington, who has just turned thirty. Pitchford has constructed a one-stringed guitar and achieves on it a sound very similar to that of some West African lutes. He has been playing this instrument since he was a teenager and more recently has begun playing a regular six-stringed guitar. He has studied the records of older Mississippi artists, such as Robert Johnson, and has apprenticed with Johnson's old partner and stepson Robert "Junior" Lockwood. Lonnie Pitchford is clearly an artist to watch in the future. Another artist still in his thirties is Jimmie Holmes of Bentonia. Holmes performs on electric guitar in the style of local blues greats Skip James and Jack Owens, with his brother on second guitar or bass, but their rhythm has a more modern feeling somewhat reminiscent of the records of Jimmy Reed. Holmes is also a blues entrepreneur, sponsoring other local artists at a café he manages in town and at picnics on his family farm out in the country. He has a college degree and an intellectual respect for the blues tradition combined with a deep personal involvement with it since he was a child.

Another Mississippi artist with strong blues roots and an original sound is Jessie Mae Hemphill of Senatobia. Music has been a part of her family for at least four generations, and both her aunt and grandfather recorded before her. She sings original blues that she creates herself out of life experiences but also drawing from the shared tradition of folk blues. Her electric guitar style is strongly rhythmic and dance-oriented, based upon insistent riff patterns drawn from the rhythms of fife and drum music in which she also participates. She sometimes plays a tambourine with her foot, and her rhythms are consistent with the use of a drum set, lending her music a quality that is contemporary yet traditional at the same time. She has performed at many festivals in the South and toured in Europe. At home she plays at picnics and house parties and has recently begun playing on Beale Street in nearby Memphis.

R. L. Burnside of Holly Springs is best known away from home for his solo performances with acoustic or electric guitar, which display a repertoire that combines traditional blues in the riffing style and recreations of downhome blues records from the 1950s. Burnside has toured throughout the United States and many times in Europe as a solo blues artist. At home, however, he can generally be heard on weekends at country juke joints, house parties, and picnics with his band, the Sound Machine, comprised of his sons and son-in-law on electric guitar, bass, and drums. The younger musicians have been influenced by more contemporary popular blues and soul music, but the drummer has also participated in fife and drum music. Sometimes their style seems to clash with the older Burnside's conception of blues, but on many songs the result is a very exciting synthesis of traditional and modern elements. Burnside has some younger sons who are developing as musicians and who seem more oriented toward the traditional side of his repertoire.

Junior Kimbrough and the Soul Blues Boys, also from Holly Springs, have achieved a remarkable sound, truly that of an electric country blues band. Kimbrough performs almost entirely his own compositions, which feature unusual and different structures and are built up from riff patterns. Usually one associates this style with solo artists, but Kimbrough has trained a second guitarist, bass player, and drummer to play his pieces with him and develop complementary melodic lines to his own guitar playing. It is a unique sound in Mississippi blues and one with great potential for further development. Although he made one brief European appearance, Kimbrough rarely performs outside Holly Springs and Memphis and has recorded only two 45s. His blues deserve to be better known.

Perhaps the most unusual blues band in Mississippi, if not the entire United States, is Hezekiah and the House Rockers. The leader, Hezekiah Early, lives in Natchez, while the other two members live across the Mississippi River in Ferriday and St. Joseph, Louisiana. Early sings and plays drums and a harmonica taped to his vocal microphone. His harmonica style was learned from the great Papa Lightfoot, while his drumming was influenced by the sound of local fife and drum bands. Guitarist James Baker, who was born and raised in Natchez, contributes boogie bass lines. The other lead instrument is the trombone of Peewee Whittaker, whose musical experience goes back to the ragtime era and includes stints in circus bands, dance bands, minstrel shows, jazz, and rock and roll groups. Whittaker also contributes a few vocals in a traditional style. The band's repertoire is basically blues but also includes some numbers from country music, rock and roll, and rhythm and blues. The members of the band represent three generations with musical influences ranging from ragtime to disco. The band has appeared at a number of festivals in America and has toured in Europe, but it still deserves to be better known among blues fans.

The mainstream of contemporary blues is not heavily represented on the local level in Mississippi. When I last saw him in 1981, Arkansas harmonica bluesman Willie Cobbs had settled in Greenwood and was fronting a youthful nine-piece disco band. They were managing to make a precarious living touring in a modern version of a regional "chitlin' circuit" of clubs in the larger towns and small cities like Greenwood, Columbus, Hattiesburg, and Meridian. Blind Jackson harmonica player and former Ace recording artist Sam Myers works mostly with white backup musicians and gets plenty of work playing at white clubs and college fraternity parties. He recently recorded an album with white Texas blues guitarist Anson Funderburgh. With the exception of Cobbs and Myers, the main sounds of contemporary blues in Mississippi are provided by touring artists, some of them former Mississippians like B.B. King, and blues artists who record at studios in Jackson. Since 1982 Malaco Records in Jackson has had enormous success in reviving the careers of veteran soul-blues artists. Most of these artists are not originally from Mississippi, but they now spend a great deal of time in the state, and the company has developed an identifiable studio sound which emphasizes the role of a bluesy lead guitar. Many of the best songs on the label were composed by former Mississippian George Jackson. Of all the blues artists on the label, Little Milton has the strongest ties to Mississippi and probably the strongest adherence to a pure blues sound. Another company based in Jackson, LaJam records, has had considerable success with artists like Nolan Struck and especially Bobby Rush, whose original and often humorous pieces are among the most innovative sounds in contemporary blues. All of these recording artists tour nationally, often recruiting show bands from Mississippi to provide their backup and giving young musicians from the state some valuable experience in performing blues.

A number of factors have combined in recent years to bring Mississippi blues to the consciousness of people of all social levels in the state as well as audiences throughout America and the world. The earliest serious research and rediscovery of pioneer blues recording artists seems to have had little direct impact in the state during the 1960s. The only Mississippi-born researcher in the early part of that decade was Gayle Dean Wardlow, but his work was published mainly in collectors' magazines and album notes to reissue records that were unavailable in Mississippi.

More effective in reaching a statewide audience has been William Ferris, whose work was much less historically oriented than Wardlow's and more concerned with blues as a living tradition in the state. Ferris began his fieldwork in the Delta in 1967, and by the early 1970s the results were being disseminated in Mississippi through a series of films and his book *Blues from the Delta*. Coming from a socially prominent Vicksburg family, Ferris received his Ph.D. degree from the University of Pennsylvania, then taught at predominantly black Jackson State University for a few years. During this time he became a co-founder of the Center for Southern Folklore in Memphis, which served as a publication outlet for his films. He went back north to teach at prestigious Yale University for a few years and returned to his home state in 1979 to become the Director of the Center for the Study of Southern Culture at the University of Mississippi. Ferris had the perfect background to bring respect to blues music in a state that had historically not given much respect to anything associated with its black community. He has used this background well and received massive support from the university administration. The university has acquired B.B. King's personal record collection and used it as a basis to set up the nation's first Blues Archive, which promises to become an important research center. The university has also become the publishing headquarters for *Living Blues* magazine, which in turn provides a bi-monthly forum for publicizing internationally the many blues activities at the university and in the state. The university has also begun a documentary record album series that includes some of Ferris's blues recordings.

In the same year that Ferris came to the University of Mississippi, Sid Graves inaugurated the Delta Blues Museum at the Carnegie Public Library in Clarksdale. This museum provides an impressive permanent display focusing on Mississippi blues and is supported by a strong collection of literature and audiovisual material. The museum has also sponsored concerts and a number of prominent speakers on the blues. It has attracted visitors from all over America and the world, a fact that guarantees strong support from the community. The museum and the music it highlights have literally put Clarksdale on the cultural map. Another educational institution in the state, Jackson State University, has for the past three years held a one-week summer symposium on blues. Organized by Professor Joseph Goree, the seminar presents classes and concerts oriented especially toward secondary and college teachers, designed to increase their knowledge of this musical tradition that has been so prominent in the state's cultural life.

Various blues and folk festivals in the state have combined the functions of education and entertainment. The oldest and largest of these is the Delta Blues Festival, founded in 1978. It is run by Mississippi Action for Community Education (MACE), a black community organization in Greenville. Held in an open field, the festival regularly draws an audience of over thirty thousand, about an equal mixture of black and white, with many coming from long distances. Over the years the program has moved from highlighting mainly Mississippi folk blues artists to a showcase for nationally known talent. Nevertheless, there are always several top Mississippi and former Mississippi artists on the program. Just as important, the festival has received widespread support from political, social, and business leaders in the state and is viewed as a symbol of black accomplishment and cultural pride. The Medgar Evers

Homecoming Festival was organized in honor of the slain civil rights leader and first held in 1979 in his home town of Fayette. Later it was moved to Jackson. It features mainly nationally known blues and soul talent, with many of the artists having former ties to Mississippi. The B.B. King Festival in Indianola is similar and honors the nation's top blues artist who grew up in that Delta town. The Oxford Folklife Festival has been held since 1982. Sponsored by the University of Mississippi, the festival always presents several Mississippi and other Mid-South blues artists and symbolizes the university's commitment to the study and preservation of the region's folk culture. Other blues festivals have been held in Columbus (since 1984) and Chunky (1985), featuring mostly Mississippi talent. One of the most impressive festivals in the state is the Northeast Mississippi Blues and Gospel Folk Festival, held every year since 1980 on the campus of Rust College in Holly Springs. Some excellent blues talent from surrounding Marshall County appears at this festival along with other artists from the state and region. There is a strong emphasis on traditional styles of blues. The festival's organizer, Professor Sylvester Oliver, has also built an archive of audio and video recordings of local artists performing blues and other forms of folk music. What is especially noteworthy about these festivals is that most of them are organized by black community leaders and organizations and that they draw large black and sometimes mixed audiences.

Mississippi artists have also performed in concerts and festivals outside the state in recent years, but most of this touring has been elsewhere in the South and occasionally in Europe. Although there was formerly great interest in Mississippi blues in the Northeast, Midwest, and West Coast, today's Mississippi blues artists have rarely appeared in these parts of America, which now mostly hear the sound of Chicago blues. Mississippi artists do appear fairly often at festivals in Memphis and have been doing so since the pioneer blues festivals of the 1960s. The prestigious New Orleans Jazz and Heritage Festival has also usually had one or two Mississippi blues artists appear every year. Several artists from the state also performed at the World's Fairs in Knoxville, Tennessee, in 1982 and in New Orleans in 1984. At the National Downhome Blues Festival held in Atlanta in 1984, five of the twenty-three acts were from Mississippi, and several others had grown up in the state. Son Thomas and R. L. Burnside have toured most extensively in Europe, but Jessie Mae Hemphill, Ranie Burnette, Johnny Woods, Elmore Williams, Frank Frost, Hezekiah and the House Rockers, and Junior Kimbrough and his band have also appeared on the continent. European interest in Mississippi blues appears to be growing, and it seems likely that more artists from the state will cross the Atlantic in the near future.

Mississippi artists have also reached new audiences through visual media and sound recordings. The films of William Ferris have been viewed widely since the 1970s. In 1978 Alan Lomax returned to Mississippi and produced a television program called *Land Where the Blues Began*, which has been shown throughout America. Excerpts from the 1984 National Downhome Blues Festival will also be shown on national television, including several performances by Mississippi artists. Television and film crews from France have visited the state in recent years and brought back documentary recordings for showing in Europe. In 1986 Mississippi blues will gain major popular exposure through an appearance by Frank Frost and his band in a Hollywood film entitled *Crossroads*. The most commercially successful phonograph records have been those of the Jackson-based Malaco and LaJam labels, although most of their artists are not from Mississippi and perform on a national level rather than a local or regional one. These records have received heavy airplay on radio stations in the South that reach primarily black audiences. In 1979 I produced the first records for the High Water label, which is a division of Memphis State University. The first four releases were 45s by Mississippi blues artists Raymond and Lillie Hill, Jessie Mae Hemphill, R. L. Burnside, and Ranie Burnette. These have been followed by 45s of Junior Kimbrough, Hezekiah and the House Rockers, and a second release by Ms. Hemphill. Most of these records received radio airplay and appeared on juke boxes in Mississippi and Memphis, helping raise respect for traditional blues in the region and putting it on an equal basis with more commercial forms of music. High Water has also produced albums by Hemphill and Burnside (with his band) for Vogue Records of France and has further albums by Hemphill and Hezekiah and the House Rockers scheduled for release. Memphis State University offers an undergraduate degree in Commercial Music, and many students in the program have participated in High Water sessions as recording engineers in the university's twenty-four-track studio. The university also offers M.A. and Ph.D. degrees in Ethnomusicology with a specialization in southern regional music, providing advanced students an opportunity to do original research on blues and related musical traditions of the South. A few European record companies have shown a continuing interest in Mississippi blues in the 1980s. The Swingmaster company based in the Netherlands has released albums by Son Thomas and R. L. Burnside, while the Italian Albatros label has released albums by older artists Jack Owens and Eugene Powell along with individual tracks by other artists from the state. The German L+R label has also issued a number of tracks by Mississippi artists on its "Living Country Blues USA" series of albums. Various other companies in America and Europe have individual releases by Mississippi artists.

The preceding survey should be enough to indicate that there is plenty of variety and quality in the Mississippi blues in the mid-1980s and that much is taking place in research, public performance, and recording. The tradition is alive and well and in better shape than it has been in thirty years.

Bibliography

Charters, Samuel. *The Country Blues*. New York: Rinehart, 1959.

———. *The Bluesmen*. New York: Oak Publications, 1967.

Evans, David. "Afro-American One-Stringed Instruments." *Western Folklore* 29 (1970): 229–45. Reprinted in *Afro-American Folk Arts and Crafts*, ed. William Ferris (Boston: G. K. Hall, 1983), 181–96.

———. *Tommy Johnson*. London: Studio Vista, 1971.

———. "Black Fife and Drum Music in Mississippi." *Mississippi Folklore Register* 6 (1972): 94–107. Reprinted in *Afro-American Folk Arts and Crafts*, ed. William Ferris (Boston: G. K. Hall, 1983), 163–71.

———. *Big Road Blues: Tradition and Creativity in the Folk Blues*. Berkeley: University of California Press, 1982.

Fahey, John. *Charley Patton*. London: Studio Vista, 1970.

Ferris, William. *Blues from the Delta*. Garden City, NY: Anchor, 1978.

Handy, W. C. *Father of the Blues*. New York: Collier, 1970.

Leadbitter, Mike. *Delta Country Blues*. Bexhill-on-Sea, UK: Blues Unlimited, 1968.

Mitchell, George. *Blow My Blues Away*. Baton Rouge: Louisiana State University Press, 1971.

Odum, Howard W. "Folk-Song and Folk-Poetry As Found in the Secular Songs of the Southern Negroes." *Journal of American Folklore* 24 (1911): 255–94, 351–96.

Oliver, Paul. *The Story of the Blues*. London: Barrie & Rockliff, 1969.

Palmer, Robert. *Deep Blues*. New York: Viking, 1981.

Sawyer, Charles. *The Arrival of B.B. King*. Garden City, NY: Doubleday, 1980.

Zur Heide, Karl Gert. *Deep South Piano: The Story of Little Brother Montgomery*. London: Studio Vista, 1970.

INDEX

Lightning Source UK Ltd.
Milton Keynes UK
UKHW01f1632170518
322764UK00001B/40/P